Water Village

The Story of Waterville, Maine

By Earl H. Smith

Published by North Country Press
Unity, Maine

Cover photograph and design by Gary Green

All photographs and images used with permission

ISBN 978-1-943424-43-6
Library of Congress Control Number: 2018957903
Smith, Earl H. – 1st Edition
Water Village: The Story of Waterville, Maine
Includes bibliographical references and index

Printed in the United States

North Country Press
Unity, Maine

FOR PAUL AND GARY

DEAR BROTHERS AND FELLOW SONS OF WATERVILLE

CHAPTERS

Prologue

The land where the great Kennebec River drops to greet two of her tributaries was the perfect place to build a village. The native people had known it for 10,000 years, before the English came and took it over. In but a century, the invaders harnessed the feeder stream called Messalonskee and lined its banks with mills of every kind. The natives had named the place Teconnet for the big river falls nearby, but the English called it Kingfield, then Winslow, and when the time came to create a separate west bank village, they quite sensibly named it for the water itself.

The story of Waterville and its surrounds is one of astonishingly rapid growth and prosperity. The city flourished on the wave of the Second Industrial Revolution. Its ever-multiplying mills drew workers from around the world, and its streets were filled with merchants of every kind.

The boom, of course, could not last, and before the end of the 20th century Waterville had barely anything to do with the water at all. The once-thriving industries were all gone, and the proud river city, like so many others in the north, began a long struggle to reinvent itself and recover its missing pride.

1

First Things

1498-1802

The earliest European explorers of the Kennebec valley were merchants who began poking into the river's mouth soon after Christopher Columbus stumbled upon the new land. Their trading partners were the Eastern Wabanaki, "people of the dawn," a small tribe of the Algonkin Indians who lived in the vast lands of Acadia.

At first, the matter of trading bewildered the natives, for like their kin throughout North America, the Wabanaki Indians did not barter among themselves. They were from a place where no one owned anything and everyone owned everything, including the land itself.

The trading began innocently enough. The newcomers wanted fish and fur to sell for handsome profit in Europe, and the natives were intrigued by colorful beads, cloth, and all things made of iron. For the Indians, the land was never an issue, as they were sure it belonged to them. They were content to share it, but they did not grasp the designs of the intruders, who were willing to shed blood to own it outright.

Competing land claims began in the summer of 1498 when Sebastian Cabot came looking for a water route to China, and while he was about it, declared that everything from Labrador to Manhattan Island belonged to King Henry VII and England. The French disagreed, and in 1534 when Jacques Cartier discovered the St. Lawrence, he insisted that all he could see and could not see belonged to France. Samuel Champlain bolstered the French claim in 1604, and gave the name Acadia to the vast area from Cape Breton to the Hudson River. The next year, Captain George Weymouth rounded Monhegan Island and insisted once more that the mainland belonged to the British.

A full century of declarations and warring brought no resolution, and in 1607 the English attempted to cinch the matter by staking a claim at the mouth of the Kennebec.[1] The tiny settlement led by Raleigh Gilbert and George Popham collapsed and disappeared in the first winter.

Seven years later, Captain John Smith came from Virginia to map the edge of the new world, and sailed briefly into the Kennebec where he traded "trifles" with the natives for two shiploads of beaver pelts and fish. The following year, the Indians of the Kennebec and the Penobscot began a devastating border war of their own. After two years of raids and killing, neither side won. Instead, the English simply assumed all the land and promptly assembled a Plymouth Council settlement tract fifteen miles wide, spanning the banks of the Kennebec from Topsham to Cornville. Included, on the east (Winslow) shore of the Kennebec, was the native village of Teconnet, named for the tumbling falls near where the Kennebec and Sebasticook join.

> Captain Smith had already played a prominent role in establishing the first English settlement at Jamestown, and was but 34 years old when he mapped northeast America from "New Found Land" to the Hudson River. He named it New England. Smith's assertion that his life was saved by Pocahontas is often disputed, but much of his later writing from London was true and prophetic. He called the coming British slave trade "odious to God and man," and his predictions for the approaching industrial growth in the new country were insightful: "Here every man may be master and owner of his owne labour and land... If he have nothing but his hands, he may...by industries quickly grow rich."

A kind of commerce began almost at once, and by the mid-1650s there were bustling trading posts at Harpswell, Arrowsic and Teconnet Falls, providing colonists with a place to gossip and to trade for what they could not grow or make themselves. The natives came to barter as well, swapping precious pelts for guns and ammunition. They were often cheated, and when tribal leaders complained to the magistrates of the newly created government of Massachusetts that their people were being plied with "hard drink" and robbed of their furs, they were offered fair treatment in exchange for giving up their newly acquired guns. The Wabanaki balked;

---

[1] Taken from the Wabanaki name "Quinibiki," meaning "snaky monster" for the roiling water (Hell's Gates) at Sheepscot.

they had come to rely upon the guns for hunting. In August of 1676 the natives ran out of patience and raided the posts at Harpswell and Arrowsic, killed the owners, burned the buildings, and marched their white prisoners back to Teconnet. Within weeks, the entire Kennebec valley was in flames.

King Philip's War (1675-76) was only the beginning. Over the next 87 years, the Wabanaki would fight six more wars, and choosing sides was easy. The English had taken their land and treated them harshly. The French, bent on making them Catholic, were kinder and promised to share the recovered territory.

King William's War was already underway in 1693 when all the chiefs of the Kennebec, Penobscot, Androscoggin, and Saco met with English magistrates at Fort William Henry in Pemaquid and signed an agreement:

That their Majesties' subjects, the English, shall and may peaceably and quietly enter, repair, and singularly improve their rights of lands, and former settlements and possessions with the eastern parts of the said province of the Massachusetts Bay, without any pretensions or claims by us, or any other Indians, and be in no wise molested, interrupted or disturbed therein.

Scarcely had the treaty been signed when Bomaseen, a powerful chief of the Kennebecs, went to Pemaquid under a flag of peace but was captured and sent to prison in Boston as a spy. The warfare began again. The Kennebec Indians participated in the 1696 burning of Fort William Henry and would not talk of peace until three years later, when Bomaseen was allowed to return to Norridgewock. By this time, the natives had their own powerful yet unappointed leader, Father Sebastian Rasle,[2] sent by the Catholics of Quebec to Norridgewock to establish a mission. Rasle opposed the building of forts and annoyed the English by denouncing proposed treaties. In 1717, over Rasle's objections, a peace pact was finally signed with the governor of the Royal Court of Massachusetts, ruler of the troublesome District of Maine.

FIFTY YEARS PASSED, AND HEIRS OF THE ORIGINAL PLYMOUTH Company Kennebec tract asked the court to build a fort at Teconnet Falls. Dr. John McKechnie, a physician and civil engineer, had already surveyed all of the land from Augusta to Winslow, and it was ready

---

[2] Later spelled Rale.

for settlement.[3] The Indians objected and sent a delegation to ask Governor William Shirley to build no garrisons above the one in place at Richmond. They were willing to have the foreigners live among them, but they wanted no more forts. Shirley ignored them and declared that if the Plymouth Company would construct a fort in Cushnoc (Augusta), he would build one at the falls 15 miles up the river. Cushnoc got Fort Western, and a wagon road was cut along the Kennebec to the confluence of the Sebasticook, where General John Winslow oversaw construction of five buildings within an 800-foot stockade and named it Fort Halifax. The commander at Richmond, William Lithgow, was sent upriver to lead a garrison of 80 men, many of whom died from starvation and illness in the first winter of 1755. The feared French invasion never came, and the weakened Indians barely threatened. On May 18, 1757, the Teconnet made a final desperate skirmish before evaporating into the forest, never to fight again.

> The Wabanaki had been fighting the English for a full century before the killing stopped. Even then, the decimation of war did not compare to the deaths caused by the white man's diseases. Passing fishermen had infected the natives with a fatal illness as early as 1564, and an epidemic of typhoid fever ravaged their population 20 years later. When the English first came to settle, as many as 20,000 native people were living east of the White Mountains. Barely a quarter of them survived, and the illnesses kept coming: smallpox, influenza, diphtheria, and measles. By the time of the American Revolution, only a few hundred Wabanaki had survived.

In April of 1771 the English settlement at Teconnet, first called Kingfield Plantation, was incorporated by the Massachusetts Court as the fourth town in the District of Maine and re-named in honor of General Winslow.

Four years later, almost to the day, the first blood of the American Revolution was spilled at the Concord Bridge. While inhabitants of the District of Maine were at some distance from the fray, they were no less eager to revolt. Maine lumbermen suffered more than most from the strict restrictions the Royal Navy had placed on the harvesting of white pine for masts, and aside from the burdensome taxes and regulations of the ruling British, Mainers were also subjects of Massachusetts, and the struggling colonists bristled when Commonwealth merchants took advantage of their plight by raising rents and the price of provisions.

---

[3] While he was about it, the wise Scotsman reserved Lot No. 103 for himself, land that included Teconnet Falls.

4

When the war began, the new town of Winslow appointed a "Committee of Safety" and sold borrowed shingles from resident lumbermen to raise money for a store of arms. Three men were hired to scout the river and warn of any approaching British soldiers, and a petition was sent to the Royal Court asking for protection against the Canadians. Two dozen men went to fight, including a number whose names were later stamped on streets and places in the town that became Waterville: John Cool, Seth Getchell, Nathaniel Gilman, Asa Redington, Philip Thayer.[4]

THE TOWN'S ONLY REAL BRUSH WITH WAR came in the fall of 1775, when the central house of the unmanned garrison at Fort Halifax, by then a town hall and tavern, greeted Benedict Arnold's doomed expedition on its faltering way to Quebec. The feisty Arnold had convinced George Washington and the new Continental Congress in Philadelphia of a plan to storm the British garrison at Quebec. He would avoid the predictable route of the St. Lawrence River and take the back door through the wilderness, up the Kennebec and down the Chaudière.

WATERVILLE HISTORICAL SOCIETY & REDINGTON MUSEUM WHS&REDINGTON
Drawing of Fort Halifax, 1754.

---

[4] The names of those who died are listed on a memorial plaque, commissioned by the Silence Howard Hayden Chapter of the Daughters of the American Revolution and installed at the Waterville Library in 1915. Silence, the wife of Col. Josiah Hayden, was born in Brockton, MA, in 1741 and died in Winslow in 1803. She is buried in the family (Howard) cemetery in Winslow.

On September 11, Arnold marched 1100 men from Cambridge to Newburyport, from where schooners carried them up the Kennebec to Pittston to collect 200 new wooden bateaux. The boats were tested in the short, calm journey to Winslow where, on September 29, they were greeted by the enthusiastic homesteaders living near the fort.[5]

Arnold's 20-foot boats, made of green pine and ribbed with oak, were sodden and heavy – 400 pounds without provisions – and the carry beyond the 18-foot Ticonic Falls was near impossible. At Five Mile Rips the boats began to crack. When they met the first ice and faster water at the Great Falls of Norridgewock, the men began to desert.

It was almost 200 years before anyone other than the most ardent Revolutionary War historians paid any attention to the route of Arnold's 350-mile trek to Quebec City, much less tout the trail to tourists. He was, after all, a traitor. In Waterville, the Daughters of the American Revolution placed a plaque on a boulder in front of City Hall in 1917, but it wasn't until the Arnold Expedition Historical Society was formed in 1967 that travel guides dared to list the trail as an attraction.

The river place that confounded Arnold's troops also hindered the governing of the growing town of Winslow. It was difficult to collect taxes and hard to provide teachers and preachers, and in 1791 town fathers petitioned the Commonwealth to be rid of the bothersome west bank place they called Ticonic Village. Although the cross-river land had never been at the center of things (the Indians used it only as a burial ground), townspeople were reluctant to give it up, and the petition was delayed five years while they experimented with alternating town and religious meetings in the Lithgow meetinghouse on the east bank and at the home of Elnathan Sherwin (Sherwin Street, later home of Silas Redington) across the river. It was impossible. Petitioners claimed that "in the spring season, at the annual meetings held in said Town, the Inhabitants thereof living on the opposite side from where the said meeting is to be held are frequently prevented by the particular situation of said River from crossing the same to attend said meeting."

In 1801, with 800 of Winslow's 1250 inhabitants now living west of the river, the ruling court was again asked to cut the town in two. At a special town meeting on December 8, voters adopted a petition that read, in part:

---

[5] Besides a few families living at Gatchell's Corner (sic) in Vassaboro, the Winslow homesteaders were the only settlers living north of Augusta.

"That the now Town of Winslow shall be divided through the middle of the river Kennebeck (*sic*) as the river usually runs across the width of said Town" and "That part of said Town which lay on the Eastern side of the Kennebeck shall retain the name of Winslow, and the part which lay on the Western side be erected into a town by the name of Waterville." On June 23, 1802, the petition was granted, creating the new town and by local decree, a place called West Waterville (Oakland). Waterville became the 138th township in the District of Maine.

2

Water Village

1802-1821

Waterville was set to make a name for itself on the day it broke free. Less than a month after incorporation, Asa Redington, a member of General Washington's honor guard during the Revolution, called the first town meeting on July 26, 1802, at the meetinghouse in Ticonic Village.[6] Abijah Smith was elected Town Clerk and Elnathan Sherwin, Asa Soule, and Ebeneza Bacon were chosen selectmen. Nearly every other man in town was assigned to one or more town office.[7] With only 63 taxpayers to share the load, they quickly approved a $300 assessment to establish schools, and agreed to build a modest "social library." A call went out to find a preacher.

The straightforward name given to the new town spoke volumes, for the concentration and convenience of water within a five-mile radius of Ticonic Falls was unsurpassed in all of New England. The natives and early settlers reaped the bounty of the river, but no one had tapped its power near Waterville until Asa Redington and Nehemiah Getchell erected the first dam at Ticonic Falls in 1792. The rock and timber structure reached from the west shore at the falls to Rock Island (Leaman Island) in mid-river, and the

---

[6] Ticonic was the popular name of the central village within the greater town.
[7] Positions included Surveyors of Highways, Surveyors of Lumber, Caulkers of Stoves, Measurers of Wood, Sealers of Leather, Tything Men (charged with keeping order in church), School Agents, Fish Wardens, Fence Viewers and Field Drivers, Saxon, Pound Keepers, and Hog Reeves (charged with prevention or appraisal of damage by stray swine).

power it produced was used to saw lumber out of logs taken from the forests nearby. The mill's best business came when the Revolution ended and Maine farmers became sailors on the free sea and began building ships in giant crib yards up and down the river.

The many ships built on the Kennebec soon were seen around the world. From 1794 until the steamships came, two-dozen schooners, brigs and sloops were built at the wharves in Waterville. The first large ship was the 268-ton *Ticonic*, launched at the foot of Sherwin Street in the spring freshet of 1800 by Captain John Clark and his son, George. Fourteen years later, the 290-ton *Francis & Sarah* set the Waterville record.

For larger craft, river travel ended abruptly at Waterville where the treacherous falls that had cursed Benedict Arnold became a blessing. Longboats – some as large as 40 tons – were made to stop and off-load hogsheads of molasses and rum before turning back downriver, laden with all kinds of local merchandise, including lumber, potatoes, and ice.

But while being at the river terminus brought many riches, in the matter of making power, the big river had little use, as most of the year the current was too swift to manage the up-and-down wood saws and crude grist (flour) mills.

On the west bank, Waterville was twice blessed for having within its boundaries the entire length of a powerful, yet manageable, stream. Beginning at Messalonskee Lake (Snow Pond) in West Waterville and winding north four miles before turning south and then east to enter the Kennebec below Ticonic Falls, the stream drained the seven lakes and ponds of the Belgrade chain. Its cascade of 150 feet was the highest in the District of Maine, and within its three distinct falls was enough energy for seemingly endless power. Its many mills allowed Waterville to quickly outgrow its parent town of Winslow.

Like the lake of its origin, the natives had named the stream Messalonskee for its abundance of giant muskellunge (pike). The new settlers named it Emerson Stream, honoring Asa Emerson, who built the first dam and sawmill below the foot of Silver Street in the 1790s. By the turn to the 20th century, the name was changed to Messalonskee, once again. The Emerson name is preserved on the Silver Street bridge.

After the Revolution, John McKenzie built a dam near the current site of the bridge on Western Avenue, and private entrepreneurs were assigned privileges (sections) to build more. Within a half-century, dams lined the stream from one end to the other, churning out all manner of goods and materials needed for the building of the towns nearby. Water wheels turned machinery that shaped everything from bedposts to shovel handles, and from wagon hubs to doors and sashes. In all, the stream would come to host 17 sawmills, four gristmills, three plaster mills and two tanneries. Other factories made carpets and friction matches, wove cotton, and carded wool. Close by was a brickyard, a boot shop and another that made carriages and sleighs. A streamside foundry was beginning to make scythes and axes, an enterprise that would soon bring special fame to the entire area.

Pollution concerns had to do with the fish. They were so plentiful that in 1804 town fathers bore down on lax fishermen, declaring "the practice of dressing fish on the shores ... and leaving the filth and inwards of the same to putrify (*sic*), is highly injurious to the health and convenience of the inhabitants, and productive of evil consequences." They set out fines of "not more than three dollars nor less than fifty cents" for violators.

The only streets in town were Main, Silver, Mill (Western Avenue) and what is now the lower part of Front Street. A road south from Main Street along the river to Gold Street became the first business district. A simple lane running down the steep bank from Silver (Sherwin Street) ended at the ferryboat landing, and a second more precarious ferry plied the river just below Ticonic Falls. A dirt road known as Captain Bacon's Road ran along the Kennebec to Kendall's Mills (Fairfield); another went west (North Street) toward Norridgewock. In 1806 a stagecoach line began to run on the east bank of the Kennebec between Hallowell and Norridgewock, delivering the mail twice a week.

The first home on Silver Street (now No. 62) was built in 1814 by Asa Redington for his son, William. Of Federal Period design, the two-story home remained in the family until 1924 when heirs presented it to the Waterville Historical Society for its headquarters. Fashioned of hand pegged hewn timbers and featuring a spiral staircase and wide pumpkin pine floors, it became a treasured Waterville museum.

By 1809, the city's population of 1314 was nearly double that of its cross-river parent, and it was time for a full-fledged volunteer fire department. With a single tub handcart, filled and pumped by hand, volunteers were frequently tested by blazes that began from the unpredictable friction matches, sparks from the mills, and the hearths that warmed the wooden dwellings.

OTHER FLAMES WERE BLAZING FAR AT SEA. Great Britain had been at war with Napoleon's France since 1793, and both sides were raiding American ships, stealing cargo and impressing sailors for their own service. Eager to avoid the fray, in 1807 President Thomas Jefferson declared an embargo on all foreign trade. Maine shippers were outraged, and largely ignored it. With American commerce suffering and unemployment on the rise, three days before leaving office Jefferson modified the embargo to include only France and Britain, but British harassment on the seas continued. On June 18, 1812, the new President, James Madison, declared war.

By the fall of 1814, the British had occupied and burned the Capitol and the White House, and had invaded much of eastern Maine, insisting that all the land east of the Penobscot River was again part of the British Empire. Madison sent federal troops to help, but in the ungovernable lands of downeast Maine, it was difficult to sort friend from foe, and the President withdrew his men to defend more loyal places. Left alone, the small Maine militia was outnumbered, and the leaders of the Commonwealth in Boston refused to send help. There was nothing to do but wait it out, and when the war ended in February 1815, Mainers were still smarting from the Boston snub. The campaign for independent statehood heated up.

The Waterville area suffered little from the War of 1812. Increased domestic sales of the many goods coming from Emerson Stream made up for any loss of sales abroad, and the robust fishery of shad, salmon and alewives had eager markets close at hand. Lt. Col. Elnathan Sherman formed a Waterville regiment of some 70 men, but they were never called to fight, and the Kennebec valley was, in the main, unscathed by war.

The closest the local regiment came to action was an alarm raised one afternoon that an armed force was marching toward town. The "enemy" turned out to be the crew of the Unites States vessel *Adams*, which was burned on the Penobscot River by her commander in order to avoid having her fall into British hands. Local soldiers greeted the retreating crew and invited them back to town where they toasted each other far into the night at a whiskey-making bar on Silver Street.

ALTHOUGH WATERVILLE HAD ALREADY ASSEMBLED most of what was required to make it a proper town, it was still without a church. Some 20 Baptists, whose numbers included nearly every member of the town government, gathered regularly on Sundays, first at the Wood House (future site of the Elmwood Hotel) and then at the Town Meeting House (later site of City Hall), but they had no church of their own. In 1810, when the Bowdoinham Baptists petitioned the General Court of Massachusetts to establish a college in the District of Maine, local leaders quickly raised their hands. They needed a church, and nobody would care if a seminary came with it.

At the time, many thought the place was overripe for preaching. Not all the laborers who came to work along Emerson Stream were Baptists, and whether they were or not, they played as hard as they worked. Although the population was small, there were already ten bars doing a brisk business along the few streets above the river. Many felt that having college students live among them in the center of town would restore the town to some level of civility. In that vein, Dr. N. Whitaker wrote his colleague, Dr. Obadiah Williams, to say he was "agreeably affected by the noble and important design of erecting a Seminary of learning in these parts, where little skill is required to discern a too hasty return to a state of Barbarism."

The First Amendment of the new Constitution figured heavily in the discussions of the Bowdoinham petition. The protection of religious freedom meant the Massachusetts Court had to treat the Baptists as well as they had the Congregationalists (Harvard and Bowdoin), and it also required the petitioners to ask for an institution that would offer both theological *and* literary instruction. The first petition was denied, but with the help of Bath merchant William King, on February 27, 1813, the court established "a Literary Institution for the purpose of educating youth, to be known by the name of The Maine Literary and Theological Institution." The institution that would become Colby was the 33rd college chartered in the United States.

All that was left for the jubilant Bowdoinham Baptists to do was to find a place. The court awarded land in Township No. 3 near Bangor, purchased from the defeated Indians, but it was far too remote. Instead, in 1816 it was agreed that the institution could reside within the counties of Kennebec or Somerset. Waterville was interested; so were Farmington and Bloomfield (Skowhegan). A committee made visits to the three places and chose Waterville. Local merchants pledged $2000 for land and expenses. The town promised $3000 more, but another First Amendment reminder caused the town fathers to renege. Citizens quickly made up the difference, and $1,797.50 was taken from the pot for the purchase of 179 acres between the river and Emerson Stream. In 1818, The Rev. Jeremiah Chaplin brought seven students by sloop from Boston to begin classes in the old Wood House.

The very week he arrived, Chaplin organized the First Baptist Church and became its pastor.[8] In 1826, having raised $4,000 for building costs, the gathering dedicated Waterville's first church, a Federal style meetinghouse on the corner of Park and Elm streets.[9]

First Baptist Church on Elm Street, Waterville's oldest building, dedicated in 1826

Within ten years, three more Protestant churches would be formed. Universalism had come to Waterville as early as 1802, and in 1826 a small congregation was organized and in 1833 was able to dedicate a church building at the intersection of Silver and Elm streets. The Federal-Gothic Revival structure of 60 pews was topped with a two-stage square tower with a clock below the belfry where a town employee rang the bell three times a day. Following a fire in 1894, the church was rebuilt in 1921 and turned to squarely face the intersection.

---

[8] Chaplin's first sermon was entitled: *God's Love to Sinners.*
[9] An 1875 Victorian redesign of the building by Portland architect Francis Fassett today rests on part of the foundation of the original church.

Universalist Church at the corner of Silver and Elm streets, dedicated in 1833

The Methodists weren't far behind. They first gathered in Waterville in 1827, but it wasn't until 1869, with much help from local businessman Reuben Dunn, that they were able to build an elaborate Romanesque church on Pleasant Street. The Congregationalists first came together in the Waterville area 1828 and promptly built a church on Lithgow Street in Winslow. By 1836 they were able to dedicate a meetinghouse on upper Temple Street in Waterville.

Congregational Church on Temple Street, dedicated 1836

The last of the early churches to find homes was the First Unitarian Society, which organized in 1866 and three years later, dedicated a church of Italianate design at the top of Main Street (current site of TD Bank). It closed in 1936 and was later demolished.[10]

INHABITANTS OF MAINE HAD BEEN PLEADING for statehood since the Revolution, and time had only heightened their insistence. They were weary of the political dependence upon faraway Boston where their needs were ignored, and they were angry with a government that sold their public lands and made laws dictating what they could be paid for their lumber. Moreover, they had neither forgotten nor forgiven the failure of the Boston rulers to send help during the War of 1812.

The District of Maine's initial population of 90,000 had soared to 300,000, and the vast majority of them were stoutly anti-slavery. In 1819 Massachusetts finally agreed to cede some 30,000 square miles of its territory and the matter was sent to Congress, then evenly divided between the southern slave states and the free states of the north. Driven by the desire to keep things even, a compromise was struck whereby Maine and the slave-favoring territory of Missouri would be admitted into the Union at the same time. Mainers were at first tepid about the deal, but enthusiasm for being rid of the Commonwealth prevailed, and Maine became the 23rd state on March 15, 1821. Missouri waited until the following August, and the "Missouri Compromise" achieved an edgy peace that held for 40 years.

---

[10] In 1952, the Waterville Unitarians and members of the Church of the Good Shepard in Fairfield joined the Universalists on Elm and Silver streets to form the Universalist Unitarian Church of Waterville.

3

Plenty of Noise

1821-1860

The Second Industrial Revolution was underway, and the Waterville area was in the thick of it. The groan and splash of water wheels continued on, but now were joined by the clang of iron rails and the hiss of steam engines, all noises of a nation working to knit itself together. At the very same time, there were also growing grumbles of discontent and anger that would soon rip the country apart.

Community pride seemed to insist that most new things be named for the town itself. The Maine Legislature was no more than seated in Portland when The Maine Literary and Theological Institution petitioned to be rid of its awkward name and with all logic, became Waterville College (1821).[11] In 1823, the town's first newspaper began as the *Waterville Intelligencer*, a Baptist publication that within five years would become the widely circulated Zion's Advocate. And when Waterville College opened its own feeder school in 1828, it was, of course, named Waterville Academy (later Coburn Classical Institute).

Waterville had an eye toward an even bigger share of the limelight in 1827 when it made a bid to become the capital of Maine. The government had been seated in Portland since its inception, but the port city was simply too remote. The majority agreed to pick a place in the mid-section – Waterville or Augusta. After much debate, Augusta, the county seat for Kennebec since 1799, was chosen. The Legislature had to wait five years for the Charles Bulfinch-designed capitol to be completed before moving in.

---

[11] Five years later, when a leading college investor went bankrupt, local lawyer Timothy Boutelle paid the indebtedness in full and spared the new institution almost certain closure.

The first banking establishment north of Augusta had opened in 1814 under charter of the Commonwealth, and was of course named for Waterville as well. Nathanial Gilman was president of The Waterville Bank, which occupied a small, one-story building south of Ticonic Row (lower Main Street). The same building was used by its successor Ticonic Bank when it opened in 1831. Chartered as a state bank and required to pay its capital in gold and silver, it thrived as a family bank for the entire area. Timothy Boutelle, a third-generation banker, was its president. It became a national bank in 1865 and survived until the Great Depression in 1929.

> Nathanial Gilman settled in Waterville in 1802 and made a fortune as an embargo runner during the War of 1812. An ambitious trader, he moved to New York and extended his dealings in leather, lumber and fish to the West Indies and Africa. In 1858, his son, George Francis, founded the Great Atlantic and Pacific Tea Company (A&P), which from 1915 to 1975 dominated as the largest food retailer in the nation.

Cross-river commerce thrived following the 1824 opening of Ticonic Bridge, a privately-owned wooden structure where tolls were collected. The span washed out in the spring floods of 1826 and was quickly rebuilt. The worst flood occurred in May of 1832 when the spring freshet destroyed several mills and a section of the bridge, which was promptly snagged by grapple hooks in Vassalboro and hauled back upriver for reassembly. The very next month saw the first docking of a paddlewheel steamboat, The *Ticonic*, recently built at Gardiner. Over the next several years it was not unusual to see a half-dozen steamers tied up at the piers at Waterville and Winslow. The price of a passenger ticket to Boston was one dollar.

In the year following the flood, Joseph Fairbanks (of the Fairbanks Scales family) teamed with Arba Nelson to build a dam and foundry at the foot of Silver Street. In 1843, John Webber and Fred Haviland purchased the foundry, and following a fire in 1845, moved it to the bank of the Kennebec, a bit north of Temple Street. It would later flourish as the Waterville Iron Works in the manufacture of machinery and equipment for the coming railroads and giant mills. William Kendall, son and namesake of the Revolutionary War general who named Kendall's Mills (Fairfield), ran a second sawmill on Ticonic Dam, just south of the bridge. The younger Kendall is said to have invented the first circular saw in Maine. Six feet in diameter, the marvel was built of boilerplate with teeth attached by rivets. It could do the work of four reciprocating saws, and people came from miles around, willing to pay 25¢ to watch it work.

Titled "A Plan of Water-Ville," this map was drawn by the Rev. Calvin Gardner, pastor of the Waterville Universalist Church, c. 1840. Several street names and spellings have changed: Norridgewock Street (North Street), Emerson Stream (Messalonskee Stream), College Street (College Avenue), Mill Street (Western Avenue), Church Street (Park Street), and Hasty Street (Center Street). The old cemetery is now Monument Park, and the Kennebeck River has lost its last "k".

FROM 1813 THROUGH THE CENTURY, the Baptist Church and the college were as one in providing leadership for the town. At the center, of course, was the church, and high among the important causes of the Baptists were temperance and abolition.

In the battle for temperance, they were clearly losing. By 1830 the number of establishments serving alcohol in town had vaulted to 34, making an astonishing ratio to the town's population of 2200 and prompting the town council to create the first police department of 14 men who worked as a pair each night, rounding up drunks.[12] In 1834 the temperance advocates persuaded the Town Meeting to deny liquor licenses "to persons to sell wine or other spirituous liquors to be drunk in their shops or stores." The vote did not restrict taverns, but still brought a great storm of protest, and the law was not enforced.

> The issue was revisited in 1840 when the town decided not to grant liquor licenses to anybody, but it didn't deter current vendors, who went on selling just the same. In 1846, temperance advocates packed the Town Meeting and carried a vote to license two persons in the east village "to sell wine, rum, brandy, etc., for medicinal and mechanical purposes only." The conditions of the license were that the profits should not exceed 33.3 percent and that "no liquor should be sold to foreigners or persons not naturalized." When that law was ignored, the next year the town created a committee of 15 men "to furnish evidence to the town agent of all violation of the law" and the selectmen were instructed "to serve writs sued out by the town agent." The sneaking continued and the bars multiplied.

The town's stand against slavery, on the other hand, was more generally agreed upon, and the Baptists, together with the later assemblies of the Universalists and Congregationalists, joined in the preaching of abolition to parishioners who prized patriotism and personal freedom above all else. In the years leading up to the war, the entire Waterville area was fiercely anti-slavery, and many well-remembered abolitionists and patriots of the day had ties to the town.[13]

The parade of activists began in June of 1833 when the Waterville College Literary Fraternity invited the radical William Lloyd Garrison to come and speak. Townspeople joined the student body at the Baptist

---

[12] The church would at least set its own example. In 1836 it resolved theretofore to use only "unfermented fruit" for its communion.

[13] Although there were no slaves in the Commonwealth, including Maine, there were several thousand in other New England states.

Church to hear Garrison advocate for the immediate and complete emancipation of all slaves. It was an extreme view, even among abolitionists.

The previous year Garrison had helped form the New England Anti-Slavery Society, which soon became a national organization. Students were so moved by his address that on the 4th of July they called a mass community meeting and wrote a constitution for what would become the Society's first college chapter in the country. More than 150 students and townspeople signed on and then celebrated with New England rum, carrying on far into the night.

President Chaplin was not amused. "Young men who are obtaining a college education may justly be expected to have a taste somewhat more elevated than that of the common herd of mankind," he railed at chapel the next morning. "After all the pains we have taken to refine and elevate your feelings, some of you have a taste so low and boorish that you can be pleased with noises which resemble the yells of a savage or the braying of an ass." Students said he'd gone too far and demanded that he withdraw his slander of their character, but he would not back down. Students walked out. In late July, Chaplin resigned in disgust. The college did not embrace the formation of the society until 25 years later, in 1858.

There were icons of patriotism all around. In 1831, local Baptists opened a second church at Ten Lots in Fairfield, and in 1833 called as pastor the Rev. Samuel Francis Smith, who supplemented his income by teaching French at the College. As a student at Andover Theological Seminary, Smith had worked as a translator for music publisher Lowell Mason who asked him to write a special song for the coming 4th of July celebration. Smith wrote the words for "America" in one afternoon. Based upon a German or British song, *God Bless Our Native Land*, it was to become a rallying hymn for Union troops in the coming Civil War, and for a full century it rivaled Francis Scott Key's "Star-Spangled Banner" to become the national anthem, a choice not settled by Congress until 1931.

The Rev. Smith's Waterville ministry continued for eight years, during which time he baptized 170 new members. "I found the congregation peculiar," he later recalled, "being made up of three elements: the college, the village people, and the families from farms in different directions for a distance of five miles."

ONE OF THE NATION'S GREATEST HEROES in the fight against slavery was born in nearby Albion. Elijah Parish Lovejoy took his degree from Waterville College in 1826, and after a short stint as principal of China Academy, moved west to enroll in the theological school at Princeton. Upon graduation, he became editor of the Presbyterian Church's new weekly, the *St. Louis Observer*, where his editorials against slavery were not welcomed. In the spring of 1836 a mob came at night and destroyed his press. He fled upriver to Alton, in the free state of Illinois, and became editor of the *Alton Observer*. There, his second press was thrown into the Mississippi River, but he would not be silenced, and his press was wrecked yet again.

On the morning of November 7, 1837, his third press came by steamboat, and the Lovejoy haters were waiting. By evening they had become a drunk and deadly mob, and when he stepped outside, they shot him dead.

Word of the nation's first martyrdom for the free press stunned the nation. President John Quincy Adams later likened the news of Lovejoy's death to that of an earthquake. Ralph Waldo Emerson said "the brave Lovejoy gave his breast to the bullets of a mob for the rights of free speech and opinion, and died when it was better not to live." A month after the killing, John Brown attended a Lovejoy memorial service in Hudson, Ohio. At the end, Brown stood and vowed to dedicate his life to Lovejoy's memory and to the elimination of slavery. Twenty-two years later, nearly to the day, he too became a martyr, hanged for his daring raid at Harper's Ferry.

With the death of Lovejoy, the grieving community was reinvigorated with a zeal for social reform, and the Society of the Adelphi provided ideas. In 1841, the local Society invited Ralph Waldo Emerson to address its annual meeting. Previously, Emerson had used his lectures to refine his famous essays, but his talk on "The Method of Nature" was written especially for the Waterville audience. He spoke of man's need to ignore lost possibilities, and like nature, move on. It did not go well. The *Eastern Mail* said his "epigrammatic style of writing is no more peculiar than his oratory." Emerson got even by calling his audience "cool, silent, and unresponsive."

Yet another local organization bent on casting light on issues of the day was the Waterville Library Association. In 1855, six years before the war, the local Association secretary, Josiah H. Drummond, invited the African-American abolitionist Frederick Douglass to speak as part of a lecture series on pressing current topics. Drummond, an 1846 graduate of the college, was an attorney and had recently abandoned the Democrats to join the anti-slavery Republican Party of Lincoln. Douglass, a former slave, was a brilliant writer and speaker who, on every platform, gave the lie to those who argued that blacks lacked the intellect to be citizens. His speech, given at the often-used Baptist Meetinghouse, was met with broad approval.[14]

That same year, a fugitive slave named Anthony Burns was captured by Boston militia and returned to bondage. Waterville citizens were outraged and called a public meeting to see if the people "will have bells tolled in token of their sympathy." The Meetinghouse bells rang for an hour.

> The area hotbed of patriotism bore fruit through the rest of the century and beyond. James Upham, Waterville College 1860, editor of the magazine *Youth's Companion*, lobbied President Benjamin Harrison and Congress for a national Columbus holiday and commissioned his friend Francis Bellamy to write what became the Pledge of Allegiance for children to read on the first Columbus Day, Oct. 12, 1892. Katherine Lee Bates, who wrote America the Beautiful in 1895, was born in a farmhouse in the Ten Lots section of Fairfield, less than a mile from The Rev. Smith's church.

WHILE FATE HAD PLACED WATERVILLE at the business end of the Kennebec, it took more than fortune to make good its claim as the center of the newest mode of transportation that was slowly making its way into Maine. Oddly enough, the state's rail transportation did not first come from the south, but rather it began in the north woods where the Bangor & Piscataquis Canal & Railroad opened Maine's first line of tracks from Bangor to Old Town in 1836.

In 1845, the state issued a charter to the Androscoggin & Kennebec Railroad, authorizing it to touch the Kennebec at any place between Hallowell and Waterville. Augusta wanted to be that place, and with the advantage of having been the capitol seat for nearly ten years, seemed to

---

[14] Another speaker in the 1885-86 Library series was Oliver Wendell Holmes, Sr., a brilliant poet, writer, and medical reformer, but not an abolitionist.

have the political clout to make it happen. Waterville didn't give up easily, and a special town meeting was called. One of the speakers was James T. Champlin, a teacher of Greek and Latin at the college who would soon become its president. Champlin whipped the crowd into a determined frenzy, and by the time the decision was ready to be made, Waterville men had secured five seats on the board of directors. The meeting was held on July 4, 1848, in the Waterville Town Hall, where it was agreed not only to site the important station in Waterville, but also to connect the town to that portion of Winslow between the Kennebec and Sebasticook with tracks.

On November 27, 1849, the first train to leave Waterville went to Readfield to meet the train to Portland, and on its return was greeted with the roar of cannons and the ringing of bells. There was dancing far into the night. In January, the line was opened to Danville (Auburn) and two years later (1852) was connected with the Penobscot & Kennebec and its line to Bangor, opened with a new wooden railroad bridge over the Kennebec near the falls. In October 1862, the A&K and the P&K would merge, forming the long-enduring Maine Central Railroad.

> Steamboat travel on the Kennebec didn't die easily. Even as late as 1890 the last of the river steamers, *The City of Waterville*, made the trip from its birthplace in Bangor down the Penobscot, around to Bath and up the Kennebec to Augusta. It went aground before making it to her namesake town.

By 1850, the town's population had jumped by a third in ten years, to nearly 4000, and the trains were bringing more people, if only to stay a day or two. The new Elmwood Hotel was the first establishment to be named for the graceful tree that would soon provide the city's nickname, and it bustled with travelers. Because of the trains, that same year Waterville was connected to the rest of the world by telegraph. The cost, ease and frequency of using the rails drew merchants and farmers from miles around, bringing their goods to the rail station for shipment by horse-drawn wagons.

An 1874 view of the Elmwood Hotel, built in 1850, surviving until 1966

Of all the train freight patrons, it is likely that none benefited more than Charles Hathaway, who came from Plymouth, Massachusetts., in 1837 and quickly established himself as a most annoying man, pestering all he met with religious tracts, and making endless trouble for the deacons of his Baptist Church. He saw the South End as ripe for a missionary, and for a dozen years proselytized the strong Catholics there, finally seeing to the establishment of Waterville's Second Baptist Church (Water Street) in their very midst.[15] He married a Winslow woman (with the fortunate name of Temperance) in 1840 and took her back to Plymouth where he worked at his uncle's small shirt factory before returning to Waterville in 1847 to try his hand as a publisher. The *Waterville Union* was the town's eighth newspaper and like the others it quickly failed.[16] In 1853, he rented a home

---

[15] Until 1963, the church bell was alternatively used as an alarm signal for South End fires.
[16] The town's first lasting newspaper was the *Eastern Mail*, established in 1847. It became the *Waterville Mail* in 1863.

25

on Appleton Street and set out once again to make shirts. The fine apparel had a special appeal to the well-to-do men in the cities, and the trains could get them there.

The growing population required further adjustments in preparation for becoming a true city. In 1851 the town authorized the removal of bodies from the tiny burial ground in Monument Park near the Baptist Church to place them in the new Pine Grove Cemetery on Grove Street,[17] and gave $3000 to purchase an old farmhouse on a lane leading west off the road to Sidney. It became a poorhouse, where inhabitants paid their own way by building and repairing town roads.

Both the town and its political sentiments grew through the decade, and when the men went to vote in November of 1860, 504 cast their ballots for Abraham Lincoln, with 186 combined for Stephen Douglas, John Breckinridge, and John Bell. Lincoln became the nation's first Republican president with 40 percent of the national vote, but by that time seven states had already seceded from the Union.

The following February, Vice President-elect Hannibal Hamlin of Bangor came through Waterville by train and stopped at the station long enough to give a short talk to enthusiastic greeters on the platform. He was on his way to Washington and the March inauguration of a President he had never met. The Civil War began the next month.

---

[17] Monument Park was the town's second burial ground. The first was on the high ground south of Western Avenue, bordered on three sides by Emerson Stream.

4

Quick to Answer

1861-1889

On April 15, 1861, three days after the Confederate siege of Fort Sumter, President Abraham Lincoln telegraphed Maine Governor Israel Washburn and asked for 75,000 men to help quell the rebellion. Waterville was quick to answer. Three days later, Joshua Nye, treasurer of the new K&A Railroad, opened a recruiting office on the second floor of the Hanscom Block on the corner of Elm and Main. Waterville College freshman Charles Hendrickson was the first to enlist.

That same day, fellow student Frank Hesseltine stood on the steps of Recitation Hall and exhorted his classmates to join him in answering Lincoln's call. J.H. Plaisted and brothers William and Francis Heath soon opened a second office on Charles Street[18] and within a week some 40 students, fully a third of the student body, joined more than 80 local volunteers to form companies G and H of the 3rd Maine Infantry Volunteers and began conducting drills in town and along the walkways of the suddenly closed college. On their first drill, they marched to Appleton Street, where Charles Hathaway presented each man a fine French flannel shirt.

On June 4, the Waterville troops boarded steamboats to join some 10,000 Maine volunteers, who bivouacked in Augusta and Portland before heading south. With little training, the local companies met their first test in the battle at Bull Run in July.

---

[18] Running west and parallel to Main Street, Charles Street was obliterated during Urban Renewal to make room for the Concourse Shopping Center.

27

When the war ended on May 9, 1865, Maine could count 72,945 volunteers sent into Union service. More than 9,300 died; 9,000 were injured. Waterville sent 525 men; 71 did not return, and as many later died of wounds and war-inflicted illness. Of the 400 alumni and undergraduates of Waterville College, 142 entered service. Twenty-six were killed.[19]

A number of townspeople made exceptional contributions. The Penney family of Waterville sent four sons to fight; three died in battle, the fourth died at home from illness caused by war. The Heath brothers, whose names had led the list in their own recruiting office, were leaders in combat as well. Francis became colonel in command of the 19th Maine. William, lieutenant colonel of the 5th Maine, died at Gaines Mill, Virginia, in 1863. The Waterville Post of the Grand Army of the Republic was named in his honor. Charles Hendrickson, the first college boy to enlist, was captured at the initial battle at Bull Run, and when exchanged from prison, promptly re-enlisted in the Navy.

When Lincoln issued the Emancipation Proclamation in September of 1862, he asked Vice President Hamlin to find someone to organize the black volunteer regiments in Louisiana. Hamlin turned to his friend and fellow Waterville College trustee, Governor Abner Coburn, who nominated Henry Clay Merriam of the famed 20th Maine Regiment, led by the Bowdoin College professor, General Joshua Chamberlain.[20] Merriam, a Houlton native who had enlisted from Waterville College at the start of the war, accepted, and six months before the battle at Gettysburg took charge of the 73rd Corps d'Afrique, the first to plant its colors at Fort Blakeley in the siege of Mobile, Alabama. Merriam was later awarded the Congressional Medal of Honor for his "conspicuous gallantry."

Perhaps the most famous Waterville native to fight in the war was Maj. Abner Small, who joined the Maine 16th Regiment in time to enter the bloody battle of Gettysburg where, among some 400 men he was one of only 38 to survive without being killed, wounded, or captured. In August of 1863 he was captured at the Battle of Globe Tavern in Petersburg, W.V, and sent to the infamous Libby Prison in Virginia. He was exchanged in time to lead a regiment in the last days of the war. His diary contains one of the most poignant and comprehensive accounts of the entire war.

---

[19] Lorenzo Smith '50, a Vermonter caught in the southern draft while teaching in Arkansas, gave his life for the Confederacy.

[20] Four years after the war, in 1869, the Democratic Party nominated as its candidate for governor a Waterville man, Franklin Smith, whom everyone called "General." Smith accepted even though everyone knew he would lose. The Republicans had chosen Joshua Chamberlain.

Waterville provided three general officers for Lincoln's Army, including one who contributed bravely to the emancipation cause. Benjamin Franklin Butler had graduated from the college in 1838, one year behind the martyred Lovejoy,[21] and soon after the war began, Butler initiated a military policy that raised the status of former slaves. While commanding forces at Fortress Monroe in Virginia, Butler was confronted by three fugitive slaves who had been used to construct fortifications in the area. They asked for government protection, and when the owner's agent came to reclaim them, Butler refused to comply. If, as their owners claimed, the slaves were "human property," the general reasoned, he had every right to "confiscate" their property. The practice spread to other commands, and it wasn't long before the Union Army was "confiscating" a large number of grateful slaves, who came to be known as "contrabands."

Butler is often remembered in a negative light: as "Bottled Up Butler," for his military blunders; as "Beast Butler," for his stern treatment of the citizens of New Orleans; as "Spoons Butler," for the alleged corruption of his administration in Atlanta. So too, the memory of Butler's later service as a Massachusetts delegate in the U.S. House of Representatives often stops with his role in connection with the impeachment of President Andrew Johnson. Often forgotten is his consistent advocacy on behalf of black Americans, standing firmly behind the Ku Klux Klan Act of 1871 (designed to prevent a white supremacist resurgence) and the Civil Rights Act of 1871. Later, as Governor of Massachusetts, Butler appointed the first African American judge, George Lewis Ruffin.

All who fought that war were heroes, and not forgotten were the women who stayed at home and did the work of two while caring for the injured and raising money for medical supplies.

In Waterville, efforts to honor those who died began before the war was over. In March 1864, a Waterville Soldier's Monument Association was formed and charged with placing an appropriate memorial in the center of town. In addition, Waterville College commissioned Boston architect Alexander Esty to construct a memorial building on the campus.

---

[21] The other two Waterville generals were Charles Henry Smith, Waterville College '56, and Harris M. Plaisted, '53.

Memorial Hall at commencement on the old campus.

The college building was built of rubble stone quarried a mile west of the campus, and the elegant wood trimmed interior was by a local contractor, J. P. Blunt. Memorial Hall was dedicated at commencement, 1869, in outdoor ceremonies held before the imposing belfry tower, new home to the college's Paul Revere Bell, which had been calling students to classes since 1824. The chairman of the board, former Vice President and now Senator Hannibal Hamlin, presented the keys to President Champlin. It was the first college building in the recovering nation dedicated to honor those who died to save it.

The town's Monument Association chose a work by Irish immigrant Martin Milmore who had recently sculpted a large bronze statue of the common Union soldier for Forest Hills Cemetery in the Boston neighborhood of Jamaica Plain. His "Citizen Soldier" was soon being re-cast for towns and cities across the north. The association raised $2700 and the town gave $1000 more, and in 1876 the impressive statue was placed in the former graveyard near the Baptist Church, thereafter called Monument

Park. Names of the fallen, written on a scroll, were placed beneath the granite base.

The statue was the second example of Milmore's work in Waterville. When Memorial Hall was being built, Charles Hamlin of the college faculty spurred efforts to have Milmore carve a copy of the Lion of Lucerne by the Danish sculptor Bertel Thorvaldsen for installation in the alumni room of the new building. The original lion, sculpted on a hillside at Lucerne, honors Swiss guards killed in 1792 defending Louis XVI in Paris. Milmore's rendition differed from Thorvaldsen's only in size and in the insertion of the U.S. shield for that of France's beneath the dying lion's head.

> There would soon be other monuments commemorating the war dead in nearby towns. West Waterville (Oakland) dedicated its own memorial hall, designed by Boston architect Thomas Silloway, on Church Street in 1873. Winslow installed a granite statue of a soldier sculpted by I. S. Banks of Waterville at the corner of Halifax and Monument streets in 1892. Other local monuments were later erected in Fairfield, North Sidney, Clinton, East Vassalboro, and Anson.

It is often said the war deaths very nearly brought Waterville College to its end, but while the loss of students contributed to the college's plight, the institution was in financial straits even before the war began. Contributions slowed as costs began to rise, and as early as 1833 there was talk of closing the doors for good. The savior who came to rescue the place had little at all to do with the college.

Gardner Colby was born in Bowdoinham. His father, a sea captain, died when Gardner was 14, and his mother brought her four young children to Waterville, where she worked at a potash plant[22] on Silver Street. The family was often given help by the local pastor and also president of the new institute, Jeremiah Chaplin. As a young adult, Gardner worked as a dry goods clerk in Boston before opening his own business, selling women's fashions. Although unschooled, he became a success, expanding his business first to wholesaling, then importing, and finally to manufacturing woolen fabric. It was the wool that made him rich. The federal government bought as much as he could make to outfit the Union Army. In August of 1864, Colby was the guest speaker at the summer commencement in Waterville. Only President Champlin knew of Colby's plan to make a special

---

[22] Potash is fertilizer made from wood ash.

announcement, and the audience erupted when Colby said he would give an endowment of $50,000 if the college would raise $100,000 more. That January the Maine Legislature approved the trustees' petition to re-name the college in his honor.[23]

THE WAR BOTH SLOWED AND SHIFTED the momentum of Maine's economic growth. In the 40 years since statehood the population more than doubled, to 628,000, and the state was at the high point of its national influence.[24] After the war, however, Maine's industries were devastated, and its population plummeted, not only because of those killed and veterans who never returned, but also because the nation's economic focus was moving west. The shipping industry, paralyzed by the war, was further challenged by the efficiency of the expanding railroads, and new technologies and incentives invited investors to move their money from merchants to manufacturers.

Waterville found a way to keep up with the changes. In 1866, the entrepreneur George Phillips bought shore and power rights from some 50 owners on both banks of the Kennebec and formed the Ticonic Water Power & Manufacturing Company, which built the first dam across the entire river. The massive project would one day bring great riches, but at the time it very nearly led to bankruptcy.

Reuben Dunn, a recent graduate of the newly renamed Colby University and a maker of scythes and axes in West Waterville, bailed out the struggling Ticonic company and held on until 1873, when Amos Lockwood, a well-known developer of textile manufacturing, came in to reshape the town forever. As an inducement to manufacturers of cotton and wool, the town had voted in 1859 to exempt all such businesses from property taxes, and at a special town meeting in April of 1875, they agreed to extend the exemption for ten years.[25] Lockwood hastily paid off the debtors and proceeded to build a 33,000-spindle cotton mill below the falls. The first fabric was woven in February 1876, and within nine years the Lockwood Company built a second, even larger mill next door, adding 55,000 spindles.

---

[23] First called Colby University, the name soon proved too ambitious. On June 27, 1898, the institution changed its name for the fourth and final time and became Colby College.

[24] At the time, Maine had six seats in the Congress, more than Texas, California and Florida combined.

[25] In April, 1905, citizens voted 162-140 to tax the Lockwood Company for ten years for an amount not to exceed $15,000 for municipal, county and state taxes. Two subsequent popular votes to rescind the action did not pass.

They were soon consuming 15,000 bales of cotton a year, and by the turn of the century, more than 1,300 of the town's 10,000 souls were engaged in the business of making of cotton cloth. Many of them were girls who came from surrounding farms to make small nest eggs before they were married and denied work at the mills.

In the fall of 1869, a great storm carried away the old wooden toll bridge over the Kennebec, and a proposal was made to replace it with an iron bridge. Opposition came from all directions, especially from the west section of town where a bridge seemed unnecessary and the cost of $26,000 appeared outrageous. It took a special act of the Legislature to get the job done, and the new toll-free bridge was opened on December 1, 1870. Two years later, the center of town got more attention when Maine Central Railroad constructed an elegant train station on College Street, near the Colby campus.[26]

Hard feelings over the bridge dispute never went away, and some town leaders soon sought to get rid of the troublemaking west village. Proponents argued that opposing business interests of the two sections were often in conflict and that the wrangling over new initiatives was costing time and money. On February 26, 1873, a bill creating West Waterville was approved. Ten years later (March 10, 1883) the name was changed to Oakland.[27] That same year the Cascade Woolen Mill, soon a major employer, was incorporated on Emerson Stream.

With the edges of their municipal jurisdiction redefined, Waterville councilors considered constructing a new town hall, but then thought better of it and settled for a $5000 addition to the old Armory on Front Street.[28]

The invigorated economy brought other improvements in rapid fire. The Waterville Free High School opened in 1876, gas street lamps were installed in the center of town in 1874, and four years later lines were strung along the railroad tracks providing telephone connection to Portland. That same year, St. Mark's Episcopal Church opened on Center Street, and two years later the *Waterville Sentinel* began weekly publication.

FROM THE TIME OF ITS FORMATION IN 1862, the Maine Central Railroad had been adding tracks and equipment, and it was time for the

---

[26] The station was expanded in 1906 with the addition of a two-story section south of the original building.

[27] Before it became West Waterville, the greater part of what is now Oakland was called Dearborn.

[28] In a quarter century, a magnificent City Hall and Opera House would be built on the same site.

company to pick a site for the maintenance and repair of its growing stock of cars and locomotives. Most thought Portland would be the place, but Waterville officials quickly made a promise of a 20-year tax exemption, and local citizens sweetened the pot by raising subscriptions for a gift of land near the tracks. It was very near the Colby campus. Waterville won the bid, and in a single stroke became a prominent Maine railroad center.

The railroad, the cotton mill, and other new enterprises brought riches of another kind. The French Canadians of Quebec were no strangers to Maine, and were often among those who came to find temporary work in the growing industries. The first Canadian Frenchman who came to stay was Jean Mathieu, who arrived in 1827 and built a house in the south of town (134 Water Street).[29] The Kennebec Road, a wagon trail from Quebec named the Canada Road (now Rt. 201), was completed in 1830, and thereafter the French people came in increasing numbers to settle mainly in Waterville, Augusta, Lewiston, and Biddeford. Most were from the St. John's Valley and the county of Beauce, composed of the towns of St. Georges, St. Prosper, St. Francois, St. Joseph, Ste. Marie, Ste. Anne and Notre Dame. They came on horseback, on foot and even on rafts, eager to escape their struggling farms to find work along the Kennebec. In Waterville the newcomers took residence on the flat land by the river in the south of town and named it Les Plaines. The Lockwood Company built them "company homes" (Oxford, Kennebec, Green streets), but soon the newcomers made their own complete village, with churches, schools and shops. Peter Bolduc built a dry-goods market here in 1862; Frederic Pooler (once Poulin), a grocery store in 1869.

The new immigrants introduced the area to not only a new language but also a new religion. Supplied by visiting priests, they first worshiped in an unadorned chapel on Grove Street, but with sacrificial gifts, in 1874 they were able to dedicate a true church, St. Francis de Sales, at the corner of Elm and Winter streets. The *Waterville Mail* declared the Gothic brick-buttressed structure with its 120-foot spire "an ornament to the street."

There were, of course, the inevitable tensions of the assimilation of newcomers into a community long held by the descendants of colonists, but it wasn't long before the two cultures found themselves separated from each other mainly at church and in the cemeteries. By 1890, the French Canadian

---

[29] The first Roman Catholic mass held in Waterville was celebrated in this house by The Rev. Moise Fortier of St. Georges, Quebec, on July 16, 1841.

34

immigrants and their Franco-American descendants represented more than 40 percent of the city's population.

THE ENORMOUS AND RAPID GROWTH OF THE TOWN generated a raft of needs for new construction, not the least of which were bricks. With abundant deposits of clay and sand nearby, contractors did not have to look far for the millions of bricks needed to build the local mills and merchant buildings. The earliest brickyard was located west of Water Street, but by the middle of the 19th century another yard was working on the west side of Upper Main Street, just north of Hayden Brook. About 1874, a large new facility was opened below the bridge in Winslow and was soon ferrying thousands of bricks across the river for the new Lockwood mills. In 1885, the firm of Norton & Purington began operating another yard near the Fairfield line on College Street.[30] The Winslow yard was closed in 1893, and Horace Purington's College Avenue operation ran on a 12 horsepower electric engine powered by the Waterville and Fairfield Railway and Light Company that allowed the place to produce nearly four million bricks a year.

The firm of Proctor & Flood had been making bricks on College Avenue since 1892, and about 1900 Proctor joined with Bowie to make more than a million bricks a year after they reopened the old plant on the corner by the bridge in Winslow. The firm also operated a steam-powered woodworking mill for making building components, a business that thrived well into the next century.

With a population of nearly 10,000, the new brick buildings, the busy cotton mill, and trains coming and going in all directions, Waterville was beginning to look very much like a true city. The Maine Legislature had recognized its growing status as early as 1884 when it agreed to amend the charter to make it official. Citizens at first took objection to the administrative and legal obligations and entanglements that accompanied the status of a city, and at town meeting that spring turned down the offer by a vote of 344 to 223. After some tinkering with the proposed new charter, at the March 4, 1887 town meeting, voters finally approved the change, and on January 23, 1888, Waterville became Maine's 17th city.

---

[30] College Street was re-named College Avenue in 1891-92.

At a special town meeting the following January, voters accepted (975-543) an act of the Maine Legislature to amend the city charter and create a system of government that was largely a reflection of the two-chamber federal system with an alderman and two common councilors from each of the city's seven wards. Reuben Foster, a local attorney and 1855 graduate of Waterville College, was elected mayor.[31]

The bi-cameral system of governing was awkward from the beginning. For lack of space, the two bodies met in separate buildings, and the passage of ordinances and resolutions required several meetings a week. Even so, plenty of work got done. Among the first items of business was to fix the location of the trolley track from the Fairfield town line to the lower railroad crossing on College Street. (Until the track was electrified in 1892, the cars were hauled by horses.) The new government also contracted with the Waterville Electric Light and Power Company "to furnish 26 art lights at $90 per light to burn all night and every night in the year" and to appropriate $10,000 to expand the city sewer system.

That spring (1888), the new city faced its first major outbreak of typhoid fever, but it would take more than ten years to figure out the cause. Following an epidemic in 1902-03 during which 40 people died, Dr. James Frederick Hill, a Colby graduate and president of the Board of Trade, concluded that the culprit was the city's crude water system. Contrived of logs with holes bored through the core and fastened with lead collars, the system took its supply from the Messalonskee Stream, which also received sewerage from Waterville and Oakland. Hill insisted the city build an entirely new system. Local attorney and fellow Colby graduate, Harvey Doane Eaton, had already conceived the idea of multi-town service districts, approved by the Maine Legislature in 1899. The Kennebec Water District, established in 1904, was soon emulated throughout the country. It was Eaton who suggested tapping the clean water of nearby China Lake. An 8.5-mile trench was dug, and the long pipe was laid in the winter of 1904-05. The project cost $25,000.

Maine's largest city created a voluntary Portland Board of Trade in 1854 with the stated purpose "to give tone and energy to the various branches of trade," and to "consider all subjects of internal (city) improvements agitated by the community." On April 4, 1889, a little more than a year after

---

[31] Foster served as Speaker of the Maine House of Representatives from 1870-71, and as President of the Maine Senate in 1872. Specializing in real estate, he practiced law from his home on Park Street until his death in 1898.

becoming a true city, Waterville created its own Board with Mayor Nathaniel Meader, a Waterville College graduate and partner in the hardware business with W. B. Arnold, as its first president. Twenty-three years later the Board would become the Waterville Chamber of Commerce.

5

Full Steam Ahead

1889-1910

With the explosion of industries, by the turn of the century American factories were producing nearly a third of all the world's goods. Nowhere were the stars more perfectly aligned than in central Maine, where the woodlands, rivers, and rails came together to create an economic bonanza unequaled, before or since.

In 1901, the Board of Trade surveyed the heady scene and called for a grand party the following June to mark the centennial of Waterville's incorporation as a town. A volunteer committee of one hundred was charged with arrangements, including completion of the Waterville City Hall and Opera House in time for the festivities.

There would have been reason enough to celebrate if the city could boast only of the Lockwood mills, which were now providing work for 1200 cotton workers, but new industry was popping up almost every year, in Waterville and in the neighboring towns.

The paper maker Hollingsworth & Whitney owned more than a half-million acres of timberland in the state and already had a mill downriver in Gardiner when it began looking for a place to expand. Madison was chosen, but the deal fell through, and the owners settled on Winslow, where the Lockwood Company's upper power dam was still unused. The property across the river from the Colby campus was purchased, and by 1892 the H&W mills were producing 30 tons of ground pulpwood a day at the Taconnet mill and 20 tons of paper on two machines at the mill named

Mohegan. With the addition of the Algonquin sulfite mill[32] in 1899, the enterprise was able to finish 160 tons of paper a day.

Upriver in Fairfield, a tinkerer named Martin L. Keyes was experimenting with the process of making paper plates from ground spruce fiber. After suing a competitor who stole his invention, Keyes obtained patent rights in 1903, and owners of the Lawrence, Page & Newhall pulp mill in Shawmut agreed to let him rent part of their new mill to make plates. Keyes had the market cornered for a short time before new industry challengers cut prices and began to drive him out. In 1905, when his Shawmut hosts sold the mill, Keyes was forced to close.

COURTESY OF HUHTAMAKI, INC.

Martin Keyes's first paper plate machine, installed at the Shawmut mill, 1903.

Martin L. Keyes

The following year, the San Francisco earthquake and fire suddenly made paper plates popular as relief agencies began using them to feed victims, and Martin Keyes seized the moment. In 1907, with encouragement from the Board of Trade, he purchased land where upper College Avenue enters Fairfield and built his own plant along the tracks. Construction began in the spring of 1908, and by fall he was making a million paper plates a day. Through twists and turns and ownership changes, Keyes Fibre would continue as Central Maine's all-time most enduring manufacturer.

The year Keyes got his patents, his neighbor across the street claimed rights for the most significant and famous invention ever to come from the Waterville area. Alvin Orlando Lombard was a 45-year-old blacksmith when

---

[32] Sulfite is used in "digesters" to produce pure wood pulp.

he registered his patents for the Lombard Log Hauler, which, for its revolutionary impact, is often compared to Eli Whitney's cotton gin, invented a century before. Powered by steam, Lombard's tractor moved like a caterpillar on a continuous track and crawled easily over snow and stumpage, greatly reducing the time and energy required to haul logs on sleds drawn by horses or oxen. The method of moving pulpwood out of the woods was changed forever.

Alvin Lombard with an early log hauler, College Avenue factory, c. 1910

Lombard, who had made his own water-powered wood splitter when he was in his teens, went on to secure patents for several other creations, including a log de-barker and a governor to control the speed of water wheels.[33]

Lombard built 83 steam log haulers on College Avenue before 1917, and when the machines were converted to gasoline, the rigs continued to be used in the woods until the 1930s. Soon after its invention, the Lombard continuous track was adapted for use on military tanks, farm tractors, and heavy construction equipment. With skis in front, today's snowmobiles are miniature adaptations of Lombard's original tractor.

The industrial explosion in Waterville was far from over. In 1899, local citizens led by Thomas Sampson and other members of the Board of Trade, pledged $50,000 in capital stock to build the Riverview Worsted Mills close by the busy Iron Works at Ticonic Falls. The factory was up and running the next year, employing 300 workers using 80 modern looms to make wool

---

[33] Lombard later claimed he was more proud of the dam governor than he was of the log hauler.

for fine men's wear.[34] When plant ownership changed in 1909, the factory was renamed Wyandotte Worsted.

Older establishments flourished. The Noyes Stove Company foundry, in business since 1867, had moved on from forging iron kettles to making quality iron stoves that were prized throughout New England; Hathaway was using 150 ironers and stitchers, sending orders around the country by train; the Whittemore Furniture Company made Morris chairs; and the Sawyer Publishing Company, rebuilt after a devastating fire, employed 100 women to print mail order newspapers and magazines.

Workers pose outside the Hathaway Shirt Factory on Appleton Street, c. 1910

In neighboring Oakland, factories along the Messalonskee added to the industrial output. As many as eight edge-tool companies located between the head of the lake and the road to Waterville (KMD) gave the town the reputation as the axe and scythe capital of the world. Most notable was The Dunn Edge Tool Company (later North Wayne and then King Axe), which, by 1900, led the world in producing 180,000 scythes and nearly as many axes every year. The Cascade Woolen Mill, opened in 1882, together with

---

[34] At the time, it was one of 76 woolen mills in Maine.

the Oakland Woolen Company (1902), enjoyed national reputations for the manufacture of custom woolens and blends for outerwear and upholstery.[35]

One of the most successful Oakland industries was the Diamond Match division of the Berst-Foster Dixfield Company. Maker of the country's first non-poisonous matches, Diamond Match had been doing business since 1881. The Oakland plant began as Forster Manufacturing in 1913, making toothpicks and clothespins in a large factory near the railroad tracks (Pleasant Street) from 1913 into the early 1980s. At its peak, it employed 500. Locally, it was affectionately called "The Toothpick."

All the while, area demands for shipping the myriad goods from the factories led to an array of improved transportation and utility services. The Maine Central Railroad employed 1,000 men shipping 52,000 tons of goods a year and receiving 90,000 more, including 31,000 tons of coal for its own locomotives, which could be turned in a giant roundhouse with 35 stalls. The associated railroad shops had 250 hands at work repairing a growing stock of engines and cars for the entire company.

The diversified Waterville & Fairfield Railway and Light Company was providing electricity to factories and homes, and operating trolleys that carried 517,000 passengers a year between the two towns. The city soon found itself at the center of the new Wiscasset, Waterville & Farmington narrow-gauge railway that swept through a dozen tiny towns, carrying farmers' freight and passengers. Within the city itself, electric trolleys served the distant neighborhoods, including one that ran every half hour up and down Water Street.

To accommodate the ever-increasing number of overnight rail passengers, in 1879-80 the entrepreneur Reuben Dunn built the Lockwood House in a large brick block at the foot of Main Street.[36] Over the next century the hotel-restaurant would become the Bay View, and later the Crescent.

It was a time when the marvel of electricity both mystified and frightened the uninitiated, but even so, almost everyone was eager to light up the nights. Main Street had its first streetlamps in 1873, and one of the

---

[35] The Oakland Woolen Company burned in 1933. When the river factories began to close, The Cascade Woolen Mill found a special niche in the complex textile industry and continued on into the 1990s. The five-story wooden building was destroyed by arson in 2010.

[36] Dunn's wife, Martha Baker Dunn, was an author of some note. Her work was frequently published in leading national literary magazines, and her books, including *Memory Street* and *Lias's Wife*, were well received.

first three buildings with electric lights inside was the W. B. Arnold Company, a hardware store that would serve the city for 100 years.

Walter Wyman, a native of West Waterville-cum-Oakland was 25-years-old in 1899 when he quit his job with the Waterville & Fairfield Railway and Electric Company and sought backing from Waterville attorney Harvey Eaton to purchase a hydroelectric generator that was already serving some 100 customers in his home town.[37] Together, they formed the Messalonskee Electric Company. Within ten years they acquired and built several new dams, including one at Rice's Rips on the Messalonskee, and renamed their rapidly expanding company Central Maine Power.

Even with many admired captains of industry from whom to choose heroes, there is little doubt that for a number of years (1882-1909), the most revered creature in all of Central Maine was a world champion trotting horse named Nelson. Owned by Union Army veteran Charles "Hod" Nelson, the magnificent bay horse was raised at Sunnyside, a 540-acre breeding farm that sprawled on the hillside south of Oakland Road (Kennedy Memorial Drive), near the present site of the street named in his honor. In 1884 Nelson won the half-mile stake race for two-year-olds at the state fair in Lewiston, and the next year took the cup as the fastest stallion of any age. He won the New England stakes in 1887, and in 1889 some 30,000 watched as he won every heat at a meet in Boston. On October 21, 1890, Nelson carried the high wheel sulky around a half-mile track in Cambridge City, Indiana, in the astonishing time of 2.10 ¾, a world record that stood for 13 years. In 1891, Nelson and three grooms traveled in a private train car from Waterville to the American Horse Show in Chicago, stopping for throngs of admirers at Hallowell, Gardiner, Brunswick, and Portland along the way. He last appeared in public on "Nelson Day" at the Central Maine Fair in 1917.

---

[37] West Waterville town fathers had contracted with the new power company for street lighting on condition that they would not pay for power on moonlit nights.

Horse Nelson at the Central Maine Fairgrounds, c. 1895

At the urging of Alexander Graham Bell's father-in-law, Gardiner Hubbard, The New England Telephone & Telegraph Company had formed in 1878. Two years later the phone company had offices in Waterville, and by the time of the city's centennial, 439 proud local customers were connected.

With all the traffic to and from the mills on both sides of the river, in 1899 the Ticonic Company commissioned Proctor & Bowie to make piers for a pedestrian bridge at the foot of Temple Street. The 6-by-576-foot span was built on the ice in the winter of 1900-01 and many locals watched doubtfully during the spring thaw, fully expecting it to be washed away. Their predictions were off by a year. The bridge collapsed and went down river in the awful spring floods in 1902 and was rebuilt a year later at double the original price. To recover the costs, the charter of the bridge company allowed its owners to charge a two-cent toll, a fee that gave the bridge its name. The famous structure has been restored and maintained and now stands as the longest surviving wire suspension pedestrian bridge in the nation.

Things were going so well that in early January 1900, the newspapers announced, "Waterville Board of Trade members are talking of giving a banquet by which they may celebrate the prosperity of the city during the past year." The story explained that the city had not had such a prosperous time for a decade, and that the outlook for the next year was even better.

Days later, the *Kennebec Journal* took a jab at Lewiston when it noted that city's mills were able to run only 35 hours the prior week while the Lockwood Mill, along the "queen of Maine rivers," was able to run "full time with ten of the (dam) gates closed."

The Board of Trade banquet was held January 30 in the newly-decorated dining hall of the Elmwood Hotel, recently renovated and expanded to 150 rooms. The new Jefferson Hotel on College Avenue (1901) was filled to capacity.

THE BANQUET WAS BUT A PRELUDE. Eighteen months later the entire city turned out for three days (June 22-24, 1902) of wild celebration of the City Centennial. Bracing for big crowds, the planning committee widely distributed printed schedules of the Maine Central and the Wiscasset, Waterville & Farmington railroads, noting that the Waterville-Fairfield trolley would have "cars in each direction every fifteen minutes, beginning on the hour."

The gala began quietly on Sunday with simultaneous special services at all seven churches – Baptist, Catholic, Congregational, Episcopal, Methodist, Unitarian, and Universalist. Tuesday's five-division parade snaked from Elm Street to Center, then Pleasant, to Western Avenue, on Elm to Silver, then Gold, Summer, and Sherwin, back on Silver to Main, then back to Elm and Monument Park. Merchants along Main Street draped their stores with red-white-and-blue bunting that all but covered their windows. R. B. Hall's Military Band led military units, followed by the Knights of Pythias Second Regiment Band and floats with sponsors ranging from the St. John the Baptist Society to the local Bricklayers Union. In the parade, civic and centennial-event dignitaries rode in carriages followed by Hod Nelson and a cadre of trotting horses. Trailing the half-mile procession were the Waterville Bicycle Club and the Waterville Fire Department, hauling their aged tanker, "The Bloomer."

Centennial Parade, looking south down Main Street

In the afternoon, firemen held demonstrations near City Hall. Hose reel races and coupling contests were completed in time for the throngs to walk up College Avenue, where the Colby baseball team squared off against "the Watervilles." Hall's Band performed in Monument Park that night.

Born in Bowdoinham in 1858, Robert Browne Hall had become an internationally known coronet player and composer by the turn of the century. John Philip Sousa played one of his marches at the opening of a concert at the Paris Exhibition in 1900, the year Hall left his post as director of the Tenth Regiment Band of Albany, New York, to become the musical director of the Waterville Centennial. In his lifetime, Hall wrote more than 100 marches; several of the most familiar ones were created during the time he spent in Waterville. He died in Portland in 1907, and the Waterville Military Band, renamed for R.B. Hall after World War I, joined the bands that marched in his funeral procession. A long-gone R.B. Hall Memorial Bandstand was dedicated in Monument Park in 1936.

Of the many features there were to show off, citizens were most proud of the new colonial-revival city hall and its beaux-arts style opera house. Opened in time for the June celebrations, the three-story structure designed by Massachusetts architect George Gilman Adams was built in front of the armory, facing the common. It was and remains one of only a handful of the nation's municipal buildings to include a theatre, and while there was

46

much discussion and debate over timing and costs, there is no recorded objection to the notion of having the government join in supporting the arts.

New City Hall and Opera House, June 1902

The Committee of One Hundred had nothing whatever to do with the final splash of the lengthy 1902 celebrations. President Teddy Roosevelt, just weeks shy of his 43rd birthday, toured Maine by train in the late summer, and on August 8 stopped at the Waterville station to greet crowds of locals joined by Colby students who streamed across the tracks to see him. The Rough Rider was frequently interrupted by the whoops and cheers of a crowd that jammed the platform, some even perching on the cross arms of telephone poles for better views.

The 44-year-old president was being hailed everywhere for his platform of ridding the country of corrupt urban politics and for reining in corporate power, and he was using his "bully pulpit" to spread Progressivism across the country. In Waterville, he spoke against "having too many laws," and said, "each man's salvation rests in his own hands." He went on to exhort his audience: "Help the man who stumbles. Help a brother who slips. Set him up on his feet. Try to start him along the right road. But if he lies down, make up your mind you cannot carry him. If he won't try to walk himself he is not worth carrying."

In his call for self-reliance, Roosevelt took special aim at mothers when he scolded parents for spoiling their children. He might not have bothered, as surviving pictures show lots of men in bowler hats, but hardly any women at all. It was a Friday, and hundreds of local women were on shifts as seamstresses, ironers, and weavers at nearby factories and mills, most of them working in dismal conditions and always for the lowest wages. They might not have gone to see the president anyway, as politics was a man's world, and women did not yet have the right to vote.

WHS & REDINGTON

President Theodore Roosevelt visits Waterville, August 8, 1902

FACTORIES AND OTHER WORK OPPORTUNITIES GREW RAPIDLY, and the face of America changed almost overnight as some 16 million immigrants arrived in the first decade of the new century. In Waterville, the 1910 census showed that a whopping 23 percent of population was foreign born, a record that would not be beaten, but a number that would only grow in the counting of their descendants in years to come. Most of the newcomers were French Catholics from lower Quebec who first came to the area after the Lockwood Mills opened in 1873, and now began to arrive in droves.

Among the newcomers was the family of Henry Giguere, who came from Canada with his wife and their 20 children in 1921 and settled on a farm in the north end of the city. The astonishing size of the family prompted the *Sentinel* to publish a photograph of them all, with a flattering story topped by a headline that read:

Mr. and Mrs. Henry Giguere With Family of 22 Recently Arrived From Canada and Are Adding to Worries of School Department

The French were not the only ones drawn to Waterville by the opportunities in the mills and at the expanded railroad shops. Along with them now came dozens of newcomers from the Middle East, people from the Lebanon region of Greater Syria that would later gain independence (1943) and become a country of its own.

Like the French, the Syrians were escaping both tyranny and poverty. As Maronite Catholics, they had long been in conflict with the Muslim Druze and more recently, defeated and repressed by the Ottomans who forcibly conscripted them into the Turkish army. Life became more difficult when the Suez Canal opened in 1869, and traders began to pass them by. A national famine followed, and at the turn of the century, more than 100,000 – fully a quarter of the entire population – left Syria for the industrial cities of Europe and the United States. Most were traders, but some were trained as silk workers in their homeland and were already adept at weaving cloth, making them especially welcome at the new Wyandotte. Others found work in the railroad shops.

The new people made their homes in the same place as the first settlers, on a narrow strip of land along the river that the French had named Tête de Chutes – Head of Falls. Like their French counterparts, it was customary for Syrian men to arrive first and save money to bring their families.

At the same time, another population arrived to further enrich the city's growing diversity. At the turn of the century, a small number of East European Jews, mostly from Russia, settled in the North End. Many were merchants, including William Levine, an itinerant peddler who came to Waterville in 1890 and with his wife Sara, opened a dry goods store at the corner of Maple and Ticonic streets. He later moved to 94 Main Street, and in 1904 purchased the entire block at the south end of Main Street and opened a clothing store that passed on to his sons and nephew and lasted nearly 100 years.

A Jewish synagogue, Beth Israel, was chartered in 1902 but there was no place for worship, and High Holy Day services were held at the Ticonic Street Fire Station. Eventually, a piece of land with an old barn was purchased on Kelsey Street (No. 21), and a new synagogue was opened in 1905. Twenty years later, William Levine paid off the mortgage.

The Kelsey Street synagogue of the Beth Israel congregation, 1905-1958

There were new immigrants from many other nations as well. Many were Irish,[38] but there were also newcomers from other countries, including Armenia, Scotland, Italy and Poland. Commenting on the city's embracing of diversity, Maine's U.S. Senator Charles F. Johnson[39] grandly wrote in 1910:

"There are no distinctions because of wealth, so there are none of race or religion. By her industries, Waterville has attracted laborers of nearly every nationality ... who have shown their thrift and industry by building comfortable homes, and have been the source from which labor has been largely drawn ... Race prejudice does not exist and all are afforded like advantages and opportunities and accorded the respect due to their lives and work."

---

[38] At the turn of the century, the present Ticonic Street was named Irish Lane on the city maps, and was variously called Paddy Lane and St. Patrick's Street.

[39] A prominent Waterville attorney who lived on Silver Street, Johnson was defeated as the Democratic candidate for governor in 1892, served as Waterville's mayor in 1893, and lost the gubernatorial race again in 1894. He served in the U.S. Senate from 1911 until 1917, when he was appointed to the First Circuit of the U.S. Court of Appeals by President Woodrow Wilson.

6

Most Beautiful City

-1912

B y the century's second decade, Waterville was being proclaimed "the prettiest city in all of the state." It was also Maine's fastest growing city, having seen its population leap 20 percent in ten years to stand at 11,458.

Beauty was all around. Most of the public buildings, handsomely designed and built of stone or brick, were new. Grand three-story homes

WHS & REDINGTON

Silver Street looking north, c. 1890. Noyes residence, on right

51

with elaborate fretwork and carriage houses loomed on generous lots along the broadest streets, including Silver and Gold, named to reflect the elevated status of the owners. Stately elm trees, carefully planted a half-century before, now formed leafy arches over the downtown streets, giving the city a nickname that would endure even after the trees were gone.

The surge of new industry had brought a robust merchant trade, evidenced along the mostly-paved Main Street, where nearly every block was filled with stores serving not only the growing local population but also some 20,000 others from the neighboring small towns of Fairfield, Winslow, Burnham, Clinton, Benton, Albion, China, Vassalboro, Sidney, Belgrade, Oakland, Smithfield, and Rome. The crush of business brought stiff competition, and to catch the profits of advertising, beginning in 1904 the weekly *Sentinel* became the *Morning Sentinel* and published six days a week.[40]

Main Street Waterville at the Turn of the Century

WHS & REDINGTON

Main Street, turn of the century, looking north

---

[40] The old *Waterville Mail*, an evening paper, could not compete and ceased operation June 18, 1907. The *Sentinel* promptly published an added evening edition beginning June 22, but discontinued it on August 3.

Names of many of the city's establishments would ring out through many years: Joseph's Market, Poulin Furniture, L. T. Boothby & Son Insurance; W. B. Arnold Hardware, Berube Bakery, Atherton Furniture, Charles E. Morse Marble and Granite, as well as the clothing stores, Levine's, F. H. Brown, and H. R. Dunham. Now almost forgotten was the Kennebec Boat & Canoe Company on the east corner of Chaplin and Ticonic streets, which dominated sales to growing numbers of customers along the nearby lakes and rivers. Other local shops were curious and new, including the city's first automobile businesses. From the top of Main Street (south of the current fire station) The Waterville Motor Company sold Reo "commercial cars" for $750, and the Central Maine Automobile Garage on Charles Street touted itself as "the place to get oiled up and repaired," and provided service for owners of both the occasional automobile and Yale motorcycles.

The most intriguing auto of the time was the Stanley Steamer, invented by identical twins Francis and Freelan Stanley, born and raised not far up the river in Kingfield. The pair made their first steam-powered automobile in 1897, and after a much-publicized trip to the top of Mount Washington in August of 1899, began selling more than 200 cars a year out of their plant in Newton, Massachusetts. At the time, they were the largest U.S. automaker, a crown soon lost with the introduction of the internal combustion engine. In 1910, the nearest local agent was Stanley's Garage and Sales Room, located at the summer hotel in Belgrade Lakes, where there were often customers with money enough to buy them. (The Steamer could cost as much as $3,900, as compared to the Ford Motel T, at under $500.)

Waterville was beginning to make a name for itself as a hotbed of politics, as well. Overwhelmingly Democratic in a state long ruled by Republicans, the city enjoyed the rough-and-tumble of the partisan political process, and the fights ranged from the chambers of its bi-cameral local government all the way to Augusta. In 1906, the Democratic Party unanimously nominated a Waterville man, Cyrus W. Davis, as its candidate for Governor. Davis, a successful dry-goods merchant turned electric-railroad investor and state legislator, narrowly lost to Republican William T. Cobb in the fall, although he swept every major city including his home town (1250 to 750).

FROM ITS INCEPTION, THE BOARD OF TRADE had put its stamp on nearly every issue that affected trade, at home and abroad. Following the sinking of the battleship *Maine* in February 1898, the Board passed a resolution pledging support for President William McKinley "for maintaining the honor of the United States and the deliverance of Cuba."[41] At the same time the Board gave its support to the construction a $100,000 system of city sewers. During the Panic of 1896, when Colby found it hard to make ends meet, President Nathaniel Butler, Jr., went to the Board to plea for even closer ties to the city. The furniture seller, Mayor and Chairman of the Board, stood in support, "not for the intellectual and social aspects of the college, but for its financial benefit to the city." The college soon built Chemical Hall, outfitted with the finest scientific equipment of the day.

Although the Board was in favor of having a public library, it was the women of the town who saw it done. The thirst for the enlightenment from books was recognized even before Waterville separated from Winslow, when in 1801 citizens raised the then remarkable sum of $146 to purchase 117 volumes and began the Waterville Social Library.

The Waterville Public Library, corner of Elm and Appleton streets. A postcard from 1905, the year of its dedication.

Over the next 70 years, the Social Library was supplemented with "circulating libraries" at local bookshops until the Waterville Library Association was re-formed in 1873, and space was made at the Ticonic Bank (top of Main Street, east side) for the lending of books. Users paid an annual fee of $3, but there weren't enough subscribers, and both the tiny library and the Association languished until the end of the century when the

---

[41] Waterville sent 73 National Guardsmen to fight in the Spanish-American War, but they weren't needed at the front and were soon sent home. Several later saw combat in the Philippines.

collection of 1500 books was relinquished to the Waterville Women's Association.

In the late winter of 1896, Lillian Hallock Campbell took up the cause and made personal calls upon more than 50 women in town, asking for their help in re-forming the Association and building a free public library. At a meeting at the Ware Parlors[42] on Park Street, more than 20 women were elected to various committees, and their work soon led to a mass meeting at City Hall, where the Waterville Free Library Association was organized with Mayor Edmund F. Webb as president. Attorney Harvey D. Eaton offered space at his offices at 74 Main Street (now Holy Cannoli), and a public appeal was made for contributions of money and books. In the spring, the City pitched in $500 and citizens gave $600 more, along with 1,250 books, which were shelved in a room in the Plaisted Block (now Framemakers and Children's Book Cellar) on Main Street. The book lending began August 22, 1896.

In December 1901, school superintendent Elwood Wyman, eager to improve the reading resources for local children, wrote rags-to-riches steel magnate Andrew Carnegie to ask for help in building a free-standing public library.[43] Joining his appeal was Annie Grassie Pepper, wife of Colby's ninth president, George Dana Boardman Pepper, a dedicated community worker and a founder of the Waterville Free Library Association.[44] Carnegie agreed to give $20,000 if the city would provide a site and at least the promise of $2,000 a year in operating costs, in perpetuity. A place was chosen across Elm Street from the Baptist Church, and with the addition of $10,000 in public and private funds, the new Romanesque building, complete with fancy stonework and a Norman tower, was dedicated in 1905.

The library became a valuable resource for the entire community. No one profited more than the city's students, and there were plenty of them. Anchored by Colby, the city was already recognized as one of the most prominent educational cities in Maine, a distinction it would never lose.

---

[42] Located on the northwest corner of Monument Park at 12 Park Street, the Ware Parlors were built in 1889 by Harriet P. Ware and given to the Unitarian Church as a vestry with public meeting spaces. The building was demolished in 1973.
[43] Carnegie gave money for 2509 libraries across the United States between 1883-1929. Eighteen are in Maine.
[44] Her portrait by her son and noted early modernist American artist Charles Hovey Pepper, is on permanent display at the library.

While the city was gaining a reputation for its academic offerings, it was also enjoying national attention for producing athletic prowess. In 1905 Connie Mack came to watch John Wesley Coombs pitch for Colby on the diamond near the railroad tracks and signed him on the spot with the Philadelphia Athletics. They called him "Colby Jack," and in his first season with the Athletics he pitched the longest game on record, a 24-inning, 4-1 victory over the Boston Red Sox. He won 31 games in 1910, including 13 shutouts, and three World Series games in five days against the Chicago Cubs. In 1914 he was traded to the Brooklyn Robins (Dodgers) and two years later hurled the only Brooklyn win in a five-game World Series against Babe Ruth and the Sox.

Catholic teachings and the need for many hands to do the work at home made for large families of both French and Syrian people, and with growing numbers of second-generation immigrants and the overall growth of population in every sector, the demand for educational services increased each year. In 1910 the city had 3487 school age children, and while only 1630 were enrolled, the city needed eight schools and 55 teachers to keep up. A new Gothic style high school on Gilman Street, opened in 1912, cost $75,000, and was fed by four primary schools and three grammar schools, including one on Myrtle Street, said to be the finest schoolhouse in town.[45] The city education budget skyrocketed to $45,000 a year.

At the same time, the city's large Catholic population brought a growing desire for parochial teaching, first addressed in 1888 by the beloved priest, Narcisse Charland, who opened a school for boys behind St. Francis de Sales Church on Elm Street. That same year Fr. Charland brought six sisters of the Ursuline Order of nuns from Three Rivers in Quebec to found a convent named Mount Merici on Western Avenue and create a boarding school for girls. By 1912, St. Francis School was flourishing, and with 19 sisters in residence, the Ursulines were educating 500 boarders and day students at Mount Merici.[46] In 1895 Fr. Charland built a three-story wooden rectory and parish hall on Elm Street, immediately south of the church.

---

[45] North Grammar School had been built in 1888 on the southeast corner of North and Pleasant streets. South Grammar School, built on Gold Street in 1905, burned a year later and was quickly rebuilt.
[46] The Ursuline sisters eventually had 17 academies in Maine. Mount Merici is the only one remaining.

At the turn of the century, the Church of St. Francis spawned two additional Catholic parishes. French was spoken at the mother parish, and English-speaking worshipers, many of them Irish, were eager to have a church of their own. The Parish of The Sacred Heart of Jesus was created in 1906, and while parishioners waited for a building of their own, St. Francis offered one English mass among the four held each Sunday. In 1908, Sacred Heart parishioners moved into the basement of their unfinished church at the corner of Pleasant and Gilman streets, where they remained until the handsome Romanesque building was finally completed in 1930. A second new church arose from the desire of worshipers who lived on The Plains in the south of town to have a church closer to home. In 1910 they formed Notre Dame du Perpétuel Secours (Our Lady of Perpetual Help). A year later, a new two-story building off Water Street was dedicated with classrooms on the first floor and a sanctuary above. Nuns from the order of Ursuline de Jésus were called from France to teach, and a convent was established at a purchased home at 2 Gold Street. An existing home nearby (99 Water) became the rectory. The new parish building was destroyed by fire in the spring of 1913, and was rebuilt before the winter. The Ursuline de Jesus sisters returned to France in 1920, and were replaced by the Ursuline de Merici. The residence at 112 Silver Street became a convent.

Coburn Classical Institute, in operation at the edge of Monument Park for more than 80 years, had a well-deserved reputation throughout New England for excellence in education. Four governors and four of the sitting eight justices of the Maine Supreme Court had been educated at the school, including the Hon. W. Scott Libby of Lewiston, whose gift of a 12-acre tract of land (west side of Messalonskee Stream, near the present high school) made possible what was thought to be the finest outdoor athletic complex in the state. The school's elaborate main building was "one of the handsomest and most commanding structures in Waterville," and nearby, alongside the residences on Elm Street, were Coburn Cottage, a dormitory for girls, and Hanson Hall, for boys.

From the beginning, the city that flourished with commerce and industry had need of skilled men and women who could manage the offices and keep the books, and the area was over-ripe for a business school. The Bliss Business College and Waterville Business College preceded the Keist Business College, which in 1896 was sold to W.H. Morgan of New York who proceeded to "put it on the highest standard of efficiency with all modern office devices, including billing machines, mimeographs, (and) letter presses." Morgan Business College soon outgrew its tiny quarters in the

Pulsifer Block and in 1907 moved into the new Edith Block[47] next to the Savings Bank on the east side of Main Street where F. W. Woolworth and F. H. Brown occupied the street level and the college used the two floors above. In 1911 the school was purchased by John L. Thomas, Sr. of Peterborough, N.H., a railroad executive soon to become a gifted teacher. The college flourished on the fine performance reputation of its students, and it wasn't long before most every enterprise in town insisted on staffing its offices with Morgan-Thomas graduates.

> The many educational institutions and the availability of the grand Opera House heightened the city's appetite for culture and enlightenment. On May 1, 1907, William Jennings Bryan lectured at the Opera House under the auspices of a lecture course at Colby. He was entertained at the Gerald Hotel in Fairfield and by the Elks Club of Waterville. The subject of the address by the 1896 presidential candidate defeated by William McKinley was "The Value of an Ideal."

By 1910, the Waterville Board of Trade had mushroomed to nearly 150 members, and the bylaws were amended to create a smaller Board of Managers to handle the day-to-day matters of an ever-expanding agenda that now included promotions to attract tourists. High on the list was the Central Maine Fair, a four-day fall event on expansive grounds west of the First Rangeway.[48] The fair began in 1904, and by 1908 was attracting more than 25,000 spectators a day before attendance began to drop, largely because of public disdain for its indecent "carnie" shows. A new Fair Association, backed by the Board of Trade, took over in 1911 and promised "the most fastidious" of shows, that people could attend "without fear of being shocked."

---

[47] Since William T. Haines already had a block of his own at the head of Main Street on the opposite side, the new building was named in honor of his wife, Edith.
[48] Near the Chase Avenue site of the second Seton Hospital.

Central Maine Fairgrounds, with tent sign advertising "The $10,000 French Beauty Show, c. 1905

The first year under new ownership, spectators were certainly shocked when they witnessed bi-plane pilot George Schmitt strike a telephone line, spin out of control, and then walk away after the crash. Three years earlier, 25,000 watched a Strobel airship pilot plunge to his death when his dirigible balloon caught fire 500 feet in the air.

Most fair attendees came by trolley, including the new Waterville & Oakland Railway, which had an amusement park (Cascade) at the Oakland end that included an outdoor theater providing all sorts of entertainment, from concerts to vaudeville acts, from April to October.

The expanding network of trolleys and trains opened yet another opportunity for tourism in Central Maine. The nearby Belgrade Lakes were replete with large native fish – notably trout and salmon – and sportsmen and their families were arriving by the trainload from Portland, Boston, New York, Philadelphia, and beyond, eager to escape into the "wilderness" for a week or two, or even an entire summer. Guests were greeted at the rail depots in Belgrade and Oakland, and with steamer trunks loaded onto horse-drawn wagons, were escorted over rutted, dirt roads to an ever-expanding number of hotels and lodges around the lakes. For the first time, the Board advertised summer tourism and touted the lakes as "charming spots of natural interest where there are great attractions, many of which are not yet widely known."

As an adjunct to the Board of Trade, the Waterville Retail Grocers' Association was formed in 1906. Its principal purpose was to circulate lists of "bad debtors," which were hung over cash registers in stores throughout the area. In 1908 its membership was extended to all area retailers, and its name was changed to the Waterville Merchants' Association. It went on to spearhead the curtailment of retailing by wholesale houses, the appointment of a public official to guarantee the accuracy of weights and measures, the regulation of operating hours of retailers, and control of the cost of ice.

Waterville had nearly all the trappings of a proper city, but missing was a modern post office. The old post office shared the first floor of the Haines Building (Common Street) with the Waterville Building and Loan Association, and it was overwhelmed and short of space.[49] In 1910, under pressure from the Board of Trade, the U.S. Postal Service agreed to construct a new facility. A prominent site was chosen at the top of Main Street, facing the Elmwood Hotel across the five-way intersection. Costing $100,000, the new stone Greek Revival edifice with Corinthian columns and domed roof was dedicated in 1911. The handsome building, designed by James Knox Taylor to fit its sharply angled site, featured a round lobby with tiled floors and mahogany woodwork. Inkwells, blotters, and attached pens were arrayed on a large round glass-top table at the center, where patrons could write and send post cards for a penny, and letters for two. The building's roof is adorned with a replica of the Monument of Lysicrates (355 BC) near the Acropolis of Athens, honoring Dionysus, god of the theater. The feature was a fitting counterpoint to the City Hall-Opera House down the street, each bold symbols of the kinship of government and the arts.[50]

---

[49] Only the first two floors of the four-story Haines building remain. The removed top floors were once used for gathering and meeting spaces for the Odd Fellows. The Masonic Building was at the right.
[50] The building, albeit no longer a post office, still stands as one of the state's finest Greek Revival buildings and as one of 15 Waterville area buildings and locations in the U.S. National Register of Historic Places. Others are the First Baptist Church (Elm and Park), the Foster-Redington house (8 Park), the Heald house (19 West), the Redington house (64 Silver), the Lombard house (65 Silver), the Professional Building (177-79 Main), the Universalist-Unitarian Church (Silver and Elm), Waterville High School (21 Gilman), Elizabeth Ann Seton Hospital (Chase), the Two-Cent Bridge (Waterville/Winslow), the Lockwood Mill District, Fort Halifax (Winslow), and the Pressey House and Memorial Hall (Oakland).

Post Office under construction, 1911, with spire of Unitarian Church in view

The loan association was established by the city's largest taxpayer, William T. Haines, a native of Levant who began the practice of law in West Waterville (Oakland) and moved to Waterville in 1880. A Republican, he served as Kennebec County Attorney (1882-1887) and as Maine's governor (1913-1915). As governor he appointed fellow Waterville attorney and Sedgwick native Warren C. Philbrook to the Maine Supreme Judicial Court. A member of the Maine House from 1897-1899, Philbrook was Mayor of Waterville from 1899-1900. In 1913 he replaced Hannibal Emery Hamlin, son of the 15th U.S. Vice President, as Maine's Attorney General. Philbrook served on the law court from 1913-1918. His home at 54 Silver Street later became the headquarters of the local Knights of Columbus.

Governor Haines

Justice Philbrook

THE INCREASED USE OF THE U.S. MAIL was a good measure of rapidly growing commerce throughout the country. By the end of 1911, America had emerged as a leading global economic power. Unemployment

61

stood at 4.6 percent, and the nation's overall trade volume exceeded all of Great Britain. President William Howard Taft became exasperated by the barrage of advice and demands, often conflicting, from groups and associations claiming to represent U.S. business interests. On December 7, 1911, he sent a message to Congress pleading for "a central organization in touch with associations and chambers of commerce throughout the country and able to keep purely American interests in a closer touch with different phases of commercial affairs."

Taft's concerns were not without merit. At the time, the U.S. Department of Commerce reported a total of 1,968 business groups in the country, with a combined membership of more than 348,000. Boards of Trade were locally effective, but most all of them were on the Atlantic Coast, and they could not represent the interests of businesses to the west.

Members of Congress, no doubt overwhelmed by the torrent of mixed business messages themselves, agreed with Taft, and on April 22, 1912, 700 delegates from various commercial and trade organizations in 44 states met at the new Willard Hotel on Pennsylvania Avenue in Washington, D.C., and created the U.S. Chamber of Commerce. It would soon become the largest business federation in the world.

> The name Chamber of Commerce was not unfamiliar. Many chambers already existed across the country. The name was considered prior to the creation of both the Maine and the Portland Boards of Trade. The Charleston, S.C., Chamber, believed to be the nation's first, was established in 1773, the same year a newly-formed Chamber of Commerce in Boston led a raucous protest that became the Boston Tea Party.

In June of 1912, two months after the national organization was created, the Waterville Board of Trade simply renamed itself the Waterville Chamber of Commerce. Frank Redington, who had served as president of the Board (1895-1901), became the Chamber's first president, and in November 1913 the organization became a member of the U.S. Chamber of Commerce.

7

Shrinking World

-1929

Before the Great War, few Americans were interested in the back-page accounts of the troubles in southeast Europe. It was all happening so far away, and conflicts in that part of the world had seemingly been going on forever. Even after July 28, 1914, when news came that Austria-Hungary had declared war on the tiny kingdom of Serbia, most agreed with President Woodrow Wilson that the United States should stay out of it.

What began as reprisal for the Sarajevo murder of the archduke and duchess of the Austro-Hungarian Empire rapidly exploded into a world war engulfing two massive fronts; in the west, where the French and British fended off the Germans in Belgium and France; and in the east, where the Austro-Hungarian, German, and Ottoman empires fought to swallow up entire countries from the Baltic to the Black Sea. Still, Americans clung to neutrality, and nowhere were isolationist sentiments more strongly held than in the industrial cities like Waterville where so many immigrants had come in order to escape the ravages of war.

With the nation turned inward, the newly formed Waterville Chamber of Commerce was shoring up its own front. More than 125 members paid $1 a month for dues and took on a number of local projects including a pre-Christmas winter carnival-circus (declared a resounding success when it did not lose money), the creation of the Waterville Registered Live Stock (*sic*) Association, and the construction of a refrigeration storage facility along the tracks on Upper Main Street (now Railroad Square).

In its first year (1913) the Chamber published a 28-page string-bound booklet in which it extolled the virtues of living in Waterville, calling it a "thriving and growing city, located … in the midst of a great hydro-electric system, and in the centre of the busiest section of the State." A caption on a page of photographs of residential neighborhoods boasts: "Our latchstrings hang on the outside."

At its annual meeting in July, the Chamber did reach out beyond its borders when it set about to raise money for the people of Salem, Massachusetts, who had recently suffered a devastating fire that destroyed more than 1200 buildings and displaced some 20,000 workers, mostly immigrants. The Chamber took $100 from its own coffers, encouraged the city to do the same, and placed "subscription blanks" in local banks for private donations.

The empathy for fire victims was not hard to understand. There were still some who remembered the awful 1866 fire that annihilated much of nearby Portland, and more recently, the massive destruction of the great San Francisco earthquake and fire of 1906. Every city with wooden structures built close together was vulnerable to destructive fire, and Waterville leaders knew the dangers well. In 1911 the city sent a hose company by special train to Bangor to help fight a blaze that destroyed most of that city's downtown, and in Waterville that same year, Main Street fires ruined both Putnam's Smoke Shop and the Wardwell-Emery Department Store.

Both blocks were soon rebuilt of brick and stone, and at the same time the vulnerable wooden structures housing the busy Hose 1 and the hook-and-ladder company on Main Street (near current T.D. Bank) were torn down. The location of a new brick three bay station was strategically chosen at the top of Main Street, where intersecting roads fan in all directions. The new building accommodated hose companies 1 and 2 and the hook-and-ladder company, all of which were still horse-drawn on opening day, January 24, 1912.[51]

With one eye on the war, Waterville continued to grow and prosper. Factories increased production, and new neighborhoods crept slowly away

---

[51] Hose 2 had been located on Silver Street, across from the since-razed building that once housed the *Morning Sentinel*. Hose 3 was at 171 Water Street (Halde Street intersection), and Hose 4 was at 32 Ticonic Street (Brook Street intersection). In 1914, the city acquired its first motorized vehicle, a White Chemical and Hose Cart, but there were still six horses in the department in 1919. In 1923 the horse stalls and hay room at Central Station were removed. The department did not become fully motorized until 1928.

from the center of town. In 1910, the YMCA had built a 57-room hotel and restaurant near the train station to accommodate the tide of traveling rail workers and to serve as its Maine headquarters; in 1914 the local Elks Club opened a handsome Colonial Revival headquarters building on Appleton Street. In 1916 a group of businessmen, doctors and lawyers purchased 158 acres of land west of the city and built a nine-hole golf course with a shingled clubhouse. Although it was located in Oakland, they named it the Waterville Country Club.

Like many other private courses of the time, Waterville's club did not accept women, and it offered membership to only two token Jews. Lewis Rosenthal was not one, but he had no interest in the game in any case. Even so, to even things up, he promptly built his own course on land north of Roosevelt Avenue, with a clubhouse and entrance near 300 Upper Main where he had built a home for his parents and sister. His nine-hole Abanaki Golf Course was open to the public and featured one of the state's first miniature courses where children paid 15¢ to play. Waterville Country Club went in and out of bankruptcy during the Depression and World War II, and in the late 1940s lifted its membership restrictions. Rosenthal closed his course and developed Johnson Heights.

THE POPULATION HAD JUMPED MORE THAN A THIRD since the beginning of the century and was up to more than 12,000 by 1915, when the nation's entry into the Great War began to seem inevitable. Germany had declared all British waters were in the war zone, and their U-boats were sinking commercial and passenger vessels, including U.S. ships, with impunity. Americans were stunned and angered in May by news of the sinking of the British ship *Lusitania* with hundreds of U.S. citizens on board, and across the country brawls broke out between pacifists and those who wanted revenge. The debate raged for more than a year while U-boat destruction of U.S. lives and property continued.

Most peace seekers had already given up by February 15, 1917, when some 1,000 citizens filled the Opera House to hear former president William Howard Taft speak of the need to prepare for war. Out of office for four years, Taft was using his bully pulpit to encourage Americans to accept the nation's role as a world leader. In his Waterville speech he called for "reasonable" military preparedness and said the U.S. should be wary of alliances with nations "over there." He said the country had been "conscientiously neutral and void of offense, and yet we are drifting steadily toward war." The audience cheered when he finished: "God has showered us with blessings and shall we not share them with other nations? Shall we not pull our weight in the boat?"

President Taft had been to Waterville several times before and would return again later that spring as a guest of his dear friend Leslie Cornish, a Winslow native and Chief Justice of the Maine Supreme Court. An 1875 graduate of Colby, Cornish served as chair of the college board of trustees from 1907-1926. In 1922 he would join Taft, then Chief Justice of the U.S. Supreme Court, on the American Bar Association committee charged with drafting a code of judicial ethics.

The Opera House balcony was filled with Colby students the night Taft spoke, and they whooped the loudest when he urged military readiness. The next day, the men called for campus military training. President Arthur Roberts agreed, and a company of 60 was formed. The first drill was held April 4. Two days later Congress declared war on the imperial government of Germany.

By May, dozens of local men, including nearly a quarter of those enrolled at Colby, enlisted and joined some 73,000 U.S. volunteers to fight on the battlefields of France. Raymond Rogers, a Colby senior and member of the local National Guard, ran the drill company, and when he was drafted into active service, Lt. Fred McAlary of town was put in charge. In June, President Wilson ordered the conscription of all eligible single males between the ages of 21 and 31, and attorney Harvey Eaton became chairman of the local draft board. The YMCA took over the Colby ATO fraternity house on College Avenue as a dormitory for soldiers in training. When the draft age was lowered to 18 in the fall of 1918, the government established the national Student Army Training Corps (SATC) and required all male students to enroll. Colby classes were discontinued and the men's division became a "war college."

A month later, it was suddenly over. Word of the surrender came by wire to the *Sentinel* newsroom in the early morning of November 11. The siren atop Central Fire Station wailed out, and before dawn the streets were filled with joyful citizens, beating on pots and pans, building bonfires, and burning effigies of the Kaiser. The banner headline proclaimed:

THE GREATEST DAY IN HISTORY OF WATERVILLE

In all, 60 million fought in what would later be called World War I. Nine million gave their lives. Casualties included 10 from Waterville and another

19 from student and alumni ranks at Colby. The Veterans of Foreign Wars Post 1285 was named for Forest J. Pare, one of those killed in action, and on the first Armistice Day in 1919, the Common in front of City Hall was named in memory of 1st Sgt. Arthur L. Castonguay of the 103rd Infantry, the last from Waterville killed in the Great War.[52]

On June 17, 1919, three months before Congress officially chartered the American Legion, Waterville created one of the first posts (No. 5), which eventually grew to 1200 members and became the largest in Maine. It was named for 1st Lt. George N. Bourque of Sherwin Street Hill, a Colby student killed in action in France, the first from the city to die in battle.[53]

In 1924, the 30-year-old iron Emerson Bridge crossing the Messalonskee at the foot of Silver Street was replaced with a concrete-arch structure opened on Armistice Day ceremonies that year when Mayor Leon Tebbetts unveiled a bronze plaque memorializing the city's WWI veterans.[54]

On Armistice Day the following year, area WWI veterans were invited to attend an "Ex-Service Man's Muster," with a lengthy parade capped by the American Legion's presentation to the city of a German heavy field howitzer, captured at the end of the war. The 5000-pound weapon was installed in Castonguay Square, at the east end, opposite the large wooden bulletin board facing Main Street, honoring all the city's war veterans.

Locally, the public celebration of war's end in the early winter of 1918 was blamed for rekindling the Spanish flu, a world pandemic that in the United States first broke out at Fort Devens, Massachusetts, in September. Medical experts would later claim the illness was responsible for fully a third of the war's casualties. By mid-November, the epidemic was raging through Waterville. An Army private who accompanied the body of a flu victim back to the city contracted the disease himself. More than 30 Colby students were afflicted. The women were sent home, and the campus was quarantined. The Board of Health closed all public places. Many of the nation's nurses were still serving abroad, and many of those at home were disabled by the flu. The shortage made it difficult to find care, and by the

---

[52] The Common (thus Common Street) was on land deeded by the Commonwealth of Massachusetts in 1796, when Waterville was still a part of Winslow. It originally held a town church (until the Baptist Church on Elm Street was constructed in 1826) and a schoolhouse, which became the original city hall until it was replaced in 1901.

[53] The Post had its first home on the west side of Silver Street, at the intersection with Spring Street.

[54] The bridge was replaced again in 1996.

spring of 1919, an estimated 5,000 Maine people had succumbed to the flu and associated causes. Waterville and Colby lost more to the flu than had died in the war.

THE CITY HAD MEAGER FACILITIES FOR DEALING with widespread illness. In 1910, a modest community care facility, later Elm City Hospital, opened in a frame house on Western Avenue (No. 85, corner of Messalonskee), and a year later, a tiny hospital began in the north end of town in the former home of Dr. A.B. Libby on Highwood Street (off College Street, later Avenue) "in order to furnish hospital accommodations and facilities for sufferers who would otherwise have to go to Augusta, Lewiston, or Portland."

At its beginning, the seven-bed Libby Memorial Hospital was on shaky ground, and its owners, doctors Cragin and Boyer, were anxious to insure its continuation. The hospital was barely a year old when, in the summer of 1912, they asked the Rev. John Kealy, first pastor of the city's new Sacred Heart Church, to see if the Catholic order of the Daughters of Charity headquartered in Emmitsburg, Maryland, might be willing to take it over. Lewis Walsh, Bishop of the Diocese of Portland, gave his approval and a delegation of Superiors came from Maryland to have a look. The Sisters took charge on May 1, 1913, and officially renamed the hospital in honor of their U.S. founder, Elizabeth Ann Seton. (Despite the official naming, everyone simply called it Sisters, and the name stuck.) That winter, a new annex added 23 beds, but the city would not have a modern hospital until 1924 when the daughters built a $750,000 four-story brick addition to the old hospital building on Highwood Street, improving the capacity to 125 beds.[55]

The founding doctors of Libby Memorial trained their own nurses. When the Daughters of Charity arrived in 1913, they purchased a large home across Highwood Street, and it became a residence for both staff nurses and students of the first Nurses Training School in the county. The school prepared hundreds of licensed registered nurses until the mid-50s, when it became difficult for students without sufficient pre-nursing training in basic subjects to pass the State Board of Nursing examinations. Thereafter, the school trained Licensed Practical Nurses until it closed a decade later.

---

[55] The original structure of Libby Memorial Hospital was destroyed by fire in 1939, and the subsequent remodeling and additions increased capacity to 150.

When the flu epidemic came (1918-1919), what the city lacked in facilities was partly compensated for by having in residence Frederick Charles Thayer, one of Maine's most respected physicians.[56] Thayer was a Renaissance man, excelling not only as a medical doctor and surgeon but also as a public official and entrepreneur. Born in Waterville, he attended Waterville Academy (Coburn) and Waterville College (Colby) before studying medicine at Albany Medical College and Maine Medical School.[57] By the time he became president of the local Chamber of Commerce in 1918, he had already served the city as fire chief, alderman, and representative to the Maine Legislature. His eclectic business interests included the presidency of Waterville Trust and the Sawyer Publishing companies, and as a major stockholder and director of the W.W.&F. railroad.

Along with the efforts of his colleagues, Thayer's wise counsel and tireless service during the epidemic is credited with saving many lives. He lived and practiced in the house where he was born, 214 Main Street, near the intersection with College Avenue.

In 1881, Thayer had taken on James Frederick Hill as an understudy in medicine and partnered with him for a time in his Waterville practice. Hill, a native of the city and a graduate of both Coburn and Colby, went on to specialize in the eye, ear, nose, and throat. His sons Frederick and Howard and Howard's son Kevin were ophthalmologists, and earned for themselves and Waterville a broad and proud reputation for excellence in eye care that, through their successors, continues to this day.

Almost every doctor in Waterville initially practiced at the new Sisters hospital, but a rift quickly developed along the lines of religion and language. The French-speaking Catholics dominated at Sisters, and it wasn't long before the English-speaking Protestants, led by Thayer, began looking for a hospital of their own. When Thayer died in 1926, he left his home at the head of Main Street (across from the Elmwood Hotel) to Drs. John

---

[56] Thayer followed in a long line of medical doctors who had served the area since 1771, when the surveyor Dr. John McKechnie first settled in Winslow. The line continued with many others including Dr. Obadiah Williams, veteran of the Battle of Bunker Hill, who came to Waterville in 1792; Dr. Moses Appleton, who opened the first drug store in 1796; Dr. Stephen Thayer, a *Mayflower* descendant and F.C. Thayer's grandfather, who opened a practice in 1808; and Dr. Atwood Crosby, a Civil War veteran who came to practice with his local preceptor, Dr. N.R. Boutelle, in 1866.

[57] The Maine Medical School was opened in 1860 in Portland by Maine General Hospital (later Maine Medical Center) in partnership with Tufts University.

Goodrich and John O. Piper, who in November of 1930 conveyed the property to become the first Thayer Hospital.

THROUGHOUT THE WAR AND THE EPIDEMIC THAT FOLLOWED, the country was also absorbed in two disparate social issues that would bring much demonstration and debate before they were finally settled with amendments to the U.S. Constitution. One would ban alcohol. The other, give women the right to vote.

The 18th Amendment, prohibiting the manufacture, sale, and consumption of alcohol, was approved by Congress and sent to the states for ratification in January 1917. Maine voted two-to-one for the amendment on January 8, 1919, and within a week the requisite two-thirds of the states had approved. The law, together with the enforcement provisions of the Volstead Act, went into effect on January 16, 1920.

Had proponents of a national prohibition been versed in Maine history, they might have known the social experiment wouldn't work. Many towns, including Waterville, had liquor laws as early as 1834, but enforcement was impossible. The state adopted its first prohibition laws in 1846, which were strengthened in 1851 and then replaced with a more limited version five years later.[58] In 1856, Waterville citizens overwhelmingly approved a local ordinance "to restrain and regulate the sale of intoxicating liquors, and to prohibit and suppress drinking houses and tippling shops." In 1883 Maine became the first state in the nation to amend its constitution to "forever prohibit" the sale or use of intoxicating liquors.[59] In Waterville, the amendment carried by a vote of 563-238. When the national Temperance Party was formed in 1869, the new state organization nominated Joshua Nye of Waterville as its candidate for governor. He received 309 votes in the entire state, not one in Waterville.

None of the state or local laws did much to impact the manufacture, sale or consumption of alcohol, and now it seemed the great national social experiment was destined to fail, especially in mixed industrial and agricultural areas like central Maine, where factory workers were bent on ending long, hard days with libation, and where farmers were adept at distilling their own. The proximity of Canada and the Atlantic coast made it

---

[58] In an attempt to enforce the law, the Maine Liquor Commission was created in 1862.
[59] Apple cider was exempted.

all but impossible to deal with rum-runners, and the growth of local police departments merely added to the number of eyes that looked away.

In Waterville, as in other immigrant cities, ethnic backgrounds and the instruction of the two dominant religions, Protestant and Catholic, converged as one to oppose the evils of alcohol, but at the same time, the culture and Catholic church teachings also led to the continued suppression of the rights of women.

On August 26, 1920, seven months after the 18th Amendment was put in place, the 19th Amendment giving women the right to vote was settled as well. As with the battle for Prohibition, the women's victory came at the end of a very long fight. It had begun in 1840, but was put aside through the Civil War. Susan B. Anthony, a campaigner for both the abolition of slavery and against alcohol, renewed the cause for women in 1872. A suffrage amendment was proposed to Congress as early as 1878, but it languished nine years before it was voted down in the Senate on the first vote.

In 1914, the General Federation of Women's Clubs marched on the White House to confront President Wilson with the question, but he dodged it by claiming it was an issue for the states to decide.[60] Taking him at his word, in 1916 Maine proponents of suffrage gathered signatures to amend the state constitution, set for a vote in September 1917. In February, at a meeting at her Winter Street home, Mrs. T.B. Ashcraft was elected president of the newly formed Waterville Suffrage League, and members set out to find support among the men who would do the voting.

The nation was in the midst of war, and fewer than half the number who had voted to settle the liquor question turned out for the women. The initiative failed with barely 20,000 votes in favor and nearly 39,000 against. In Waterville, the gap was even wider, with 625 voting against and 317 in favor. In the heavily Catholic Ward 7, only 25 voted in favor while 229 said no.

A year later, President Wilson got on board, and in 1919 the U.S. House and Senate passed the 19th Amendment and sent it to the states for ratification. By August 1920 the requisite three-quarters of the states had already agreed, and in September, making what was then a moot point, Maine reversed its position of three years before and ratified the amendment as well.

---

[60] Wyoming, Colorado, and Utah already had women's suffrage, written into their constitutions when they were admitted to the Union.

On June 4, 1920, only months before the 19ᵗʰ Amendment was ratified, General of the Armies John Pershing, commander of the American Expeditionary Force during the war, stopped in Waterville while on a whirlwind tour of Maine. He was the guest of honor at a lunch at the Elmwood Hotel, and then was escorted up College Avenue to the Zeta Psi fraternity house, where the front porch had been draped in patriotic bunting. He said it was "a pleasure to speak on a coed college campus, for without American women, America could not have accomplished what it did in the World War." That fall (September 3), 38-year-old Secretary of the Navy Franklin D. Roosevelt made a campaign stop as Democratic candidate for Vice President under James Cox. Roosevelt was given an auto parade from the train station down College Avenue to the steps of City Hall where he spoke to supporters for a half-hour. In November, the Cox ticket lost to Republican Warren G. Harding, who swept 37 of the 48 states, including Maine, where there was strong sentiment favoring his VP candidate and New Englander, Calvin Coolidge. Maine and Vermont would go on to become the only two states to rebuke Roosevelt in all four of his presidential elections.

Perhaps it was their new status as full citizens that made women every bit as enthusiastic as the men to make the nation roar during the 1920s. Men wore wingtips and gangster garb to mock Prohibition, women shortened their skirts and bobbed their hair, and both sexes binged on jazz, delightedly snubbing their noses at convention. It was a kind of youthful rebellion that would not happen again for another half-century.

In Waterville, adding to the glamor of the age and giving Main Street a hint of Broadway, was the new Haines Theater (built in 1917), complete with a sidewalk ticket booth, flashing overhead lights, leather-cushioned swinging doors, and a popcorn machine. Built by the local attorney and prior Maine Governor William T. Haines, the modern theater thrilled packed houses for a decade of silent movies until *The Jazz Singer* came in 1927.

The Haines was Waterville's third moving picture theater. The Opera House at City Hall (1902) often showed films on the dates between live performances, [61] and the Silver Theater (No. 14 Silver Street), opened in 1913, sold tickets at a cheaper price and kept its name until it changed hands and became the State Theater in 1941. By that time, Ulysses Ponsant had

---

[61] The silent movies were commonly accompanied by a live piano, and the Opera House had the advantage when Blanche (Letourneau) Dubord was in the pit. Dubord played by ear or sight and delighted theatergoers with the drama she added to accompany the images that flickered on the screen. In 1917 she was the new bride of F. Harold Dubord, who would become Waterville's first French mayor in 1928.

added the city's fourth movie house. The Maine Theater and Launderette (67 Water Street) sold tickets for a dime.

The top of Main Street got even more of a big-city look in 1923 with the completion of the new four-story Professional Building (No. 177-79) at the Appleton Street intersection. The bravely modern Art-Deco structure with store spaces on the street level and three flights of offices above was the pride of the town. Adding to the building's attraction was the city's first passenger elevator, complete with a uniformed operator who jiggled the brake at every stop to make the cage floor match the hallway.[62] Not to be outdone, the other end of Main Street added a stroke of modern elegance with the Federal Trust Building, complete with art deco motifs, in 1926.

THE WORLD WAS SHRINKING. The recent war had much to do with it, and the growing marvels of radios and airplanes were making distances seem smaller still. The feeling of closeness was certainly true in the cities, large and small, where the mid-town areas were crowded with offices, shops, and automobiles. By 1920, Henry Ford had built nearly ten million Model T's, and members of the city council thought that altogether too many of them were clogging up downtown Waterville. Six days a week shoppers parked diagonally along both sides of Main Street, and there was rarely an open space. Heavy traffic at the intersections often brought a chorus of 'ooga' horns and a crescendo of crunching metal. Something clearly had to be done, and the city council decreed one-hour parking on Main Street, installed the town's first traffic lights at the head of Main Street and the Temple Street intersection, and opened municipal parking lots in Lockwood Park, on Charles Street, and behind City Hall. The Merchants Bureau of the Chamber, fearing the regulations would discourage shoppers, begged for a repeal of restrictions, but to no avail.

The need for new laws was the price of success, and the good fortune kept coming. The national textile industry saw demand fluctuate in the post-war period, and the local Lockwood and the Wyandotte mills made their workers nervous by adjusting production outputs to suit the day. At the same time, the paper and railroad industries flourished, and immigrants

---

[62] The Professional Building has been well maintained and occupied, and its elevator is still run by a human operator.

continued to arrive. The Chamber formed an Americanization Committee charged with finding volunteers to help teach English to the newcomers.

The heady time also brought about the formation of service clubs, not only to provide social opportunities for making business ties, but also to join together in efforts to give back to the community and improve the lives of others. Waterville's Rotary Club led the way, holding its first meeting at the Elmwood Hotel on Feb. 11, 1918, when Colby president Roberts was elected the first president. The Kiwanis Club was formed in 1923, and the Lions Club, in 1924.[63]

The swelling population brought increased demands on the city to keep pace, and in 1922, the old high school building on Pleasant Street was torn down to make room for a new junior high school. Costing $195,000, the Colonial Revival structure included an auditorium, a gymnasium and specialized classrooms for textile design and automotive repair.

> The area had not lost its penchant for creative genius. William T. Bovie, a physicist on the faculty at Harvard University, worked at his home on Summit Street in Fairfield to develop a surgical knife that could cauterize as it cut. He sold his invention for $1, and when Harvard denied him tenure, he returned to Fairfield and taught at Colby from 1939-1948. The Bovie knife, patented in 1926, is still in use.

AS THE DECADE DREW TO A CLOSE, the city faced a new crisis brought on by its own success. When Waterville people first went looking for a place to put their new literary and theological institution in 1813, they must have thought they'd found the perfect place when they chose the long plateau along the dirt road beside the river, just outside of town. They could not have known that in 50 years the campus would find itself trapped between the railroad and the river, and by the turn to the 20th century, held hostage by the very things that gave the city its economic strength.

Many of the college buildings were nearly 100 years old, sadly out of repair, and heated by aging and finicky coal furnaces. The campus had suffered three serious fires since 1920, one of them taking the lives of four students,[64] and the once bucolic campus had become so beleaguered by its close neighbors that students and faculty became accustomed to closing the

---

[63] The local Exchange Club was formed in 1936.
[64] The Lambda Chi Alpha house burned in December 1922. Charles Treworgy, the fraternity president, escaped the building but died when he returned in a vain attempt to save three of his brothers. A dormitory (first a fraternity house) on the Mayflower Hill campus is named in his memory.

windows to wait for the noisy, soot belching trains to pass and to dull the stench of sulfur from the paper mill across the river.

One man was about to lead the way out of trouble. Franklin Winslow Johnson was no stranger to Waterville when he came to serve as Colby's 15th president in 1929. He had been headmaster at Coburn Classical Institute for 11 years before he was lured to the University of Chicago, then Teachers College at Columbia, where he became a national leader in secondary education.

There was talk of moving the campus even before Johnson took office, and in May (1929) the president-elect asked his friend and Central Maine Power founder Walter Wyman to quietly secure land options on 1500 acres of farmland on the ridge between Waterville and Oakland. He told Colby trustees of his plan on the eve of his June 15 inauguration, and while there were many doubters, Johnson was able to make his case for considering the idea by sharing a preliminary report on a survey of Maine educational institutions prepared for the University of Maine, and Bates, Bowdoin and Colby colleges. With regard to Colby, the report was damning. The college could not survive unless it moved "to a new and adequate location" as quickly as possible.

The first to suggest Colby move its campus was Waterville native and Colby graduate Herbert Philbrick, a dean at Northwestern University who had been Johnson's choice for the Colby presidency. In 1928, after Philbrick declined in favor of Johnson, the two met in Chicago where Philbrick made it clear that he felt the college needed a new home.

Trustees appointed a special committee to study the matter, and at a meeting in July the group toured the existing campus before lunch. Afterward, Wyman showed them Mayflower Hill. When they reconvened at the Elmwood Hotel at the end of the day, the vote to recommend a move was unanimous. The committee was set to make its report to the full board in August, but Johnson asked to delay a final vote until the following June, by which time he hoped the college would own Mayflower Hill and have a sense of how they might raise the three million dollars it would need to construct the buildings.

On October 29, eight months before Colby trustees were set to make a decision, the stock market crashed and the nation began to slide into depression. In Waterville, where the pending question of Colby's move was well discussed, two attitudes prevailed. One was that the national economic crisis would quickly pass. The other was that whatever became of Colby, no one would even dare to think about moving out of town. They were dead wrong on both counts.

8

Against the Tide

-1939

B y 1930, the telling of the story of America was ever more centered on the extraordinary confidence and optimism that marked its people. Little wonder. In a mere century and a half, a new society of disparate immigrants had tamed much of the vast land by turning forests into farmland and rivers into gold, and creating the greatest democratic nation on earth.

The month before the stock market crashed, the Dow-Jones industrial average hit an all-time high,[65] continuing a nine-year bull market fed in large measure by investments made with borrowed money. Americans had big dreams, and outrageous things were coming to pass. Charles Lindburgh had already flown solo over the Atlantic, and remarkable records were being set with the construction of the world's tallest building in New York, the world's longest bridge in San Francisco, and the world's biggest dam in Colorado.

Mill cities were still magnets for those who dared leave their farms and seek their living in factories. Waterville's population had soared more than 15 percent since 1920, standing well above 15,000 by 1930, and while the stream of new immigrants had slowed, there were still jobs in the mills that assured opportunities by the service and merchant trades. Improved roads and affordable automobiles produced a steady traffic of visitors and businessmen. In celebration, the owners of the Elmwood Hotel were

---

[65] The mark of 381.17 would not be reached again until November 1954.

emboldened to build an extravagant new dining room and name it for the Palace at Versailles. Schools and churches were filled, and after 21 years of worshipping in the basement, Sacred Heart Church finally opened its handsome new sanctuary upstairs in the sunshine. Even as Colby was considering a move, the college dedicated its new Alumnae Building across College Avenue on Main Place and announced plans to construct a bigger gymnasium on the north end of the old campus, below Shannon Observatory. The summer of 1930 also saw the opening of a swimming pool and bathhouses on North Street, a gift of the Waterville Kiwanis Club that would also be used for skating in the winter.

Despite the prosperity, it was not hard to find warning signs. Textile towns in New England had been under threat as far back as Reconstruction, when manufacturers first began to lure the industry south with the promise of low wages and cheaper transportation. Farmers had been hurting since the end of World War I, when agricultural prices fell and failed to recover. Automobiles were already taking away the business of trains.

In the days following the October crash, most believed the economy would quickly rebound, but in a month the market lost a whopping $30 billion and the Great Depression began to unleash a reign of poverty and heartache that would last a decade.

If there were any optimists left by June 1930, one of them was surely Colby's president, Franklin Johnson. Trustees were set to meet to make a final decision on moving, and there were plenty of doubters, even on the board. The very idea of transplanting an entire college was preposterous enough, never mind trying to do it in the midst of the worst financial upheaval the country had ever seen. Many called the idea "Johnson's Folly," but his stubborn defense was always the same: "Anything that ought to be done, can be done."

In April, Johnson had received a letter that rallied the support he so desperately needed. William H. Gannett, publisher of four Maine newspapers including the local *Sentinel,* wrote to invite Colby trustees to have a look at Ganneston Park, a 450-acre family-owned parcel of land near the capitol in Augusta. If they liked it, he said they could have it. Hoping to stay in Waterville and having options on the Mayflower Hill land already in his pocket, Johnson was nonetheless eager to give the Augusta invitation straight-faced consideration. On June 8 trustees agreed to move, but they didn't say where.

News of the Gannett offer brought howls from town, and suspicion that the new Colby president was behind the treacherous Augusta proposal prompted a rally cry that captured local sentiment: *Keep Colby, Move Johnson.* Within days, a Citizens Committee of One Hundred was formed to see what could be done. The clothing merchant Herbert Emery led the group that included Mayor F. Harold Dubord; his predecessor as mayor and well-known editor of Colby's alumni magazine, Herbert C. Libby; and Chamber of Commerce[66] president and manager of the *Sentinel*, Caleb Lewis. At its first meeting, the committee pledged to raise $100,000 to buy Mayflower Hill, and the group met 15 times over that summer before deciding to call a mass rally of citizens at the Opera House on September 23. A full-page advertisement in the *Sentinel* urged that it be "the largest meeting ever held in Waterville," and declared "sickness is the only excuse any should have not to attend." The editorial page chipped in, calling for full participation and adding: "There's no place for slackers or whiners in this situation."

The Opera House meeting was jammed with more than a thousand citizens. Redington Funeral Home brought extra chairs, bands played, and the uniformed American Legion Auxiliary Glee Club sang. Judge Harold Marden presided, and Dr. F.C. Hill urged pledges of support "so that the trustees will be slow indeed to pull up the roots of a 100-year-old institution and endanger its future growth by planting it in foreign soil."

Mayor Dubord made the longest speech, citing the practical outcomes if Colby should disappear. He said property values would depreciate 25-30 percent, and although the college was tax exempt, the departure of faculty and staff would leave "empty rents and empty houses," making a need for a tax increase and creating a bonded debt for the city that "would surely and quickly exceed its legal limit."

Professor Julian "Judy" Taylor spoke at the end and shocked the audience by announcing he was prepared to purchase land abutting his own property in the city's South End and present the entire package to Colby for a new campus.[67] The Taylor land (abutting Pine Grove Cemetery) was, in fact, a gravel pit, and even with the addition of adjacent land, not suitable for a college. Even so, Taylor's generosity gave impetus to the coming local campaign.

---

[66] The Waterville Chamber had recently joined forces with its cross-river parent town to become the Waterville-Winslow Chamber of Commerce.

[67] Julian Taylor's father Daniel was one of Waterville's earliest settlers. In 1931, Taylor was in his sixty-second year as a teacher of Latin at the college, the longest tenure of any college professor in the country. The beloved professor was known affectionately to his students as "The Old Roman."

Trustees met on November 21 to deal with a divided report from the special committee. The majority favored staying in Waterville; a minority recommended moving to Augusta. The 16-5 vote to stay in Waterville was made unanimous before the meeting adjourned.

Although no specific site was chosen, three were under consideration: The Peninsula (Taylor) property of about 300 acres in the South End, where the Messalonskee meets the Kennebec; the Mountain Farm on the ridge between Waterville and Fairfield Center (Upper Main), and the Mayflower Hill site of about 600 acres including a place called Beefsteak Grove on the crest of the hill near the Second Rangeway (Washington Street). After consultation with engineers and architects, the Mayflower Hill site was chosen.[68]

The Committee of One Hundred received five pledges of $5,000 each almost instantly, but in that long first winter of the Depression, the rest came slowly. Chamber president Caleb Lewis, who got his ink by the barrel, used his daily *Sentinel* column, "Ima Wanderer," to hype the effort, and in the last week of the campaign the newspaper printed the names of all who had given with the hope of shaming those who had not. The money trickled in. (Johnson later liked to tell the story of meeting a mill worker on Main Street who wished him well and pressed a quarter into his hand.)

By the time of the final meeting on Saturday night (April 11, 1931) at the Savings Bank on Main Street, the committee had $97,406 in gifts and pledges in hand. Federal Trust officials pledged to make up any shortfall of less than $500, and committee members dug in for additional gifts. Before the night ended, the goal was topped at $101,376. By prearranged signal, the Central Fire Station siren began to wail and two bands stepped out to march down Main Street with dozens of horn-tooting cars behind them. From Castonguay Square, the revelers marched onto Front Street and up College Avenue to the President's House (No. 33[69]) to play for Johnson, who had gone from goat to hero in ten months time. A week later, at a special ceremony at the Opera House, Mayor Dubord presented Johnson the deed to Mayflower Hill.

---

[68] The property was less than half the size of that for which Wyman had taken options. There were ten principal parcels, owned by Alonzo Morrell, Ralph Stanley, the heirs of W.H. Stanley, Elmore Hustus, Philippe Poulin, Wilfred LaPointe, Roy Page, Thomas Labbe, William Lannigan, and Mount Merici Convent.
[69] Originally the home of Nathanial Boutelle.

THE COLBY VICTORY MADE SPIRITS SOAR, and barely a month later (May 5, 1931), in full celebratory fashion, the first airplane landed at the still unfinished Waterville Airport. The pilot of the two-wing Fairchild, H. H. Talbot, was quick to declare the landing field "as good, or perhaps better," than the one in Portland.

Two years earlier, at the urging of the Kiwanis Club, Dr. George Averill put up $4700 to purchase 106 acres of flat pastureland south of the Oakland Road, within sight of the Second Rangeway. He gave the city the first option to purchase or lease the land, and proceeded to construct a new quarter-mile connecting road to the landing strip.

The Waterville Airport was not the first airfield in the area. There had been a crude airstrip in Winslow since 1919, located on property adjacent to the locally famous "Round Barn," owned by James Lowell Dean (later Corbett Farm) on the corner of Benton Avenue and present-day Dean Street (current Heartland Estates). A civil engineer who worked on the construction of the Hollingsworth & Whitney plant in Winslow, Dean was also the designer of the well-known barn, listed on the National Register of Historic Buildings until it was destroyed by fire in 1991. George Maxim was the fixed base operator at Dean Field, offering sightseeing trips and pilot training. In 1925, Charles Treat came from Rockland to operate the field "on weekends and by special appointment." Wesley Marden was base operator from 1929-1930 and took over in Waterville when the new field was complete.

The Haines Theater received its first films by air on June 24, 1931, and over the next three days the airport was christened in a gala celebration that included stunt flying, parachuting, and fly-ins by more than 40 aircraft.[70] That summer, manager Marden established Airways Incorporated Flying Service with one pilot (himself) and one plane (his Waco). Two planes crashed in the following year, one carrying Elizabeth Arden, who survived on the way to her famous Maine Chance resort and spa in Mount Vernon (now a veterans' retreat operated by the Travis Mills Foundation). The city quickly got help from the Work Project Administration (WPA) to improve the runways.

In August 1933, more than 5,000 people came to greet the famed aviatrix Amelia Earhart when she flew in to help celebrate the establishment

---

[70] The new airport consisted of four runways (two of 2000 feet, two of 1800 feet), a 40x16 foot hangar, and a small administration building.

of Boston & Maine Airlines (later Northeast), which had begun flying routes connecting Waterville, Bangor, Rockland, Portland and Boston, and established these cities as the first in New England to have regular air service. Earhart, the first woman to fly solo over the Atlantic, piloted one of the two 10-place, tri-motor Stinson aircraft purchased by the Boston & Maine and Maine Central railroads to cover the route. Standing by the hangar out of sight of much of the crowd, she spoke over a loudspeaker of the thrill of flying and urged listeners "to become interested in this mode of transportation ... especially women, who are finding aviation a welcome diversion from the hustle and bustle of the home."

COURTESY OF WESLEY MARDEN, JR.
Airport manager Wes Marden with his new amphibian Sirioa, the first airplane to land and take off from Messalonskee Lake (Snow Pond), c. 1933

The city began leasing the airport from Dr. Averill in 1934 for $2000 a year. Within two years, Marden's Airways Inc. had 11 planes and six employees, and there were often as many as 18 planes on the field at once, stacked on their props at night in an enlarged hanger.

THE PURCHASE OF AN AIRPORT WAS BUT ONE EXAMPLE of the generosity of George G. Averill, an often-forgotten Waterville hero whose many gifts in the first half of the 20th century helped shape and enrich both the city and the college. Born in Lincoln, Maine, he began his career as a physician in Cambridge, Massachusetts. Poor health forced him to leave medicine; and he and his wife, Mabel, moved to Waterville, where he became general manager of the Keyes Fibre Company, the molded pulp firm founded by her father. Mabel died in 1918 and in 1921 Averill married Frances Moser of Bangor. He sold his Keyes interests in 1927 and invested in real estate and oil wells in California.

> In 1926, Keyes directors discovered that national sales director John Hart had been secretly working with a former plant employee, Merle Chaplin, to devise significant improvements on the Keyes process. In March 1927, Hart and Chaplin offered their five patents in exchange for 3000 Keyes shares. Averill negotiated to retain his majority holdings, but Keyes stockholders said no to the offer. The competitors returned with a $4.5 million offer to buy the company outright, and shareholders agreed. The new Rex Pulp Products Company kept the famous Keyes name and named Maine's leading industrialist, Walter Wyman, as president.

Childless, the Averills preferred giving their money to help young people. In 1924, when Colby students and football teammates Frank Goodrich and George Hawes spearheaded the effort to establish the Waterville Boys Club, the Averills helped by purchasing the 1842 estate on Temple Street (opposite the Congregational Church) built as a wedding gift to his daughter by the prominent attorney, banker, and railroad investor, Timothy Boutelle. Averill also established public land and playgrounds on North Street (site of current Alfond Youth Center), promptly named Averill Park in his honor.

As chair of the Colby board, Averill gave $100,000 when the college launched the campaign for the new campus, and his lifetime gifts to the college exceeded $1 million (approximately $18 million, current value). In 1941, with the college on the move, the Averills gave the city $75,000 to purchase the Alumnae Building on Main Place and gave it to the Boys Club, which, in turn, relinquished the Temple Street property to the YMCA.

The Averills lived at 104 Silver Street, and in John D. Rockefeller fashion, when Averill walked about town he would often give coins to the children he met along the way. The North Street ball field is now gone, as is a grade school (between Mathews and Oakland streets) that carried his name. A Colby dormitory and a street in town (Averill Terrace) are among the few reminders of the man and his wife who were at once the richest and most generous people in town.

George Averill with the key given to him by Colby President Seelye Bixler at the dedication of the Keyes Science Building, 1950

Those who profited most from the Averills' generosity to young athletes were, at the time, inspired by the prowess of two Waterville-born athletes, each then in the midst of remarkable high school careers. Polish-American Frank "Touchy" Gaul starred in three sports at Waterville High before attending Notre Dame, where he was a star football quarterback and baseball catcher. The baseball field near the high school on Messalonskee Avenue is named in his memory. Gaul later coached at John Carroll University in Ohio, and helped recruit Eddie Arsenault from Winslow High School, who had managed to excel in football, hockey, basketball, baseball, and track and field. After attending Colby for a year, Arsenault transferred to John Carroll University where, as a halfback, he earned the sobriquet "The Flying Frenchman," and proceeded to break most of the school's rushing records. On the ice, he set all scoring records and led the team to a 15-0 season his senior year.

THE YEAR 1932 WAS THE WORST OF THE LONG DEPRESSION. Fifteen million Americans were unemployed; more than a million were transients, roaming the country looking for work, standing in bread lines, eating in soup kitchens. Waterville's riverfront factories were struggling to stay open. Neighborhood grocery stores were often short on staples. There were fewer customers downtown, and some shops were closing. Children could be seen carrying sacks along the railroad tracks, looking for stray bits of coal.

84

President Herbert Hoover was confident the economic ship would right itself, but it didn't, and when Franklin Roosevelt stood against him in the fall elections of 1932, the Democrat won in a landslide.[71] The ballot had been a referendum on Roosevelt's New Deal, and in Waterville, the largely French population was also drawn to the U.S. Senate candidacy of its popular five-term mayor and FDR supporter, F. Harold Dubord, who narrowly lost to Republican Frederick Hale (49.7 - 50.1 percent) in statewide balloting. In 1936, Dubord lost to Lewis Barrows in a bid for Governor, and lost again in 1938 in an attempt to unseat the incumbent Republican Congressman Clyde Smith (husband of Margaret Chase Smith). In 1955, Dubord was appointed to the Maine Superior Court by Gov. Edmund Muskie, and a year later was named to the Maine Supreme Judicial Court where he served until 1962.

Justice Dubord

The most prominent local politician of the day was Republican Congressman John Edward Nelson. Born in nearby China, Nelson attended Waterville schools, graduated from Colby in 1898, and practiced law in Waterville for a time before moving to Augusta. He served five terms in Congress (1922-1933). As a member of the Anti-Communist Hamilton Fish Committee in 1930, he was the lone dissenter in a report that called for the outlawing of the Communist Party in the U.S. and denying of citizenship to naturalized communists. In his minority report he denounced the communist "hysteria," insisting: "Our best defense against the red shirt of the Communist and the black shirt of the Fascist is the blue shirt of the American workingman."

Across the country, discouraged and desperate citizens were willing to put their fate in the hands of the confident new president, and within the first 100 days an astonishing number of recovery initiatives went largely unchallenged and were quickly put into effect.

On March 6, 1933, after only three days in office, Roosevelt closed the nation's banks to stem the tide of closings (nearly half had already failed)

---

[71] Maine was one of only six states to support Hoover (he won by 12 percent). Waterville and the state's other industrial cities chose Roosevelt.

and give Congress time to adopt controls to restore banking confidence. Waterville's Ticonic Bank, already a century old when it merged with Peoples Bank in 1931, did not reopen, but in 1934 reorganized as First National Bank (later a branch of Depositors Trust) and honored all of its deposits.

By July of 1933, the new recovery programs were beginning to work. Henry Ford was the first to initiate the 40-hour work week in his automobile assembly plants, and FDR wanted other manufacturers to do the same as part of his National Recovery Program, arguing fewer hours would bring higher wages and more jobs. The paper plate manufacturer Keyes Fibre, now owned by Maine investors led by CMP founder Walter Wyman, was on the verge of bankruptcy before he and his successor president, Wallace Parsons, expanded the product line to include all sorts of pulp fiber products including plant pots, berry baskets, apple trays, and packaging for eggs, bottles and light bulbs. In partial response to the government call, Keyes shortened its workweek from 48 to 42 hours and quickly hired 100 extra workers. Lockwood, bound by an agreement across the textile industry, dropped to 40 hours and took on 300 new hands. When the Hollingsworth & Whitney paper mill owners considered following suit, the initiative was hastened by the brief walkout of 60 women in the plant's finishing room who were making less than $2 a day and demanding more.

Among the many things that weren't working well in 1933 was Prohibition. Even those who had once favored the alcohol ban admitted the law had done little more than create a nation of bootleggers and speakeasies while turning loose a torrent of corruption and crime. Franklin Roosevelt knew bringing back legal alcohol would provide thousands of much needed jobs (not to mention that he himself enjoyed a martini), and he ran on a platform favoring repeal. Congress sent the 21st Amendment to the states in February 1933. Certain of ratification, in June the Maine Legislature authorized the licensing of distilleries, and the first taste was set for July 1. The day before, 14 carloads of 3.2 beer arrived at the Waterville train station, headed for 22 of the city's restaurants and reopened beer parlors. Asked if he was worried about having 8096 pints and 37 barrels of beer suddenly on sale, police chief Albert Poirier shrugged; "Let 'em have it." The entire stock sold in a day.[72] Utah became the 36th state to ratify the amendment on December 5, 1933, the effective date of repeal. Maine voted the following day. The results in Waterville were 4057 in favor, 1533 opposed.

---

[72] Within the week, state police raided a still in Vassalboro that was capable of producing 100 gallons of booze a day. It was said to be one of the largest moonshine operations ever in Maine.

Despite adjustments in policy and production, northern textile mills continued to suffer. Southern plants were by now producing nearly three-quarters of the nation's fabrics while paying workers 40 percent less than their northern competitors. In Maine, manufacturers began to "stretch out," speeding production by adding looms and paying piece rates to workers. When the National Recovery Act required the shortened workweek, owners insisted on the same weekly production as before. Although job insecurity often kept workers from joining unions, the Recovery Act nonetheless guaranteed workers the right to organize, and the United Textile Association of America quickly grew stronger. On Sept. 1, 1934, it called a general strike of the nation's cotton workers, and within four days, 4000 of Maine's textile workers had walked out.[73]

In Waterville, all 413 of the Wyandotte workers were union members, and the mill peacefully closed on the strike schedule. Lockwood cotton mill workers were not organized, and when the mill stayed open it became a target for union activists. Over the next six days, union membership grew as workers wilted in the face of taunting picketers. Still, there were more than 450 willing to run the gauntlet through the gates and keep the mill running.

Wyandotte workers, c. 1930

---

[73] It was not Waterville's first labor strike. Car shop workmen at Maine Central Railroad walked out for three months beginning in July 1922 protesting lowered wages and the company's policy of contracting work from the outside. The railroad refused to negotiate, but when it was over, all but a few of the strikers were rehired.

Violence erupted shortly before dawn on September 19 when more than 300 men and women strikers moved in under cover of heavy fog and suddenly stormed the mill, grappling with a small force of local police in an attempt to get at the strikebreakers. Six arrests were made before the mob retreated. By noon, Mayor Robert M. Jackson had Company G of the 103rd Maine Infantry on the scene, wielding bayonetted rifles and carrying tear gas. That evening, strikers tested the guardsmen by throwing stones and breaking more than 100 windows. The militia responded with tear gas. Additional militia came from Portland and Lewiston.

Although the number of strikebreakers dwindled to 50, the mill stayed open, and when union leader George Jabar arrived at the tense scene later that night, he sent the picketers away. The strike was over by late July, but tensions between labor and management continued, and hard feelings between strikers and those who had crossed the lines lasted for lifetimes.

George Jabar, a first generation Syrian (Lebanese)-American from Waterville, was a key figure in the organization of Maine's factory workers. He had worked at the Lockwood mill and then at the Wyandotte before joining the new government-protected labor movement in 1933. Brash and unyielding in defense of workers, Jabar enjoyed their loyalty and support, and although management did not often sing his praises, he earned their respect. At the time of the strike he was head of the Maine Textile Council representing union organizations throughout the state. Speaking at a labor meeting early that September, he called for unity among workers and said their biggest enemies were "the communists, the capitalist, and the fellow worker who becomes a scab." He marched with the Lockwood picketers in the days leading up to the violence, gaining more than 125 new union members, but the mill never became fully organized, and that would weaken the hand of the local cotton workers 20 years down the road.

For Waterville, the labor troubles were not over. In the spring of 1937, the women stitchers and the men cutters at C.F. Hathaway threatened to walk out unless the company agreed to recognize the Amalgamated Clothing Workers of America (ACWA) and its local union. The factory owners, Ellerton Jetté and E. K. Leighton, refused, and on April 6 police were called to Appleton Street to face picketers demanding $13 a week, a 40-hour workweek, and union recognition. A counter-offer of a 10 percent raise and a 45-hour week was refused, and both sides dug in. Workers, represented by the indefatigable Jabar, claimed 200 of Hathaway's 302 employees were off duty; Jetté claimed 200 were still at work. The stalemate continued until April 14 when, in a surprising turn, a committee of workers went to management to say they would renounce ACWA if they could be represented by a union of their own invention, the Waterville Shirt Makers Association. That same day, Jetté agreed to a 5 percent raise and a 40-hour week, and on April 20, soon after a near unanimous vote to sign on with the new Association, the strike ended.[74]

Even in the midst of strife, there were those in Waterville who were brave enough to begin new ventures. In 1935, Louis and Ceila Shiro opened a new hotel on busy College Avenue and named it The Jefferson. Offering all manner of entertainment, the hotel managed by "Ma" Shiro was famous for its dining room, which featured the finest Chinese cuisine for miles around.[75] At the same time, Kennebec Federal Savings bravely organized as a customer-owned bank and, faced with overcrowding of the high school, the city itself dug into limited tax dollars and got WPA funds to plan an expansion of the Gilman Street building by adding a manual arts training wing on the west end and a gymnasium and auditorium wing to the east.

As if financial catastrophes weren't bad enough, weather tragedies made the hard times even worse. Most would remember The Great New England Hurricane of 1938 as the worst regional weather event in history, but the storm that took the lives of 682 people that September lost its deadly force before reaching Maine. Two years before, in March of 1936, two weeks of steady rain flooded much of the eastern United States, killing more than 200, leaving 14,000 homeless, and causing $100 million in damage. The Kennebec River flooded behind giant ice jams, discharging at its peak 150,000 cubic feet of water per second[76] and destroying the 100-year old Ticonic (Waterville-Winslow) Bridge. The bridge was quickly rebuilt.

NOT ONLY WERE THE SCHOOLS CROWDED, but the streets were clogging up as well. The freedom and convenience of the automobile collided (often literally) with the scheduled electric streetcars that most believed would run forever. When owners of the Waterville, Fairfield & Oakland Railway announced they were losing money, wails came from both those who had forsaken the streetcars for their automobiles and those who relied on the trolleys to get to work. Promotions and discounted tickets failed to attract enough customers, and the last electric streetcar ran on October 11, 1937. That same day the city began running buses along most

---

[74] The local union was of little use, and in 1945 it was dissolved and Hathaway workers signed on again with Amalgamated.

[75] The hotel burned in 1945, was rebuilt, and survived under Shiro family management until 1977 when it became John Martin's Manor and continued another 30 years until it closed in 2007. The city's first off-track betting parlor continued to operate in the building's basement until 2012.

[76] In the record flood of 1987 the river discharged 194,000 cubic feet per second at its crest.

of the old routes, stopping for passengers at telephone poles marked with yellow bands of paint, but like the trolleys the buses got little use, and the service eventually withered as well.

On November 8, 1937, Herbert Hoover came to speak at the Baptist Church on the occasion of the 100th anniversary of the martyrdom of Elijah Lovejoy. The speech was carried nationwide on the NBC radio network. A somewhat nervous Colby president, Franklin Johnson, made the introduction. "Ladies and gentlemen," Johnson said, "it is my distinct pleasure to introduce you to that extinguished gentleman, The Honorable Herbert Hoover, former President of the United States." Johnson's face turned red. Undaunted, Hoover plunged into his prepared remarks.

HAVING ESCAPED THE GREAT DEPRESSION with relatively few scars, in 1938 Waterville could justifiably celebrate its 50th anniversary as a city, and in 1939, at the end of the first of his record-breaking six one-year terms as mayor, Paul Dundas said in his annual report that the city "has progressed in an exceptional manner." He boasted that the city's bonded indebtedness had been cut in half, to $75,000, in a year. He also cited a rise in new home construction, the building of a new street in the North End (Johnson Heights), the laying of two miles of new asphalt sidewalks, and the opening of a new public skating rink (Whipple Bowl) behind the Public Works Department garages at the end of Wentworth Court.

As if to underscore the returning vibrancy of the city, on October 7, 1939, Sisters Hospital announced the birth of 14 babies the day before, a new city record. Sadly, that same day, headlines from Europe brought news that Poland could no longer resist the invasion of Hitler's Nazi Germany and the winds of a second world war were in the air.

9

All in the Same Boat

-1949

Pearl Harbor!
Until December 7, 1941, most Americans didn't know much about the place, or even where it was. Afterward, its mention would resonate above the Alamo and the battleship *Maine* as a name that rallied the nation to a level of unity and patriotism unequaled before or since.

The surprise Japanese attack came on a Sunday, shortly after 8 a.m., Hawaii time. It was early afternoon in New York, and a radio announcer broke into the Dodgers-Giants football game to announce the news. Others first heard it when they dialed to the New York Philharmonic concert at 3 o'clock on CBS. Stunned listeners left their radios on to keep the tubes warm, and ran to tell their neighbors. By dusk, there was barely a soul in the country who didn't know the United States was going to war.

The local *Sentinel* went to press early, and by early Monday morning, lines had formed outside the Silver Street headquarters, waiting to grab still wet copies of an edition that blazed the sobering headline:

JAPS DECLARE WAR ON U.S.

As details trickled in, the truth was wrenching. The heart of the American naval fleet had been caught off guard. Eight battleships were damaged or sunk; more than 2400 had perished. The first reaction was one of confusion. Except on the west coast, where anxious eyes had been trained on the Pacific, most Americans believed their worst enemy was Hitler's Germany. Although they wanted retribution for the Japanese attack, they were even more anxious to put the *Führer* in his place. In Waterville, angry feelings toward the Nazis were especially intense. Germany had

91

overtaken France the year before, and the city's large French Canadian population, albeit twice removed from their homeland, was eager for revenge.

President Franklin Roosevelt quickly declared war on Japan, and then, fearing Congress would not abide a fight on two fronts, took a pause. Hitler forced the question three days later (December 11) by declaring war on the United States. FDR responded in kind.

Over the next few days, the *Sentinel* published photos of more than 20 local service members who were on duty in Hawaii at the time of the attack.[77] Against the odds, none was injured or killed. Around the country, enlisted reserves (ages 28-35) were called to active duty, and dozens of local men trekked off to the nearest enlistment office at City Hall in Augusta to sign up. The country was on its way to building an armed service that would eventually number 12 million troops.

Before Pearl Harbor, U.S. war plans were mostly on paper. Afterward, every national effort instantly focused on making them real. The automobile industry began making airplanes and tanks, and hundreds of other manufacturers tooled up to meet the demands of war. Nearby, Keyes Fibre prepared to make pistol grips, shell caps, and valve wheels, and to use its patented KYS-ITE product to make serving trays with plastic fiber instead of precious rubber or aluminum. When many southern cotton mills converted to manufacture nylon for parachutes, Lockwood and other northern factories stepped up production of much-needed cotton cloth.

The war was barely three weeks old when the 500 workers at the Wyandotte, already sharing around-the-clock shifts, volunteered to work for no pay on New Years Day and send their wages to help build a bomber aircraft. Across the river, Hollingsworth & Whitney began to re-tool to make heavy "tabulator" stock to meet the government's exploding need to keep records.

Neighbors everywhere pulled together. Victory gardens replaced back lawns, and families flattened tin cans, peeled the aluminum foil off gum wrappers, and stirred yellow dye into lard to make it look like butter. Unconcerned about marking homes where the men were gone, mothers of those in service proudly posted blue stars in their windows and prayed they would never have to be changed to gold.

---

[77] The list included a single woman, Nellie Stuart, a military nurse who lived on Maple Street.

Mayor Clinton Clauson and actress Dorothy Lamour sell War Bonds at the Waterville Railroad Station, 1943

East coast towns were on high alert, even as far as 50 miles inland. Within weeks, more than 1800 residents signed up for local Civilian Defense teams. Older men volunteered as air raid wardens, fitting eyebrows over the tops of headlights in order to patrol the roads safely at night, and walking through neighborhoods, watching for violators of the frequent blackout curfews. The plucky wardens also took shifts in hastily-built wooden towers to watch for enemy planes.

The first tower was on the Hapworth Farm in Winslow; another was built near the train overpass on the Belgrade Road in Oakland. No one ever spotted an enemy plane, but more than once, diligent observers called a false alarm on friendly Piper Cubs from the Civilian Pilot Training Program (CPTP) at the Waterville Airport. The program had begun in 1938 to address the national shortage of trained pilots, and in May of 1942, in cooperation with local airport management, Colby was asked to manage a local CPTP to train pilots as instructors for the naval training school at

Pensacola, Florida. All private aviation was re-located to Pittsfield, and the private Heart of Maine Flying Service moved to Dexter.[78]

Gasoline was rationed (three gallons a week), and tokens and stamps for scarce commodities were doled out in a complicated, ever-changing system that neither merchants nor their customers ever fully understood. Locally, doctors Thomas McCoy and Blynn Goodrich gathered contributions and built the state's first fully-manned mobile field hospital.

At the same time, two local physicians, husband and wife Clair and Nora Brown, met with colleagues who bravely agreed to establish the city's first osteopathic hospital. The group purchased the old Elm City Hospital on Western Avenue and proceeded to do much of the renovating and remodeling work themselves. It opened on September 6, 1943, and received 668 patients the first year. Philadelphia surgeon Edward Drew, D.O., was the first administrator and chief of staff. In October 1945, the Waterville Osteopathic Hospital became a public entity.

The few who had gasoline enough to splurge on a Sunday ride up Mayflower Hill had little to see. The only completed Colby building was Lorimer Chapel, finished in 1939, a full eight years after the decision to move. Since then, progress had been painfully poky, more so because the college's inclination was to pay as it went, buying building materials with cash as gifts came in. When the war began, work continued only until the supply of beams and bricks ran out. By 1942, they had managed to complete two women's dormitories, Mary Low and Louise Coburn.[79]

Colby could not have used dormitories for men if it had them. The enrollment, which stood at 435 men and 267 women in the fall of 1941, fell in a single year to a total of 282. Students, mostly women, were shuttled between the two campuses in a decrepit former school bus called the Blue Beetle. The women's union was finished in 1943, but eight other skeleton structures stood starkly against the treeless hillside landscape for the duration. The most prominent unfinished building was Miller Library, which would one day stand as the most iconic symbol of the handsome campus. It was the gift of Merton Miller, graduate of the class of 1890, who had made a

---

[78] During the war, more than 1400 CPT schools across the country trained nearly a half-million pilots, including 19-year-old John Glenn of Ohio. The Waterville program was discontinued in 1944. The Civilian Air Patrol (CAP) was an offshoot of the CPTP. The program of volunteer pilots who patrolled the local skies was abandoned in 1951 following a Fairfield Center crash in which pilot Paul Paulette was killed.

[79] Mary Low was Colby's first woman student. She was admitted in 1871, making Colby the first previously all-male college to become coed. Louise Coburn, niece of Governor Abner Coburn, joined three other women in the Class of 1876.

fortune from the gold mines of the Philippines. At first, he sent $50,000 a month for construction costs. In 1941, when the Japanese took the islands and flooded his mines, the payments stopped. He resumed them again when the war was over, but the building was not dedicated until 1947.

With enrollment dwindling, the college made a successful bid for assignment of a military training unit of the Army Air Force that began in early 1943. The College Training Detachment (CTD) plan called for 100 men to be enrolled every month (up to 500) and receive four months of classroom instruction and a month of flight training before being commissioned. It didn't work. Many enlistees were not qualified for college, most were called to service before they finished, and only one group ever completed the program. A year later, the 21st CTD was disbanded.

> Progress on Mayflower Hill was so discouragingly slow that there was a moment in 1944 when trustees were tempted to accept an offer from the U.S. Navy to lease the entire new campus and convert it into a 1000-bed hospital. It became a contest between the pragmatists and those who stubbornly clung to the hope of completing the move. The dreamers won, and the college declined the offer.

For five long years, those at home desperately sought any diversion from the worries of war.[80] The government, eager to keep morale high, encouraged Hollywood to churn out movies. Most were about war. Servicemen Clark Gable, John Ford, and Jimmy Stewart became instant stars, and GIs carried photos of Betty Grable, folded into their Bibles. Theaters filled with patrons who came not only to see the features, but especially to catch the heavily-censored *Movietone News* that preceded every showing and provided the only chance to see action images from the battlefronts.

For those who couldn't afford the 25¢ movie ticket, there were other distractions. Neighbors often walked together into town and strolled down

---

[80] The dreariest winter of the war was 1942-43, the year of double daylight savings time with a second hour added to the customary summer one-hour fallback and both hours continued into the winter. In Maine, already doomed to long nights of darkness, it seemed darker even longer.

The Main Street Haines Theater embellishes its marquee with patriotic slogans while promoting the 1943 classic comedy film, *Heaven Can Wait*

Main Street to gawk through shop windows. Others went to the train station on College Avenue to watch and wave as troops came and left. Sometimes they caught glimpses of German prisoners, headed to one of Maine's four POW camps in the north.[81]

OF THE MANY ACTIVITIES THAT WORKED to bring the community together, local sports were high on the list. In Waterville the enthusiasm had once been split, north and south, between ice hockey and basketball. By 1940, the fan bases had begun to meld.

The Canadians had brought hockey with them, and the joy of the game became infectious. Backyard rinks were everywhere, and children prayed for freezing temperatures. The city kept the Whipple Bowl in the North End, and Arthur Gagne ran the South End Arena (52 King Street), home to the high school Purple Panther team, which, when war began, had won all four state championships since 1938. Everyone knew the names of the local

---

[81] Some 4000 German prisoners were detained at Maine camps in Houlton, Princeton, Seboomook Farm (near Moosehead), and Spencer Lake. They were required to pick potatoes and harvest pulpwood.

heroes. Tops among them was Ray Lemieux, a member of the 1932 U.S. Olympic team who made his career in Waterville and along the way, taught hundreds of local youngsters in a vibrant Pee Wee hockey program that he founded and worked tirelessly to sustain.

In the winter of 1943-44, it wasn't hockey that galvanized the community; it was basketball. The high school team included a number of Lebanese Americans who had honed their skills at the Boys Club on Main Place, near their Head of Falls neighborhood. By the time the boys first met high school coach Wallace "Wally" Donovan, they had already spent endless hours drilling in the tiny club gym under the tutelage of Dutch Bernhardt. Brothers John and Norman Jabar and John and Paul Mitchell[82] teamed with Ted Shiro, Len Saulter and others to win all 27 games in the regular season before trouncing Portland for the state championship. After defeating Somerville, Massachusetts, in a three-game New England tournament, the team returned to Waterville to find hordes of adoring, cheering fans waiting at the train station.

Coach "Wally" Donovan was a sports hero in his own right, having earned 15 varsity letters at Waterville High, where he captained teams in football, basketball, and baseball. Local fans followed to watch him play at Colby, where he succeeded as a student and as an athlete. As a running back he was All-Maine, All-New England, and All-American honorable mention, and as a scholar he was president of his class and shared the top commencement prize (Condon Medal). Following graduation, he returned to Waterville High where he served as coach and athletic director over a career that spanned 38 years. His football teams won state titles in 1937 and 1944, and after taking the New England title in 1944, his basketball teams repeated state championships in 1945 and 1949. The high school gymnasium is named in his memory.

WHEN WORD CAME THAT PRESIDENT ROOSEVELT HAD DIED (April 12, 1945), the nation was swept with grief. For the past 11 years, the father-like giant had led the country through its worst economic crisis and its most destructive war. Now, he was suddenly gone, and grieving citizens stood on the streets and wept. Although the war was going well in Europe, without Roosevelt the future seemed uncertain. To make matters worse, no one was at all sure his successor, Vice President Harry Truman, was up to the task.

---

[82] John "Swisher" Mitchell was the star. He and Paul were two of four brothers, least famous of whom was George, who later went on to make something of himself as a diplomat and politician.

It took three days for the train carrying FDR's body to wind a thousand miles from Warm Springs, Georgia, to Washington, D.C., and then to Hyde Park, New York. Mourners lined the tracks the entire way. The April 15 funeral was not broadcast, and local memorial services were put together in towns and cities across America. At 2 p.m., as his funeral was beginning at Hyde Park, factories halted production, and telephone operators pulled the switchboard plugs and stood in silence. In Waterville, citizens jammed the Opera House, where a portrait of the fallen President was placed on a center-stage easel, flanked by a flag-bearing honor guard of the American Legion. Mayor George J. Doyle presided, there were many eulogies, and the high-school band played. The service lasted two hours.

Roosevelt had lived to see the miraculous invasion of Normandy and the advance of Allied troops toward Berlin, but the country was still mourning his death when Berlin fell and Nazi Germany surrendered on May 8, 1945. Celebrations were muted, since the war in the Pacific raged on. By June, the Allies had reclaimed Okinawa and the Philippines, but the Japanese were determined to defend their homeland to the last man. In early August, faced with the probable loss of thousands of additional lives on both sides, President Truman unleashed the atomic bomb on Hiroshima and Nagasaki; and on August 15, Emperor Hirohito surrendered.

The news triggered a national party. Crowds danced on the White House lawn, and two million people cheered as they waded through six inches of confetti in Times Square. In Waterville, hundreds of people headed downtown. Cars – all pre-war models and most all of them black – clogged Main Street in both directions and had to be cleared for a hastily arranged parade. Veterans from every branch, including Waterville's Company G of the 103rd National Guard infantry, lined up at Post Office Square and headed down Main Street. Cheering spectators dangled their legs over the eaves of the rooftop of the Appleton Inn and stood four deep on the sidewalk across the street in front of Parks Diner and the Red & White food store.[83] Spontaneously, the revelers began to fall haphazardly in line behind the well-aligned troops. By the time the parade reached Levine's store at the foot of the street there was barely a soul left on the sidewalks to watch.

---

[83] Opposite the historic railroad diner, the Haines Theater was playing *Out of this World* starring Eddie Bracken and Veronica Lake, a romantic comedy whose title, if not the story, seemed to fit the mood.

Main Street parade, VJ Day, August 15, 1945

Waterville counted more than 2000 of its men and women who went to fight, and 59 who gave their lives. Among the casualties was 22-year-old Army Air Corp Captain Robert A. LaFleur of Kennebec Street, missing in action in Africa in June of 1943. Nicknamed "The Blond Bomber," LaFleur was an exceptional athlete at Waterville High and at Colby. In 1947, the growing Waterville Airport was renamed in his memory.[84]

Membership of the Bourque American Legion Post, named to honor the first local man to die in World War I, suddenly grew to more than 1200 to become the largest in Maine. Contributions for a new home came easily, and in 1949 construction began on a handsome new facility on College Avenue (No. 21). The original tiny quarters at the corner of Silver and Spring streets were abandoned. At the dedication, the new post was renamed Bourque-Lanigan, adding the name of Seaman Arthur W. Lanigan,

---

[84] LaFleur's body was never recovered. His name is inscribed on an MIA memorial wall in Carthage, Tunisia.

99

the first Waterville casualty of World War II, who died in January, 1942, when USS *Houston* was sunk.[85]

THE WAR BROADENED AMERICANS' VIEW of themselves and of each other, and the gaps between the sexes and social classes narrowed. The military draft gave no favors to any class, and everyone shared in the sacrifices at home. For the women, the space might have narrowed even more if they had held onto the jobs they managed to land when the glass ceiling was cracked by war, but few women had aspirations for careers in the workplace and fewer men thought they should. Instead, voluntarily or otherwise, they surrendered the better positions to the returning men and went home to build the kinds of lives both men and women had dreamed of through the war.

In 1941, the federal government had been spending $3 million a day on Depression recovery programs, and eight million people were still out of work. By Victory Day, the country had spent an estimated $245 billion on the war; and 66 million, including five million women, had jobs. Roosevelt's nation-saving New Deal paled in comparison. In places like Waterville, where factory jobs were still the foundation of the economy, the future seemed rosy. The developing Colby campus was a magnet for new neighborhoods beyond the Messalonskee, and new streets and homes began popping up on the edges of town. The graveled Gilman Street extension above the bridge was paved and renamed Mayflower Hill Drive, a mecca for those who dreamed of moving up.

Gas rationing was gone, automobile plants were making cars once again, and Americans were madly buying up the new models and taking to the roads everywhere.[86] The Maine Turnpike Authority, established in 1941, began to build a north-south toll highway, and by 1947 the first 50 miles were open, from Kittery to Portland. In Waterville, citizens became embroiled in the first of an endless series of parking and traffic control arguments when city officials – claiming downtown workers were hogging Main Street parking spaces all day long – talked of installing parking meters. Merchants, certain the gadgets would drive customers away, howled in

---

[85] By 2017 the Post membership, although still the largest in the state, had dropped to 583 members and the College Avenue facility became needlessly large. The Post moved into a smaller building on Drummond Avenue, formerly occupied by the Waterville Humane Society. The College Avenue building was set to become a Children's Museum.

[86] In the decade of the 40s, the Waterville-Winslow area had 6187 traffic accidents, 51 of them fatal.

objection. When 268 meters finally went in, most workers continued to park in the same places and simply skipped out of shops and offices every hour to feed nickels to the city, while customers found free spaces on the already-clogged side streets and kept coming.

A rowdy debate over parking was as good a subject as any for a city that dearly loved its politics. While membership in the Democratic and Republican parties was most often determined by the color of the voter's collar, there were enough who strayed to the opposite parties to make every election campaign colorful. Citizens enjoyed the fray, and it was a rare election when both parties didn't fill the ballots with candidates for every office, from mayor to clerks and constables. Through it all, the city clung to the federal-like bicameral system of government, established in 1888. Almost every municipal question took weeks to sort out as resolutions passed back and forth between the Common Council and the Board of Aldermen for multiple readings, debates, amendments, and votes.

FROM THE TURN OF THE CENTURY until 1948, the city had elected 23 mayors – 12 Democrats and 11 Republicans. Popular shop owner and bank president Russell Squire evened the score for the GOP when he squeaked out a victory (3287-2853) over 34-year-old Democratic upstart, Edmund S. Muskie. A Polish-American from Rumford,[87] Muskie had moved to Waterville in 1940 and was practicing law upstairs over Fidelity Insurance and across the hall from the Waterville Women's Association at 131 Main Street. Already a member of the Maine House of Representatives when he ran for mayor, Muskie had begun to travel up and down Maine in an attempt to invigorate the Democratic Party, a statewide underdog since Reconstruction. His defeat by Squire was the last political race he would lose for another 20 years, when he was defeated in the race for Vice President of the United States.

Squire was an outspoken but persuasive and unifying leader. He accomplished much of what he wanted to achieve, except to build an enduring airport. He knew what having more air traffic could mean and urged Waterville and Augusta to come together and consider a single airport somewhere in between. He was hooted down in both cities, and his vision never got off the ground.

---

[87] His father, Stephen Marciszewski, changed the family name soon after arriving in the United States.

THE MOST EFFECTIVE UNIFYING DEVICE of the war had been the now-ubiquitous radio. Roosevelt used it for his "fireside chats;" state and local officials used it to spread vital information; merchants used it to tout their wares; and listeners used it both to keep up with the news and to relax. Waterville area listeners, on the fringes of the coverage area of WLBZ radio in Bangor, were forced to fiddle and fuss amid the vagaries of atmospheric conditions to tune it in.

The static suddenly cleared up on July 19, 1946, when the city's own station, WTVL (1490 Mhz) went on the air. Mayor H. Chesterfield Marden presided at opening ceremonies, and that evening listeners heard the ABC network broadcast of Joe Lewis's defeating Billy Conn in defense of his world heavyweight boxing title in Yankee Stadium. [88]

The new station was the creation of Carleton D. Brown, photographer and entrepreneur, whose fascination with radio began when he built his own crystal receiver as a child. While a student at Colby, Brown was an announcer at WLBZ's tiny Waterville satellite station that opened in 1929. Located in a back room of Choate's Music Store on Main Street, the station was tied to Bangor by a Western Union line that ran alongside the Maine Central Railroad tracks to Bangor. The Waterville studio contributed a few hours each week to the mother station, including a *Colby at the Mike* show that Brown produced and announced, and his freewheeling Saturday morning *Sidewalk Interview* program, staged in front of the Haines Theater and sponsored by the Bolduc Baking Company (makers of Bambi Bread).

In 1935, the feeder station was moved to the second floor of Brown's photography studio (50 Main), and two years later WLBZ took over the Augusta station (WRDO) and tied it to both Waterville's satellite and WCSH in Portland, to establish the first radio network in Maine.

Brown was severely crippled by polio as an infant, but neither he nor anyone who knew him would ever think to say he was handicapped. Determined to have his own station, in 1941 Brown organized the Kennebec Broadcasting Company, and with the help of investments from friends, purchased a vacant home at the head of Silver Street (No. 36), rented out the upstairs, and made a studio on the main floor. He found a second-hand transmitter and a 110-foot tower, bought a high plot of land on Benton Avenue in Winslow, and proceeded to help with the

---

[88] Ironically, the fight was also the first to be televised.

construction. When it was up and running, the new station boasted 250 watts of power and covered a 15-mile radius.

In the years following the first broadcast, WTVL and its owner received broad recognition as models of community-service broadcasting. Listeners long remembered the popular network offerings (*Don McNeil's Breakfast Club*, Betty Crocker, Paul Harvey, Howard Cosell, *The Green Hornet, Gang Busters*, and more), but the most endearing programs were locally produced. They included Allison Day and her popular *Luncheon with Allison*, Edgar Poulin's *Mélodie Française, Variété Française* with Joe Bulger, and local sports coverage with Bob Woodbury. Best-known of all was retired Colby dean Ernest Marriner's *Little Talks on Common Things*, a weekly 15-minute program that continued for 1672 consecutive broadcasts (1948-82) to become the nation's longest-running radio program under a single sponsor, the Keyes Fibre Company.

COURTESY OF DAVID BROWN

10

Sunshine and Shadows

-1959

The decade had barely begun when the nagging Cold War suddenly got a whole lot colder, and then warmed up again. In February 1950, the egomaniacal Wisconsin Senator Joseph McCarthy claimed that 205 communists were working for the State Department, and in June, 80,000 North Korean troops struck the Republic of Korea like a cobra. Adults began thinking Reds might be hiding under their beds, and children were taught to duck under their desks.

The capital, Seoul, fell within days, and the United Nations, barely five years old, agreed for the first time to meet aggression with force. American troops led NATO forces into battle on June 27, and President Truman assured a war-weary nation that the U.S. role was only a "police action." Over the next three years, the country would suffer 100,000 casualties.

The light focused on the war in Korea was less intense than the one that had shone on the recent world war, but the fear of communism was rampant. By coincidence or canniness, McCarthy's tirades were perfectly timed to feed the hysteria, and his baseless accusations fed an American mood all too eager to find evidence of its worst fears. Even in Congress, where McCarthy's narcissism and drunken outbursts were well known, members felt threatened and stood by and watched as innocent lives were ruined.

Among the first leaders to speak up was Maine Senator Margaret Chase Smith, from nearby Skowhegan. Having served four terms in the House of Representatives, the popular Republican became the only woman U.S. Senator when she won the seat by a whopping 71 percent margin the year before. On June 1, 1950, she delivered a 15-minute *Declaration of Conscience* speech on the Senate floor in which she defended the right of Americans to criticize and hold unpopular beliefs, but called the Senate "debased" for stooping to "the level of a forum of hate and character assassination." McCarthy's treacherous talons had cut too deeply for the wounds to heal soon, but there is no doubt Smith's brave speech turned the tide toward his downfall in disgrace.

Maine U.S. Rep. Clyde Smith died in 1940, and his wife Margaret Madeline Chase Smith won his seat in a special election. She was re-elected four times, and in 1949 ran for the Senate to become the only woman ever to serve in both houses of Congress. Sen. Smith's place in the House was taken by a Waterville native, Charles P. "Charlie" Nelson, son of John E. Nelson who held the same seat from 1922 to 1933. The younger Nelson was born in Waterville and like his father, graduated from Colby before attending law school. Charles Nelson served in the Navy during WWII. Discharged in 1946, he returned to Augusta, where he was twice elected Mayor before running for Sen. Smith's Congressional seat. Re-elected to the House four times, he served from 1949 to 1957.

DESPITE WARS HOT AND COLD, in 1950 Central Maine enjoyed a robust economy firmly anchored on 5 paper-related mills, 18 textile and apparel factories, 25 food-processing plants, and 8 shoe and leather makers.

Waterville's population had jumped ten percent in a decade (to 18,287), and the city issued an average of four new building permits a week to keep up. A dozen homes were already built on Mayflower Hill Drive, and work on a dozen more paused only long enough for the Waterville Sewerage District, established in July, to lay pipes ahead of the new pavement. [89] Several new streets in the west of town were in various stages of completion. Mayor Dubord's prediction that by saving Colby, Waterville would strengthen itself, was fast coming true.

Nowhere was the vibrancy more easily seen than from the foot of College Avenue, at the five-way intersection with Main, where two of the city's four traffic lights drew constant honks from altogether too many cars. Across the way sat the classic post office and on the right stood the Elmwood Hotel, exactly 100 years old, its front yard recently relinquished to

---

[89] The City built the Sewerage District as a quasi-municipal public utility serving most of Waterville and nearby towns. It was incorporated after the fashion of the successful and once unique multi-town Kennebec Water District. When the project was finished, 85 percent of the city's homes were connected, and no longer did the homes along Burleigh Street "straight pipe" waste into the Messalonskee.

an Esso Service Center. Across the street, the Central Fire Station blasted a curfew every night at 9, to test the horn and get the kids off the streets.

Near the Waterville Savings Bank with its chiming sidewalk clock was the popular 24-hour Parks Diner, and across the street Enrico Conte sold frosted mugs of root beer for 20 cents. Leo Diambri's fruit stand had a lunch counter specializing in spaghetti, and Evariste LaVerdiere's drug store was fast becoming a chain. The burly Tom Georgantas could be seen through the window of the candy store named for his wife Bea, pulling taffy from hooks hung over copper kettles. At the Harris Bakery outlet, women clerks wore starched uniforms with tieback caps and white gloves to serve the drooling customers. W.B. Arnold's hardware store had expanded in 1948, and at the foot of the street, Saul Mandell's Waterville Hardware competed with an inventory that ran the gamut.

Parks Diner, W.W. Berrys, and Cottles Red & White, top of Main Street, west side, c. 1949

While merchants offered all kinds of goods, the street was a mecca for clothing. At Levine's, a fixture on the street since 1896, Pacy and Ludy catered to men and boys. Near Castonguay Square, George and Herbert Sterns ran a small version of Selfridges, complete with an escalator and a fluoroscope (x-ray) for fitting feet to shoes. Across the street, facing the

106

square, the classic-designed white limestone front of Emery-Brown's[90] invited shoppers into 12,000 square feet of sales space on four floors. Dunham's sold Hathaway shirts, pricey at $3 a shirt, and did a brisk mail-order business in the back room. Alvina & Delia[91] catered to women with means. Butlers and Fishman's suited everyone. Most stores ran tabs for faithful customers on tight budgets.

On the corner by Temple Street, above Bob Dexter's Drug Store and next to a Chinese restaurant, Al Corey, fresh from the Army, ran a tiny music studio, selling reeds and strings and giving lessons. He would soon move downstairs and then across the street, where he continued his business into the next century.

> Al Corey's "Big Band" orchestra provided almost weekly dances and concerts, indoors and out, with visiting dance bands whose names read like Broadway marquees: Tex Beneke, Les Brown, Tommy Dorsey, Gene Krupa, Woody Herman, Sammy Kaye, Stan Kenton, and Vaughn Monroe. Another Waterville music group, The Elders, played throughout the state. It customarily featured Fred Petra (trumpet), Bob Marden (trombone), Don Nelson (tuba), Richard Dubord (clarinet), John Guptill (drums), Stan Wheeler (base), and Gerry Wright (piano).

Beyond Main Street, the broader city had more to offer. In less than a mile in every direction was a city-wide total of 72 grocery stores, 16 meat markets, 38 restaurants, 11 hotels, 23 gas stations, 13 automobile dealers, 18 appliance and furniture stores, 15 clothing stores, 8 shoe stores, and an array of other service and retail shops. The grandest retailer of all, Sears & Roebuck, was about to open on the corner of Elm and Center streets, near the heart of town.

As throughout its history, the city had no shortage of bars, and while the locals could hold their own, having a residential college in their midst further broadened the sale of beer. Conveniently, the new flood of war veterans improved the plausibility of students who claimed to be of age, and for the rest, helpful local cops tipped off bar owners when the state liquor inspector was in town. Arrests for burglaries, larcenies, and auto thefts

---

[90] Herbert Emery came from Fairfield, and was a leading figure in almost every local charity. Harry Sanford Brown was born in Winn, Maine (Penobscot County), graduated from Colby in 1899 and 12 years later partnered with Emery to open the well-known department store that specialized in custom tailoring for women.

[91] The shop was owned and shared by two women. Alvina Lewia sold fashion and furs and Delia Bouchard sold hats. Edmund Muskie's wife-to-be, Jane Gray, worked as a clerk.

numbered merely a half-dozen each in 1950, but in that same year 135 citizens were apprehended for drunkenness and another 31 for drunken driving.

WATERVILLE MARKED ITS 150TH ANNIVERSARY as a town in 1952, most memorably with a parade where the men of town showed off moustaches and beards as "Brothers of the Brush" in honor of the pioneers who built the town. The full decade was, in fact, highlighted with celebrations. St. Joseph Church on Front Street was dedicated in 1951, joining the city's other three Catholic churches in offering a total of 16 Sunday masses, five more on weekdays, and afternoon vespers as well. The local Unitarians united with the Universalists in 1952, making an even dozen Protestant churches, including the Pleasant Street Methodist Church where a new sanctuary was opened with high praise for contractor Henry T. Winters, who paid for most of it. In 1958, Beth Israel Synagogue moved into a new temple at the top of Kelsey Street, at the corner of Main. Congregation president David Gray led the building effort, achieved with the generous help of many, including the Levine brothers, and shoemaker Harold Alfond and his wife Dorothy.

Waterville's reputation in the sphere of education was growing as well. Enrollment at Morgan-Thomas College increased every year, and in 1950, with the founder's son, John L. Thomas, Jr., as president, the name of the business school was changed to Thomas Junior College, and the State Legislature approved the granting of associate degrees. In 1956 the 62-year-old college would move from its upstairs home on Main Street (over F. W. Woolworth) to its first proper campus in the Silver Street home of the late John Ware, founder of banks and railroads. The original buildings were renovated and a new classroom building was put up.

In 1951 the city celebrated the new Thayer Hospital on North Street, on land given by hospital trustee and benefactor Lewis Rosenthal. After two decades in Dr. Thayer's old house on Main Street, the hospital opened a modern $1 million 63-bed facility near the back door to the new Colby campus. It would join the city's other two hospitals in greeting 600 new babies in the coming year (and treat 33 cases of whooping cough and 133 of measles). Thayer's chief physician, Frederick T. Hill, put his friend and colleague, Registered Nurse Pearl Fisher, in charge.[92]

Presiding at the ceremonies was board chair Franklin Johnson, nearly ten years retired from the Colby presidency. Standing on the front steps of the new building, he could see on his left Johnson Heights, a street named in his honor, recently extended the full length from Upper Main to North Street.[93] Whatever pride the street naming or the hospital dedication might have brought him, nothing could compare to his elation a year later when the dream of his life came true. Colby had completed 14 buildings in the seven years since the end of the world war (bringing the total to 22), and when the fall term began in 1952, the college was fully settled on Mayflower Hill.

> Not every building on the new campus was of Georgian design and made of brick. Four plain gray barracks buildings purchased from a Rhode Island shipyard were hastily re-assembled across the road from Johnson Pond to provide 32 apartments for the flood of married veterans taking advantage of the GI Bill. Both the field house and neighboring headquarters of the Buildings and Grounds Department were war-surplus airplane hangars, and an old farmhouse, once at a corner of Miller Library, was moved behind the new tennis courts and became a tiny theater (later the Hill Family Guest House). Both the B&G (now Physical Plant) building and the guesthouse remain. The veterans' apartments were meant to be temporary, but they remained in use until 1958 and were not torn down until the early 1960s. The field house facilities survived three major renovations and a fire before being replaced by an entirely new athletic facility, planned for completion in 2020.

With the college needing every nickel for the new campus, the old one was all but forgotten, and the neglect annoyed townspeople who had come to love it. Colby suddenly began to seem a long way off, and while most faculty still lived in town and many students remained involved in local causes,[94] the most visible remaining tie with undergraduates was at "Colby Corner," at the intersection of Gilman and Pleasant streets near Sacred Heart Church, where they gathered in bunches to hook rides up the hill.

---

[92] Fisher and a succession of Mothers Superior at Sisters Hospital were the only women chief executives in town.

[93] Soon after the decade ended, Eustis Parkway, nearer the hospital, was named for Arthur Galen Eustis, who died in 1959. He had served as Colby's administrative vice president through the precarious financial times of building the new campus.

[94] In the summer of 1951, William Bryan, assistant dean of men and president of the Junior Chamber of Commerce, Colby graduate George Beach, and baseball team captain Art White formed the city's first Little League program. Managers of all four teams were Colby students.

Before the move, Colby hoped it might sell the old property to the railroad company that had crowded the college off the riverbank, but Maine Central Railroad wasn't interested, and in 1952 a large sign went up on College Avenue advertising the sale of eight buildings and 38 commercial lots. A piece on the corner by Front Street became a filling station, and a paint store went into buildings south of the station. The Phi Delta Theta fraternity house became a supermarket. Robert Drapeau bought Mary Low Hall on the corner of Getchell Street for his furniture and appliance store. Melvin and Meverett Beck took two lots near the river on Champlin Street to expand their metal roofing business, and across the way Yvonne Mathieu bought land for a family enterprise in auto repair. Sears & Roebuck rented part of Memorial Hall for storage, and Sacred Heart Church purchased Foss Hall on the Avenue to establish a parochial school in 1953.[95]

Waterville still had no venue for large events, and the state chipped in to help the city buy the north end of the old campus ($150,000), including Shannon Observatory, the Woodman Stadium and football field, and the field house, near the river. The field house was renovated and soon became the site of a number of well-attended events, including the annual Kiwanis Club Sportsmen's Show and the popular Harlem Globetrotters basketball team. The building was razed in 1962. Throughout its short life, great clouds of dust rose from the dirt floor and dimmed the already weak lighting, and the glass roof leaked like a sieve. The concrete stadium crumbled, became unsafe, and was torn down.

WHEN IT CAME TIME TO PREPARE THE INTRODUCTION to the City Directory for the 150th anniversary in 1952, someone gave the pen to the outspoken attorney and community activist Harvey Doane Eaton. Eaton clearly enjoyed the assignment and rambled on in a freewheeling, often irreverent style. He included the town of Winslow in his survey of local topics, broadly ranging from sanitation ("an obligation in human relations") to friendliness ("our park benches have a seating capacity of 144").

His report also included a section labeled "Failures" (the inclusion of which must surely have startled his editors) in which he facetiously chided the town's founders for making streets too narrow for automobiles, and

---

[95] Sacred Heart School became the city's Consolidated Catholic School in 1969. Administered by the Ursuline Sisters, it closed at the end of the 1973-74 academic year. The building was sold in 1978.

then went on to upbraid the Chamber of Commerce, of which he was a prominent member. "It is not very good [and] it has fluffed a lot of chances to do good service," and wrote tersely before urging "an action program adequate for our needs and opportunities."

The Chamber had indeed languished during the distress of World War II and had never gotten back up to full steam. Throughout its first 41 years it had been an informal entity with no legal standing, but on July 10, 1953 – perhaps moved by Eaton's barbs – a number of local luminaries (all men) met at the Elks Club and voted to incorporate the Waterville Area Chamber of Commerce with the State of Maine. Its stated purpose was "to establish a body of recognized authority" that would "encourage the growth and advocate the business prosperity of the City of Waterville and the towns of

---

The Korean War ended July 27, 1953, when an uneasy truce was declared along the 38th Parallel where it had all begun. The war without victory took more than 33,000 American lives, 233 of them from Maine. Waterville's four casualties[96] included the city's most decorated – and least well-remembered – war hero of all time. David B. Champagne was the son of Bernard and Anna (Osborne) Champagne, second generation Franco-Americans from St. Georges, Quebec. As a member of the 1st Battalion, 7th Marines, Corporal Champagne was badly wounded while leading his fire team against an enemy position. He refused medical help, and when an enemy grenade landed near him he threw it back to protect his comrades and was mortally wounded in the explosion. He was posthumously awarded the Congressional Medal of Honor, the Purple Heart, and six other medals from the U.S., NATO, and the Republic of Korea. His family was living in Fairfield at the time of his birth, and later moved to Warwick, R.I., before returning to live on Merrill Street in Waterville. Cpl. Champagne is buried in the family plot in St. Francis Cemetery.[97]

---

[96] Besides Cpl. Champagne, Marine PFC Herbert Corrigan, Jr., was also killed in action. Army PFC Roland Richard Carey and Army Cpl. Reginald E. Gervais both died in service.

[97] The tiny nearby town of Benton has two Medal of Honor recipients: Frank Haskell was killed in the Civil War, and Brian L. Buker, in Vietnam.

Winslow, Oakland and Fairfield and surrounding areas." Among the signatories were soon-to-be governor Edmund Muskie, former mayor Russell Squire, current mayor Richard Dubord, and soon-to-be mayor Cyril M. Joly, Jr. The Chamber opened an office on College Avenue, opposite the old campus, and retired state police officer Francis McCabe became executive director.

THE OLD STEAM LOCOMOTIVE #470 made its final passenger run on June 13, 1954, and throngs of nostalgic rail enthusiasts were on hand at the Waterville station to bid it farewell. It was soon to be deactivated and in October 1962, on the occasion of the 100th anniversary of Maine Central Railroad, it was presented to the city "to be preserved as a monument to steam travel." In 1969, then former Mayor Donald Marden, who had led the effort to preserve it, rode in the cab for the last few yards to its resting place near the railroad shops on College Avenue. Welded to a "dummy" section of track near the railroad shops, it was never properly preserved, and Maine weather and vandals took their toll. In 2018 the city sold the engine to the New England Steam Corporation for $25,000. The locomotive and tender were trucked separately to a site at Washington Junction in Ellsworth, owned by the State of Maine and operated by Downeast Scenic Railroad, where it was stored, subject to possible restoration.

The retirement of #470 came long after the introduction of diesel-electric locomotion. The streamlined stainless-steel-clad Flying Yankee, built for the Maine Central and Boston & Maine, had begun passenger service in 1935 and was soon running on a hectic six-day, 750-mile schedule, with stops from Boston to Bangor. In its later years, the articulated three-coach Flying Yankee drew more admiring spectators than paying passengers when it stopped in Waterville. Just as the trains had taken travelers off the rivers a century before, automobiles and new interstate highways were now taking travelers off the rails. By the time #470 was retired, the Flying Yankee had but a few more years to serve. It was retired in 1957, and by 1959 Waterville had no passenger rail service at all. [98]

---

[98] The Flying Yankee is now owned by the State of New Hampshire and is stored in Lincoln, N.H., where it, like the 470, awaits sufficient funds for restoration.

112

Maine Central Railroad Yards, full steam ahead, c. 1950

A fire on the night of February 22, 1955, brought yet another sign of regrettable change. The blaze began on the top floor of the imposing central building of Coburn Classical Institute, and firefighters, hampered by freezing temperatures and brisk winds, could not keep it from burning almost to the ground.

The alma mater of hundreds of area residents, the institute had been a source of community pride since 1829, when an earlier Latin school was established as Waterville Academy, a feeder for Waterville College-cum-Colby. The handsome four-story brick building with its domed belfry had loomed magnificently over Elm Street and Monument Park since 1884, when it was built as a replacement for the original schoolhouse. The new building came as a personal gift from Maine Governor Abner Coburn of Skowhegan, in memory of his brother and nephew, who had died in a swimming accident in 1881. In gratitude for his gift, the institution took the Coburn name. [99]

---

[99] The school existed under a succession of names: 1820, The College Latin School; 1829, Waterville Academy; 1865, Waterville Classical Institute; 1883, Coburn Classical Institute; 1970-1989, Oak Grove-Coburn.

A winter scene of Coburn Classical Institute, from Monument Park. Civil War memorial sculpture in the foreground, on right. Steeple of St. Francis Church, background, on left.

At the time of the fire, enrollment stood at 95 students, 12 of them in residence. By shifting classrooms to other buildings, the school managed to survive another dozen years under the gritty leadership of Principal Charles O'Reilly. There was talk (c.1966) of constructing a new school on the Ridge Road, but it was not to be, and in 1970 Coburn merged with Oak Grove School on the Augusta Road in Vassalboro. Oak Grove-Coburn operated until 1989, when it closed for lack of funds.

The decade brought natural disasters, as well. The blizzard of 1952 set records, and while a pair of hurricanes (Carol and Edna) in the fall of 1954 became tropical storms before hitting Central Maine, they caused flooding, damaged buildings, and felled trees, many of them stately elms already weakened by Dutch elm disease.

Caused by a fungi spread by elm bark beetles, Dutch elm disease was first discovered in the U.S. around 1920 and is believed to have come from a shipment of logs from the Netherlands. By 1930, three-quarters of the country's estimated 77 million trees had died. Waterville, The Elm City, began the 1950s with 3361 elms, but over the next two decades most of them would succumb to the disease. With annual treatment, the city has managed to keep alive a single tree in Castonguay Square. The 75-foot tall specimen is thought to be more than 175 years old.

WATERVILLE'S FIRST HINT OF THE COMING WAVE of buy-outs and mergers among the nation's large companies came in 1954 when the giant Scott Paper Company paid $38 million to purchase the 64-year-old Hollingsworth & Whitney plant and its vast Maine timberlands. H&W's 1680 Winslow paper workers held their collective breath, but there was nothing to fear. Scott sent only top management from its Philadelphia headquarters, and the workers kept their jobs. The new executives bought homes in town and were soon engaged as leaders in community affairs, and almost every school and community event listed Scott as a sponsor. The single biggest change came when the factory retooled and began churning out miles of toilet tissue.

The city's most crushing industrial blow came in 1955.

Northeast cotton makers had been in trouble since the end of World War II. Their equipment was old, and the advent of acrylic fibers was fast eating into the demand for cotton. Mills in the south were cutting prices, and foreign manufacturers were undercutting everybody. The year before, New England owners demanded and got a ten-cent an hour pay cut, a concession to keep the mills running, and the average wage for Maine workers dropped to $1.03 an hour. Now, owners were asking for a cut of eight cents more. On April 11, the AFL local #2658 of the United Textile Workers agreed to join with the broad-based CIO, which wanted a seven-

The Hollingsworth and Whitney Paper Mill, soon to be Scott Paper Company, c. 1950.

cent raise and threatened to stop work all along the eastern seaboard on April 15 unless an agreement was reached.

Newly elected Governor Ed Muskie and Mayor Dubord joined negotiators on the last day, but the talks collapsed. At 11:30 p.m. on April 14, Lockwood managers gave workers half an hour to pick up their belongings before turning off the lights and locking the doors. Some 850 jobs representing 30 percent of the mill work force on the Waterville side of the Kennebec, were suddenly gone. Twenty-three thousand textile workers at 22 other Maine mills were out of work as well.

For a time, some believed the frightening loss could be recovered, but their hopes were short-lived. In June, the Lockwood Company was liquidated, and the looms were sold. Kennebec Mills in Fairfield and American Woolen in North Vassalboro followed, and by mid-summer the number of lost area textile jobs soared above 1000.

Not every local enterprise was suffering. C.F. Hathaway was selling more shirts than ever, and its plant on Appleton Street was bursting at the seams. Its success was to the credit of a single man, Ellerton M. Jetté, who had been a lead investor in the 1932 purchase of the plant. Now, as president of the country's oldest shirt maker, Jetté wanted to march Hathaway onto the national scene, and in 1951 spent most of his meager advertising budget to hire the New York marketing guru David Ogilvy. Ogilvy put a black eye patch on a man wearing a Hathaway shirt,[100] and Jetté paid $3,167 to buy a single ad in the *New Yorker*. Within a week, every Hathaway shirt in New York City was sold, and within a month, shirt production at the tiny Waterville plant doubled. In 1957, with Hathaway employing some 800 people, the company purchased Lockwood Mill No. 2 and moved in.

Ogilvy took credit for the idea of the man with a patch, but so did Jetté's wife Edith, who later told the story of the two being on a cruise ship when an elegant man with an eye patch walked into the dining room. Edith claimed she turned to her husband and announced she had found the Hathaway man. Ellerton Jetté could well have been the Hathaway man himself, as he was as elegant as the fine shirts he sold. He made friends easily and never seemed out of place driving the only Rolls-Royce in town. He was obsessed with quality and had a bent toward the flamboyant. Unlike Charles Hathaway, Jetté liked big buttons, with three holes for added

[100] The model's name was Louis Douglas. His eyes were fine.

116

distinction. His innovations included oval collars, square-cornered cuffs, single-needle stitching, and one-piece sleeves. He led the shirt industry into the world of exotic fabrics and color: silk and madras from India, gingham from Scotland, prints from France, broadcloth from Japan, and Lochlana from Switzerland.

The Man With the Patch

THE CHAMBER OF COMMERCE MIGHT NOT HAVE BEEN AS LIVELY as attorney Eaton wished, but members were on their toes when plans were made for Maine's section of President Eisenhower's new interstate highway project. Despite the wailing about having too much traffic, the Chamber joined local officials in making a special plea to have the new highway come as close to Waterville as possible. When the Maine Highway Commission unveiled its initial plan in August of 1956, the supplicants began to think they should have been more careful about what they wished for. Drawings showed the four-lane highway laid out between Mount Merici Academy and Colby's campus, across the foot of the front lawn of the new President's House, over fields east of Mayflower Hill Drive,[101] and on to a North Street overpass near Thayer Hospital.

The city was outraged. Colby president Seelye Bixler sent letters to alumni. Mayor Clinton Clauson signed a City Council resolution

---

[101] The college had already made use of the land east of Mayflower Hill Drive for tennis courts, playfields and parking lots, but in 1992 it built the Lunder Admissions Office and later surrounded the Colby Green with other major buildings.

condemning the plan, and the Chamber lobbied state officials, top to bottom.

> Well-known Maine author Kenneth Roberts was furious. Earlier, when British historian Arnold Toynbee wrote that Maine was "a backward state, rich in nothing but woodsmen, watermen, hunters, and not much besides," Roberts wrote a scathing rebuttal. Now, Roberts said, if the Highway Commission committed this "contemptible sin," he would have to write Toynbee and apologize.

The Commission was accustomed to laying out roads by dead reckoning, and at first refused to budge, but by September its members agreed to have another look. Engineers suggested three alternate routes, unveiled at a public hearing at Averill School. One of the plans took the road farther west, behind the campus. It required no land from Mount Merici or Thayer Hospital, but would re-locate the Second Rangeway and take a chunk of 27 acres out of Colby's back yard.

That plan made the most sense, and everybody signed on except the U.S. Bureau of Public Roads, which had the final word. The Bureau said no, arguing the alternate route would increase distance and costs for motorists. Colby vice president Eustis said the change resulted in a mere addition of $44/100^{th}$ of a mile and the college would cover the extra cost ($230,000) by reducing its claim for land acquisition. Appeals for help in swaying the Bureau went to government officials, newspaper editors, college presidents and even judges. Some claim the highest tap was on the shoulder of Sherman Adams, President Eisenhower's Chief of Staff. Others believe Bixler reached out to his fellow college president, Milton Eisenhower, recently settled in as the president of Johns Hopkins, who spoke to his brother. In any case, the Bureau surrendered and the new road got a wrinkle.

THROUGHOUT THE DECADE, Waterville was blessed with strong leadership, often in high places. The local lawyer, Ed Muskie, finished his term as governor in January 1959 and went off to his first term in the U.S. Senate. His successor in the Blaine House was another adopted Waterville son, Clinton A. Clauson. A native of Iowa, Clauson came to town to establish his practice as a chiropractor and served as mayor in 1956-57.

Clauson's term as governor was cut short when he died after only 11 months in office.[102]

Waterville had steady leaders, as well. Popular Democrat Albert Bernier succeeded Clauson as mayor, serving four years until 1961. Republican Cyril M. Joly, Jr., took his place, and Willard "Bill" Arnold, whose family had helped lead Waterville from the beginning, became president of the Chamber.

The good leadership was much needed, for the city was a much different place from what it was when the decade began. Now there was no college on College Avenue, no Coburn near Coburn Park, no passenger trains at the train station, no regional airport, no cotton mill on the river, and many fewer elms on Elm Street. People were beginning to say it was time for some urban renewal.

---

[102] Among those attending his Waterville funeral was young Robert Kennedy, already known nationally as chief counsel to the Senate Labor Rackets Committee, where he publicly challenged Jimmy Hoffa over Teamster Union practices. At the time of the funeral, he was leading his brother's 1960 campaign for the presidency.

11

Urban Renewal

-1978

O nce cited as Maine's most beautiful city, Waterville was suffering both the plagues of old age and the curses of modern times. Its crown was slipping. The oldest housing in the poorest neighborhoods was dilapidated and unsafe, downtown was clogged with cars, traffic circulation was a labyrinth of narrow streets, and parking was all but impossible. As the 1960s neared, the best hope was an all-out program of Urban Renewal,[103] and while the effort achieved many good and necessary things, it also brought more controversy than the city had ever seen.

Some improvements were underway before Urban Renewal began. The railroad crossings on College Avenue had always been a bother, and with Colby safely up the hill, it was time to straighten out the top of Front Street and put College Avenue under the tracks. In 1955, new Governor Ed Muskie, Mayor Dubord, and city engineer Ralph Knowlton proposed a study of eliminating the crossings, and that winter Dubord and State Representative Albert Bernier convinced the Maine Legislature to approve planning money. It took six years for the federal government to agree to pay 90 percent of the $2.6 million cost.

---

[103] The term Urban Renewal was introduced into the American lexicon in 1955 when the federal Housing Act of that year provided for the use of eminent domain in acquiring property to partner with cities to demolish sub-standard buildings and construct new housing.

Nowhere was the crush of automobiles more apparent than on Main Street, where the narrow driving lanes, unsynchronized traffic lights, and diagonal parking often brought long lines of cars to a horn-tooting standstill. In 1957, the State Highway Department recommended that the street become one-way, north to south, with most parking parallel to the curbs; and make Front Street one-way in the other direction, with barely any parking at all. Howls came from everywhere. The hardware merchant Willard "Bill" Arnold, chair of the new Waterville Merchants Association,[104] was in favor of the change, but most members were opposed, fearing motorists would simply zip in one end of Main Street and out the other, without stopping. The City Council thought it was a fine idea, and the local *Sentinel* agreed. The Opera House was packed with more than 600 citizens when Arnold bravely presided over a noisy public hearing on the question. When the dust had settled, Council members agreed to give the plan a try.

VOTERS APPROVED THE CREATION of an Urban Renewal Authority (URA) in December 1959. Mayor Albert Bernier appointed three Democrats and two Republicans to serve as officers, as well a 15-member advisory board of citizens at large.[105] It would be two years before the first project began, but the Authority already had a detailed downtown plan to consider. In 1958, the new Merchants Association joined with the city in commissioning a city improvement study from Morton Braun and his firm, Planning & Renewal Associates, and the report was ready in June 1960, just as the URA was getting down to work.

Most striking among Braun's recommendations was that the entire Main Street be closed to traffic and turned into a pedestrian way, divided by extending the grass of Castonguay Square across the street. A widened Front Street would continue to handle traffic south to north, the report suggested, and a lengthened one-way Charles Street would take care of travel from Post Office Square to Silver Street. The project, thus named for Charles Street, would provide ample space for parking alongside both arteries, leaving an attractive and uncluttered shopping oval in the middle.

---

[104] The Bureau was an offshoot of the Chamber of Commerce, guarding the interests of downtown retailers.
[105] All the appointees were men. Members were Democrats Raymond Lemieux, Omer Richard, and Ralph Knowlton, and Republicans Willard Arnold and Lester Weeks. Citizens Committee members were Howard Gray, Carleton Brown, Joseph Noel, John Jabar, Bernard Begin, Onesime Bolduc, Samual Shapiro, Reginald LaVerdiere, Welton Farrow, Eugene Bolduc, Carl Dubord, Lester Weeks, Joseph Ferris, Saul Mandell, and William Cottle.

The report went on to say it would be nice to have a second bridge over the Kennebec below Winslow to handle through traffic from busy Route 201.[106] Failing that, a rotary circle at the foot of Main Street would give motorists choices in four directions, including west on an extended Spring Street, where traffic lights would lead to Silver and Elm.

The URA had plenty of time to tinker with Braun's recommendations. In the end, it adopted his scheme for handling traffic from the bridge, but rejected the bold notion of making Main Street a pedestrian zone. Instead, the Authority decided to obliterate the entire street for which the project was named, and in its place, mimic the new scourge of downtown merchants everywhere and build a shopping mall.

In January 1962, the Authority named local insurance man Paul Mitchell as executive director, and chose Bradford Wall, recently retired as superintendent of Scott Paper Company's logwood division, as chairman. The two set up shop on the third floor of the Levine Building on Main Street (No. 131). The genial, capable, and hard-working Mitchell was a solid match for the job ahead. Long active in civic affairs, he was stepping down as a member of the Board of Aldermen, a position from which he had followed every detail in the development of the URA plans. As a member of a respected Waterville family known especially for its love of competitive sports, he was also well equipped to handle the various roles of point guard, referee, and coach in a rough-and-tumble game where most everyone in town stood in the stands and booed as often as they cheered.

That December, Senator Muskie announced the federal approval of the Charles Street Project (Me. R-6), providing a capital grant of $1.6 million and a loan to the city of $2.6 million. In January 1963 the Opera House was again filled for a lively public hearing on the final plan. Mitchell had the charts, graphs, facts, and the persuasive powers to fend off noisy critics. The Board of Aldermen, sitting as municipal officers, voted 5-2 to approve, and before the year was out, the Federal Housing and Home Finance Agency sent a check. Within days, the URA acquired its first piece of property, a dilapidated Charles Street building once used by Lincoln Stores as a boiler room. Other acquisitions followed quickly, and the long transformation began.

---

[106] It would be nearly four decades before the bridge was built. State Representative Donald V. Carter of Winslow was the principal proponent and got the Legislature to agree before his death in 1990. When it was opened in 1997, the bridge and its connecting roads from beyond the end of lower Water Street to the Augusta Road were named in his memory.

Work could not go fast enough. Many of the older buildings were not only unsightly, but also dangerous. Five children died in a house fire on King Street in 1954, and in March, soon after the Coburn fire, two died in a tenement blaze on King Court at Head of Falls. In April, fire destroyed the downtown Templeton Hotel and Elms Restaurant, and in 1958 a succession of blazes ruined three businesses on College Avenue and took the life of a tenant in an apartment house on Water Street. In 1962, just as Urban Renewal was getting underway, a massive fire in the connected buildings on Main Street severely damaged 41 businesses.

By 1960, a challenge of a different sort was already coming up the road. President Eisenhower's interstate highway system, begun in 1953, was by then completed all the way from Florida to the ramps in Waterville.[107] Local planners had only to look over their shoulders to know the four-lane marvel had spawned shopping centers at nearly every urban exit along its 2000-mile way. Not surprisingly, when the Waterville ramps began spewing out 8000 cars a day, a new mall was already in place to greet them.

The genesis of Elm Plaza on Upper Main Street came in the early 1950s when local entrepreneurs and developers Lewis Rosenthal and his son, Robert, dropped in at the New York City headquarters of W. T. Grant to see if the retail giant might be interested in opening a Waterville store. Grant executives already had their eyes on the city, and said they would come if the Rosenthals acquired the Main Street building of Emery-Brown (presently Days Jewelry Store) at the right price. When the pair returned with the purchase option in hand, they were told the deal was off. Hereafter, the Grant people said, they would open new stores only in shopping malls near the highways. The Rosenthals already owned land on Upper Main, and they offered to build a shopping center there if Grant would come. The company agreed on condition that a supermarket came with them. First National signed on, and Mammoth Mart was close behind.[108] Advertisements for the new Elm Plaza Shopping Center touted its "comfort and convenience." Shoppers agreed, and slowly began turning their backs on Main Street.

---

[107] *Parade Magazine* called the Maine segment of I-95 "America's most scenic highway."

[108] The Plaza opened with 84,000 square feet of store space and soon added 45,000 square feet with Mammouth Mart. At the time, Waterville had the clear jump on its retail rival, Augusta. Although the Plaza eventually grew to 300,000 square feet and other smaller malls were opened, the capital city by then had an insurmountable lead in shopping malls, outlets, and retail space.

The story of Lewis Rosenthal is quite literally one of rags to riches. Born in Russian-ruled Divinishok (Dieveniskes), Lithuania, in 1896, he was still a toddler when his father Hyman, faced with conscription into the Czar's army, fled to the United States (c.1901), and soon sent for his wife Leah and their three children. The family settled in Princeton, N.J., before moving to Waterville, where Hyman opened a junkyard. Lewis was barely nine years old when his father was taken ill, and Lewis left Brook Street School to run the family business. His father recovered, but when Lewis returned to school he was told he had to repeat the third grade. He refused, and instead continued his horse-and-buggy rounds of area mills, where he soon discovered that waste from wool was more profitable than scrap iron. Factory "sweeps" and tiny bits of cloth could be sold to make less expensive fabrics, to blend with roofing shingles, to add to grease for the axles of train cars, or to wind as the core of baseballs. By age 15, Lewis had earned enough money to purchase the Boutelle Farm, a large tract of 100 acres extending from the present Eustis Parkway to south of Noyes Street, and build a home for his parents. Too young to make legal contracts, his father signed for him. His success continued, and after returning from U.S. Army service in France during World War I, he expanded his real estate holdings on both sides of Upper Main Street, southeast to May Street and Drummond Avenue, and north beyond the current I-95. When the wool market suffered during the Depression, he began to acquire mills and make his own blankets to sell. In the years before the American woolen industry collapsed altogether, he became one of the country's largest wool waste dealers, owning four mills in Maine and others in Vermont, Massachusetts, and South Carolina.[109] As a real estate speculator, he laid out his first Waterville street in 1920 and named it for his hero, Teddy Roosevelt.[110] During and after World War II, when most investors shied from housing investments, he purchased or built more than 300 north-end houses, often making loans to buyers when the banks would not. Throughout his life, Rosenthal purchased a number of businesses, including the Waterville Iron Works, the city's oldest manufacturing company. In 1953, when his son, Robert, returned from the Air Force, the two became involved in commercial real estate. Elm Plaza was first, followed by shopping centers in Brunswick, Lewiston, Millinocket and Belfast. Lewis's entrepreneurial zeal often put him at odds with city officials and others, but no one ever doubted his devotion to the city he loved or the contributions he made as an agent of positive change in the city's North End.

[109] Rosenthal's first office manager in his Skowhegan office near his mill was a young woman named Margaret Chase, who left the position when she married the prominent local politician, Clyde Smith. Rosenthal and the woman who became a U.S. Senator were friends throughout their lives. After the war, she called him to Washington to testify to Congress on his feelings about the Marshall Plan. He said it would be unfair to send new woolen mill equipment to Europe because U.S. manufacturers, with older equipment and higher wages, could not compete.
[110] In time he would build three more streets and name them for two Colby men he admired, Franklin Johnson and Galen Eustis; and for his late sister, Henrietta Rupert.

The Charles Street Project encompassed 20 acres of downtown real estate and included 83 buildings marked for destruction. It was, far and away, the most complex undertaking among the four areas designated for renewal. Progress was painfully slow, and among those most frustrated by the plodding pace was the conservative mayor, Cyril M. Joly, Jr., who came to office just as the downtown project began. In his second inaugural address in January 1964, he railed at the URA for the delays, which he claimed were creating hardships for landlords and merchants whose futures were uncertain.

WHS & REDINGTON

Temple Street east of Main is leveled to make room for the Concourse, 1965

Joly had a point. One of the slowest tasks was the delicate business of acquiring property. Nearly everyone was familiar with the exercise of eminent domain in the matter of clearing the way for highways, but the taking of private property to remedy urban blight was a new idea. The government's offers of compensation, usually diminished by the poor condition of the structures, were often unacceptable to the owners. A leading Waterville opponent was Rose Warren, a resident of Spring Street who owned a number of apartment houses, cheek-by-jowl on nearby Temple Court. The tiny, crowded street ran parallel to Charles Street and was in the way of the new mall. She was offered $48,000 for her land and buildings, but she refused, and took her case to the Supreme Judicial Court of Maine.[111] She held that there had been illegalities in the condemnation procedure, and that the taking of her property by eminent domain was unlawful and thus invalid. The URA countered that her buildings were "old, deteriorating, and dilapidated," and the taking was necessary "in the interest of public health, safety, morals or welfare of the residents [of Waterville]." In an often-cited landmark decision (May 1965), the court found for the Authority.

> Utilizing accepted criteria for measurement, the Braun study concluded that 15 percent of the city's housing units were either deteriorating (809 units) or altogether dilapidated (110). Even though Warren's properties were clearly blighted, many of her tenants supported her court fight. Mostly older French Catholics who did not own cars, they enjoyed being able to walk to the downtown shops, Cottle's Grocery, and to St. Francis Church, and were fearful of being forced to move.

Not all of the complainers were stakeholders. Those with sentimental attachment to the old properties were uneasy about the aggressiveness of planners. While fingers were often unfairly pointed at the URA, the Authority had little to do with the railroad-crossing project on College Avenue. In fact, the old wood frame station with its two-story hipped roof jutting out over the rail platform was not in the way of the improvements and did not need to be taken. Even so, as happened to the vacated railroad stations elsewhere, Waterville's archetype building was leveled in 1963.

A bigger crime was about to happen across the street. After the move, Colby officials hoped to sell the entire abandoned campus to a single developer, but there were no takers, and the college began selling lots and buildings piecemeal. When it was apparent the old campus would soon be isolated on an island surrounded by new roads, the college gave the southern sector of the campus to the city. Included was the 100-year-old Memorial Hall, the handsome rubble-stone edifice said to be the first structure in the North built to honor those who fell in the Civil War. Long vacant and often occupied by vagrants, the unkempt building became a liability, and the city inspector said it had to come down. Mayor Joly pleaded

---

[111] Former mayor Harold C. Marden was a justice on the high court (1962-1970) and recused himself.

for money to rescue it, but his efforts failed, and in the summer of 1966 the unique memorial fell to the wrecking ball.[112]

Downtown, the URA Charles Street Project was also running into historic buildings that stood in the way. The initial Braun proposal called for upper Temple Street to be preserved, even widened to make room for plantings. The new scheme called for the street to end in the parking lot of the new shopping mall. A block north, Appleton Street was to be extended across Main, passing dangerously close to the Library, and intersecting with Elm Street.

At the top of the now-doomed Temple Street were two iconic buildings. The handsome 130-year-old First Congregational Church stood on the south side, almost exactly where the new mall buildings were to go. The URA offered to move the entire structure to the corner of Elm Street and Western Avenue, but church elders decided instead to rescue the stained-glass windows, pews and altar, and build a new sanctuary at the Main Street end of the new Eustis Parkway (1966). A private developer purchased the four white columns of the church portico for a new home in Winslow, and the 130-year-old building was demolished.

Across from the church stood the grand Italianate home built in 1842 by attorney Timothy Boutelle as a wedding gift to his daughter, Helen Noyes. The Noyes estate later became headquarters of the Waterville Fraternal Order of Eagles,[113] and in 1924, the city's first Boys Club. Since 1941 it had been the home of the YMCA. With the building set for demolition, the YMCA raised money to build new quarters on the southeast corner of North and Pleasant, a place made vacant by the demolition of North Grammar School (1964).

The effort was championed by one of Waterville's most beloved leaders of the time. George Keller, a tireless counselor and advocate for youth, became YMCA director in 1957 and served for 20 years. His legacy was a number of new association initiatives, including a summer day camp (Camp Tracy) program on nearby McGrath Pond.

---

[112] The four-ton marble Lion of Lucern and its accompanying plaque etched with the names of the fallen was moved to Miller Library on the new campus in 1962. The rare Paul Revere & Son tower bell that once called students to classes was moved to the portico of Roberts Union. It later was damaged and moved to safe storage upon its repair.

[113] Founded in 1898 by touring theater troupes, the goal of the national order of Eagles was "to make human life more desirable by lessening its ills and promoting peace, prosperity, gladness and hope."

Some of the old buildings were hauled away in one piece. In 1965, the Spring Street residence of physician Rudolph Pomerleau was lifted onto a flat-bed and slowly moved to Oakland, down Elm and Silver streets, across Emerson Bridge, and out the Oakland Road, already widened to four lanes and that same year renamed John F. Kennedy Memorial Drive in honor of the martyred President.

Although not at the hands of Urban Renewal, old landmarks seemed to keep on disappearing. The Elmwood Hotel, the city's most recognizable building since the beginning, briefly changed its name to the Elmwood Motor Hotel to compete with the new motels, but it went bankrupt just the same. Furnishings were sold to satisfy creditors, and in 1966 the iconic structure was reduced to rubble.[114] Soon after, the elegant Haines Theater on nearby Main Street burned (1967), and was never rebuilt. Adding insult to injury, the U.S. Postal Service was beginning to talk about auctioning off the classic limestone Post Office at the head of the street and moving somewhere else.

Meanwhile, the Charles Street Project slowly came to an end. Downtown shoppers filled the spacious new parking lot before it was even paved (September 1966), sending great clouds of dust into the air in celebration. That winter the place was named The Concourse,[115] and in the spring, the discount chain, Zayre, began construction of its anchor store, joining Cottle's Market in utilizing 74,000 square feet of retail space laid out in true strip mall style: long and low, flat roof, cinder-block walls, and glass front. The grocery store, sixth in a chain operated by William T. Cottle, replaced his recently demolished store on Spring Street and was touted as the largest supermarket in Maine. Before the two stores opened, work began on an adjacent complex (later named The Forum) to accommodate five relocating firms.[116]

---

[114] That same year, Urban Renewal claimed the city's popular – although hardly historic – Majestic Restaurant, at the corner of Temple and Charles.

[115] Marjorie Hales of Silver Street won the naming contest and received a $50 U.S. Savings Bond.

[116] A.W. Larsen, The Yardgoods Center, Admor Cleaners, Rossignol Jewelers, and Diambri's Restaurant.

When drawings for the overall complex were first revealed, there were some who begged for an added bit of charm. Suggestions to sacrifice a few parking spaces in order to have a green strip between the sidewalk and the parking lot were dismissed by merchants who insisted shoppers be able to pull up to their very doors. When a local official wrote Zayre to plead for something smaller than the large neon signs routinely put over their stores, the front office proudly replied that the local sign would be the smallest in their entire chain, but the resulting 12-foot letters were still the largest Waterville had ever seen. With its back to The Concourse, the *Sentinel* building, with its giant presses and linotype machines, was too big and too expensive to move. In the hope of disguise, the brick walls were painted a creamy yellow, but the four-story structure still stuck out like a giant lemon on a sea of asphalt.

By the time the Charles Street Project was completed in 1971, work at Head of Falls had already begun. Ranging the length of Front Street east to the river, the 80-acre project (Me. 17) was four times the size of the Charles Street venture and involved nearly three times as many buildings (240). When work began, fewer than 20 families still lived along Head of Falls Road and its tiny side alleys. The acquisition was easy, and the work was straightforward demolition. When it ended in 1976, all that was left of Waterville's oldest neighborhood and first home to hundreds of French Canadian and Lebanese immigrants was the venerable Two-Cent Bridge and the vacant Wyandotte woolen mill.[117] Everything else was deemed blighted and came down. Still listed on the city books as an industrial zone, the vacant plain was used for years as a dumping place for the snow and random waste from plowing city streets. Mounds of slush and debris were often still visible in June. When the dumping practice stopped, the space became a rarely used, unpaved parking lot.

The federal Urban Renewal initiative merged with the Model Cities Program in 1974, and thereafter, much of the city's continuing redevelopment effort was supported by grants from that program, managed by the U.S. Housing and Urban Development Department (HUD).

---

[117] The Wyandotte Mill closed in 1969 and moved to a new plant on the Sidney (now West River) Road, two miles south of Emerson Bridge.

The Two-Cent Bridge, c. 1955

Waterville did not pursue major funding for public housing, but a succession of mayors worked with the URA, planning boards, and city development directors to secure redevelopment funds. Mayors Malcolm Fortier (1966-67), Donald Marden (1968-69), Richard "Spike" Carey (1970-78), and Paul LaVerdiere (1978-1982) each battled tight budgets but found ways to move the city ahead.

Elaborate community centers designed for both ends of town were never built, but grants helped to renovate the closed South Grammar School on Gold Street for low-income housing and build a center for senior citizen services next door, later named for Senator Muskie. The South End also got a facelift with the removal of dilapidated tenement buildings on Water Street, dangerously close to the flood zone along the river. In the North End, federal funds helped to build a new elementary school on Drummond Avenue, first named Brookside. In 1976, the Catholic Diocese of Portland backed a federal loan to build the 100-unit Seton Village on Carver Street, providing "supportive housing" for the low-income elderly.

The Waterville Urban Renewal Authority ended in 1978. By any measure of its original goals, it had been a ringing success, most notably in its principal effort to revive the center of town. From the beginning of the Charles Street Project to the opening of The Concourse, downtown employment jumped nearly 20 percent, and retail sales escalated from $37.9 to $82.5 million. In that same period, the service sector nearly doubled.

Throughout the 17-year effort, director Mitchell and chairman Brad Wall had worked closely with city officials and others to bring together widely disparate interests and complete the massive job with numerous victories and without a hint of the kinds of scandals that plagued similar projects elsewhere.

Even so, there was grumbling. Some in the South End felt isolated and abandoned; some in the North End felt left out and cheated; almost everybody had strong and varied opinions about the configuration and appearance of The Concourse. In many ways, the complaining was predictable. A city accustomed to celebrating building things up was not about to cheer about the tearing down, and people who took delight and pride in its old buildings found no joy in vast new expanses of blacktop.[118] All this criticism was fair game, but the popular blaming of Urban Renewal for the economic decline that was soon to follow, was not.[119]

Soon after the last project was completed, Waterville, much like other industrial cities throughout Maine and New England, began to suffer a domino-like series of fiscal calamities from which it would never fully recover. Domestic and foreign competition led to the closing of more river mills and brought on a steady population decline and an erosion of the city's tax base. Resulting higher taxes put an economic strain on a withering downtown retail trade that was already losing too many customers to shopping malls and big box stores. And as the mills and stores began to close, the city faced increasingly tighter annual budgets, leaving little money to continue the kind of improvements that had been provided by Urban Renewal.

---

[118] Despite the aggressive destruction, Main Street managed to retain 25 properties that in 2012 would earn listing on the National Register of Historic Places.

[119] The pejorative name "Urban *Removal*" was not coined in Waterville. Citizens wailed in almost every city where these projects were carried out, especially in places where notable buildings got in the way and were destroyed. The most contentious programs were in the historic West End neighborhood of Boston, downtown Norfolk, Virginia, and the waterfronts of Narragansett and Newport, Rhode Island.

12

Scattered Clouds

-1975

Waterville's census grew every year after 1873, when Amos Lockwood came to build his cotton mills. By 1960, the newest record stood at 18,696 souls, and there was every reason to believe the number would keep going up. Renovations were under way to remove downtown blight and make room for traffic, expanding services and shopping malls were luring visitors at a rate five times the city's population. Although 5000 people were still working along the river, the population had climbed as high as it would get for the next 50 years or more.

C. F. Hathaway, newly ensconced in half of the old cotton mill, employed 750 workers making four million shirts a year, and in 1960, Hathaway's success impelled the giant textile corporation, Warner Brothers Company, to take it over. The shirts still carried the proud name made famous by the man with the eye patch, but the ownership went out of town. Following the sale, the creative genius, Ellerton Jetté, stepped down as president, and Waterville native Leonard Saulter took his place. Warner Brothers became Warnaco in 1968, and with continuing mergers and acquisitions, managed to turn a small profit.

Across the river, Scott Paper Company's Winslow mill was still taking logs from the river each spring and piling the pulp in a man-made mountain near the plant, where some 1300 workers tended paper machines that rolled around the clock. Scott was the most profitable paper company in the nation in 1961, when the soap maker, Proctor & Gamble, entered a market that Scott once had almost all to itself. By the end of the decade, the

132

number of tissue-making competitors grew even larger, and in 1967 Scott went on the offense and bought out S.D. Warren, a maker of fine papers, and began building a modern $138 million mill in Skowhegan (later Sappi). The timing might have been better. A recession was about to slow slick-paper advertising, and government cuts in educational funding sent the textbook market into a slump.

For more than 80 years before the Clean Water Act of 1974, Maine paper mills held annual spring log drives to retrieve pulpwood from the northern timberlands. Often, the rivers were filled from shore to shore. This photograph shows the Kennebec, less than a mile above Ticonic Falls in Waterville, c. 1920.

The site of the new Scott/S.D. Warren plant near Route 201 had nothing whatever to do with the nearby Kennebec River. The location near the highway was chosen with an eye to the October 1976 enforcement of the Federal Clean Air Act (1972) and the Maine law that was to prohibit driving logs in the river. In preparation to receive logging trucks over the highway, the company began building a 100-mile gravel road through the wilderness from Millinocket to the Quebec border, and called it the "Golden Road."

With the elimination of passenger service and the shift of freight from rail to roads, Maine Central Railroad, once the longest line in New England, used barely 900 of its 1358 miles of track, and work at the Waterville shops was dwindling. The busy I-95 highway had become the main freight route, north and south. Seeing the promise, a group of local businessmen had collected $162,000 in private pledges in 1957 to create the Waterville Area Industrial Development Corporation, and in the early 1960s built a 30,000 square foot industrial building near the highway ramps on Upper Main Street (at Armory Road). Various tenants filled the spaces over the years, and after the turn of the century the corporation was dissolved.

Just as travelers had forsaken the rails for the roads, nobody was interested in flying either. Americans loved their cars, the bigger the better, and with gas prices hovering around 35¢ a gallon, there was no need to pay $50 for a round trip airfare to Boston.[120] Before Northeast Airlines stopped landing its DC3s at LaFleur Airport in 1960, the only customers were businessmen in a hurry. Seven years later, Executive Airlines began regular flights, and in 1969 the city built a terminal building and a two-acre parking apron for travelers. Air New England began a competing service in 1971, but within two years Executive Airlines withdrew.[121] Ray MacPhee of the Chamber of Commerce warned citizens not to neglect any possibilities that could lead to the full development of the airport,[122] but people were firmly focused on their cars, and when the popular four-term mayor Richard Carey

---

[120] Gas prices would remain stable until 1973, when the OPEC oil embargo rocketed the price at the pump to an astonishing 57¢ a gallon.

[121] Heart of Maine Aviation, providing flights for hire, was bought from George Gerry (as Heart of Maine Flying Service) by William Staples in 1967. Air New England included Waterville on its route until 1981, when commercial service in Waterville came to an end.

[122] MacPhee's time as leader of the Chamber is well remembered for his 1969 creation of the annual downtown celebration of Christmas called Kringleville, a popular month-long visit of Santa and his elves, once conducted by Waterville Main Street and now a program of the Children's Discovery Museum.

experimented with a municipal bus service that no one would use, and he quickly gave it up.

Just over the town line in Fairfield, Keyes Fibre was booming. The company's domestic sales and income had doubled in ten years (1964-1974), and by 1975 it had six American plants and subsidiaries or affiliates in eleven countries. The plant was among the first to join the growing national effort to save the environment when it announced it would use recycled paper and cartons to fill a third of its fiber needs. The gesture caught on. Helen Strider, wife of Colby's president and a founder of the Waterville Conservation Commission, partnered with Mayor Carey to arrange a regular citywide collection of newspapers. Proceeds, matched by the state, went to buy trees to replace the city's dying elms. At the same time, local high school and college students were active in lobbying the Maine Legislature for bills to ban highway billboards and to recycle bottles and cans.

Colby professor Donaldson Koons, chair of Maine's powerful Environmental Improvement Commission (later the Department of Environmental Protection), spoke in Waterville on the first Earth Day, April 22, 1970. The geologist warned, "The environmental bank is already calling its note," and said the regulations promulgated by his department could only treat the symptoms, not the disease. "The disease," he said, "is people."

Both factory closings and modernization of equipment steadily reduced the call for custom forged machinery parts, and the venerable Waterville Iron Works, in business since 1833, closed in 1970.

That same year, the Wyandotte woolen mill made a new start at its modern plant on West River Road. The abandoned mill at Head of Falls did not fit the planning vision of a park along the river, and in 1973 the city accepted a $1.4 million federal grant and chipped in $600,000 to purchase the old factory and tear it down.

WITH THE UPS AND DOWNS OF INDUSTRIES, hardly anyone noticed that the city was beginning to emerge as a statewide center for education and medical care. The last of the "baby boomers" overflowing the high school on Gilman Street were among some 3000 students who packed the city's seven public schools. Half as many more were enrolled in the parochial schools, including Mount Merici. A test of double sessions at the high school didn't work,[123] and voters approved the construction of a new building west of the Messalonskee between Brooklyn and Highland avenues on a 12-acre plot that once included Coburn Classical Institute's Libby Field. The last Gilman Street graduates received their diplomas in the spring of 1963, and the elegant new high school, designed for 1000 students, opened that fall, sending the city's annual school budget over $1 million for the first time.

The junior high building (grades 7-9), built on the site of the original high school on Pleasant Street, again followed the senior high, this time up to Gilman Street, and the Pleasant Street building became an elementary school. North Grammar, the oldest schoolhouse (1888), was torn down. With the shuffling temporarily over, the city continued to support five elementary schools until 1969, when the new Brookside Elementary (now George Mitchell) School replaced the ones on Brook and Myrtle streets.

The expansion of public educational offerings was not over. By 1967 many high school students not bound for college were dropping out, and Waterville school superintendent Buford Grant and machine shop teacher Carleton Fogg conceived a way to bring them back. Utilizing city employees as teachers and staff, they borrowed space in the evenings from the regional vocational center at the new high school and began the Kennebec Valley Vocational Technical Institute. The first classes were held in the fall of 1970 with 35 mostly part-time students. Offerings ranged from heavy equipment maintenance to health services. Manual arts teacher Fred Whitney was the first director. His colleague, Bernard King, took over in 1973.

The city added a precious dimension to its educational offerings in 1963 with the opening of Hilltop School on North Street, a stone's throw from the new Thayer Hospital, specializing in the care and training of children with mental disabilities. Beloved local pediatrician Edmund Ervin was the driving force behind the creation of the school, which played on the names of the counties it serves – Kennebec and Somerset – when it incorporated as the Ken-A-Set Association for Retarded Children. The dedicated physician (who took phone calls from anxious mothers over breakfast and made house calls in the evening) found ready and generous support from the community to create the school, and thereafter, to supplement city and state funds in providing ways to improve the lives of the young people it serves.

---

[123] Grades 11-12 attended from 7 a.m. to 12:15 p.m.; grades 9-10, from 12:30-5:30 p.m.

Both of the city's colleges gained ever-wider notice. Thomas Junior College was renamed Thomas College in 1962, and the following year the Legislature approved the conferring of four-year Bachelor of Science degrees in business education and in administration. By the end of the decade, enrollment topped 350, and the college had outgrown its makeshift campus on Silver Street. The next move – its fourth since its beginnings as the Morgan Business School in 1896 – was to a new 70-acre campus, a mile away on the Sidney Road. [124] A coeducational dormitory and a student union/dining center went up in 1970, and a year later, with the completion of townhouse apartments for upperclass students, the move was complete.

Thomas had rarely reached beyond the immediate area to attract its students, but the handsome new campus, an ever-broadening array of offerings, and the acclaimed ability of Thomas graduates to find ready employment combined to begin drawing students from throughout the state, and beyond.

The year 1963 was both the 150th anniversary of Colby College's founding and the 75th anniversary of Waterville's incorporation as a city, and the two celebrated together. The Colby party had begun a year earlier, in June, when the Ford Foundation placed the college in a group of "regional and national centers of excellence" that were given matching grants. Colby's award of $1.8 million was nearly six times larger than any gift the college had ever received. In making the announcement, foundation officials cited not only the college's academic vitality and the leadership of president Robert E. L. Strider, but also the "strong participation and support" of the local community. A Waterville area campaign succeeded in raising more than $200,000 to help match the grant, an amount twice what local people had given to keep Colby in town some 30 years before.

In the realm of education, Strider was, in a strange way, responsible for the naming of Maine's first public educational television station in 1961. At the urging of WTVL owner Carleton Brown and others, the presidents of Maine's three private colleges (Bates, Bowdoin, Colby) applied for the license, and when the time came to select the station's call letters, they agreed to flip coins to see which college would be listed first. Strider won, and CBB was named.

---

[124] John L. Thomas, Jr., Thomas College president and member of the Board of Aldermen, led the effort to rename the Sidney Road as the West River Road in 1970. Once moved, the college bought more land and doubled the size of its campus. An additional 50 acres were acquired in 2007.

Colby held a grand finale in May 1963, with a two-day convocation and speakers including Earl Warren, chief justice of the U.S. Supreme Court; and Stuart Udall, Secretary of the Interior. The next week (May 18-25) Mayor Joly's committee kicked off a city celebration that began with the dedication of the new Maine Army National Guard headquarters on Drummond Avenue, and continued with weeklong events including a barbecue and fireworks display at LaFleur Airport, a lobster bake in Castonguay Square, and a free luncheon for all citizens 75 years or older at the Elmwood Motor Hotel.[125] The party ended with a Main Street parade on Saturday, followed by a dinner dance at the Jefferson Hotel.

No one could have known that an art exhibition would be the most memorable and enduring feature of the entire celebratory year. *Maine and its Role in American Art, 1710-1963* opened quietly during the spring events, filling Colby's tiny Bixler Art Museum and spilling out along adjacent corridors. On display were works of prominent American artists who lived or worked for a time in Maine, including John Singleton Copley, Gilbert Stuart, Marsden Hartley, John Marin, N.C. and Andrew Wyeth. *Time* magazine cited it as one of the world's 12 most outstanding international shows of the year.[126] Before the summer ended, thousands had come to see it. It was the first hint that Waterville might well become a center for the fine arts.

The Silver Street campus of Thomas College was not abandoned for long. In 1970, the Maine Legislature mandated training for all law enforcement officers, and two years later the state purchased the vacated buildings to establish the first Maine Criminal Justice Academy. The academy remained in Waterville until 2000, when it moved to Vassalboro and occupied the former campus of the Oak Grove-Coburn private school, closed since 1989.

MANY SMALL CITIES IN AMERICA HAD NO HOSPITAL AT ALL. Waterville had three, and locals generally made their choice based on philosophy (allopathic or osteopathic) or religion (Protestant or Catholic). By the 1960s, the old rules and stereotypes that separated the two began to soften. For those who preferred allopathic care, the popular view held that if an ailment was complicated, Thayer was the place to go; but if tender love

---

125 It would be the last major event held at the century-old hotel.
126 Waterville jumped out on the magazine's list: "New York, Paris, London, Brussels and ... Waterville, Maine."

and care were needed, Sisters had the added bonus of angelic, white coiffed nuns. At the same time, osteopathic medicine and training had changed. While its philosophy still centered on the whole body, the hospital offered a full range of medical services, and the training and skills of D.O. physicians was on a par with their M.D. counterparts. More and more patients chose the osteopathic hospital on Western Avenue for their care, but the facility was small, old, and worrisome. With competition for customers growing, in 1961, eight years after Thayer opened its new building on North Street, the osteopaths appealed for funds to build their own 45-bed hospital on Oakland Road, soon to be brimming with traffic from the new highway. Some 9000 citizens came to inspect the new Waterville Osteopathic Hospital at its dedication on November 18, 1962.[127]

Before the decade was over, the new hospital launched another campaign to add a 33-bed wing. It opened in the spring of 1970 and was named for Charles A. Dean, whose trust fund provided the lead gift. The addition was intended for use as a long-term nursing center, but the growing number of patients made it necessary to use it for acute care. The nursing home would have to wait.

Charles Augustus Dean was president of Hollingsworth & Whitney (later Scott Paper) at the turn of the century, when the company's logging division had more than 2000 employees working in the forests near Moosehead Lake. In 1911 he built a combined YMCA and 10-bed hospital in Greenville Junction, incorporated in 1941 as the Charles A. Dean Memorial Hospital. It was replaced by a new facility in 1968, and the original building became a nursing home until a new one was built in 1984. The Dean trust, established following his death, continued to provide support for medical facilities throughout the area where the paper company's employees lived.

In 1963, the Daughters of Charity began construction of a new, six-story Elizabeth Ann Seton Hospital on Chase Avenue,[128] on the old fairgrounds west of First Rangeway. This time the patron's name prevailed, and when Seton opened in 1965, all three Waterville hospitals were new.

Set in one half of a quadrangle, the new Seton building left room for a matching building, envisioned across the mall, but it was not to be. The business of delivering medical care was changing rapidly. Patients without physicians were flocking to emergency rooms a mile from each other, and

---

[127] The Waterville Osteopathic Hospital was renamed Inland Hospital in October, 1995.
[128] Its Meissen style architecture (like Gothic) would later earn it a place on the National Registry of Historic Buildings.

rising costs were exacerbated by the expense of sophisticated new equipment. Thayer had already expanded twice, and Seton struggled to keep pace. In order to stretch scarce dollars for health care throughout the state, regulators were beginning to forbid duplicated services anywhere.

By the early 1970s, there was talk of merger. For many, especially some physicians, the idea was unthinkable. Similar discussions in Portland (Mercy and Maine Medical) had gone nowhere. In 1974, selected trustees of the two allopathic hospitals held covert meetings in private homes and found common ground. A year later, Seton and Thayer merged as the Mid-Maine Medical Center.[129]

One of several fine surgeons practicing at Thayer Hospital was Richard Hornberger. Under the pseudonym Richard Hooker, he wrote the book *M*A*S*H* about his experience as a U.S. Army Medical Corps physician in Korea. Published in 1968, it became a best seller, and was the basis for a 1970 movie as well as a popular television series that ran from 1972-1983.

THE HIGHWAY AND THE RELOCATION OF THE CITY'S COLLEGES were stretching the community both west and south. Side streets off Mayflower Hill Drive filled with new houses, and in 1972 the Fire Department opened Engine Company Five, a sub-station on upper Western Avenue, to provide quicker protection for the blossoming west end that suddenly found itself with two hospitals, two colleges, a new high school, and dozens of new streets.

Thomas College and the new Wyandotte plant opened new opportunities for development west along the Messalonskee, and the city purchased land on both sides of West River Road. Oddly enough, the first new attraction was a golf course. A national golf craze was spurred by PGA tournament telecasts that began in 1962, and locally invigorated by Waterville Country Club member, Dick Diversi, who took five successive Maine Amateur trophies from 1953-1957, and another in 1963. The golf surge emboldened the exclusive Waterville Country Club to add a second nine-hole layout in 1967. Two years later, the city built its own public 9-hole

---

[129] Each hospital had deal-breaking requirements as conditions for merger. Thayer had its Mansfield Clinic for charity care and had recently taken the struggling Dean Memorial Hospital in Greenville under its wing. Thayer wanted assurance that the outreach initiatives would continue. Seton insisted that there be no abortions in either building, and that the Catholic religious presence would continue on the Chase Avenue site.

course and restaurant on its newly acquired land on the west side of West River Road, and named it Pine Ridge. [130]

> Not everyone was enthusiastic about golf, but the entire area was caught up in the achievements of two phenomenal athletes who starred in the traditional local sports of hockey and football. In the mid-1960s, Pee-Wee hockey parents who braved the early morning cold at Colby's Alfond Arena were joined by dozens of others who came to watch the astonishing antics of left-winger Danny Bolduc, who went on to fame at Phillips Academy and then Harvard University. He was named to the U.S. National Hockey Team in 1975, and the following year played on the U.S. team at the Innsbruck Winter Olympics. As a professional, he played for the Detroit Red Wings and the Calgary Flames in the NHL, and the New England Whalers of the AHL. Ten years his senior, football linebacker John Huard had captured the hearts of local fans as a standout at Waterville High and the University of Maine (1963-1966), where he was twice named All-American. After college, he played three seasons for the Denver Broncos, and at the end of his career, for the New Orleans Saints.

The bucolic farms and pastures along the old Oakland Road had disappeared in a decade. The Penny Hill Farm garden market on the north side of the widened and renamed Kennedy Memorial Drive gave way to Furbush Chevrolet, re-located from the tangle of Urban Renewal; and Carroll Meader's horse farm on the south side above Emerson Bridge became JFK Plaza, the city's second major shopping mall (1974), with the A&P grocery chain as its anchor.

> Carroll Meader was the uncle of Abbott Vaughan Meader, a Waterville native who found instant fame with his 1962 Grammy Award-winning recording, *The First Family*, in which he gave a comic impersonation of John F. Kennedy. More than seven million copies of the record were sold. (JFK loved it, and gave copies to his Cabinet for Christmas. His wife, Jackie, hated it.) Meader's popularity evaporated following Kennedy's assassination, and the actor eventually returned to Maine to manage a pub.

Many merchants were dismayed and worried by the disruption of Urban Renewal, and let their Chamber of Commerce memberships lapse. The agency was set to move from its offices on College Avenue (across from the

---

[130] One of the area's most popular golf courses began in 1965 when Paul and Lucy Brown converted the old Fairview Farm on the Webber Pond Road in Vassalboro into a handsome 9-hole course and named it Natanis in honor of the Indian chief who guided Benedict Arnold on his trek to Quebec. In a quarter century the course would be enlarged to 27 holes, one of the largest – and patrons would say friendliest – courses in Maine.

old Colby campus) to the top floor at No. 57 Main Street (above Larsen's Jewelry), and President Walter Simcock had to struggle to find money to pay the rent and meet the payroll. He paired with W. Sanderson (Sandy) Day, the young owner of Day's Travel on Main Street, and the two knocked on doors all over town, collecting dues.[131]

WATERVILLE ENJOYED POLITICS as a form of high entertainment. The city's bi-cameral government – patterned after the system adopted by the nation's founders and copied from the British Parliament – had been the same since the city's beginning, and no one was in any hurry to change it. At every election, a long list of candidates happily vied for dozens of elected or appointed slots, ranging from Mayor and ward representatives, clerks, wardens, and constables down to myriad appointments for unpaid jobs where there was no longer any work.[132]

By the 1960s, the process of acquiring approval from both the seven-member board of aldermen and the 14-member city council, stretched on endlessly. Sometimes it took weeks to approve a single streetlight, and the shower of resolutions required for keeping Urban Renewal on pace slowed things even more. In 1967, a Charter Commission recommended a new system with a strong mayor, a city manager, and a city council with a single member from each of the seven wards. Voters approved the change and left the Massachusetts city of Everett as the only remaining municipality in the country with a bi-cameral government.[133] In January 1968, newly-elected Republican mayor Donald Marden presided over the single, seven-member council. Robert W. Palmer, Jr., was the first City Administrator.

---

[131] Day succeeded Simcock as Chamber president in 1970, and he promptly hit the jackpot when more than 600 people bought tickets for the Chamber's event honoring Edmund Muskie as its Man of the Year. In 1975, Simcock arranged for the Chamber to sponsor the famous Budweiser Clydesdales in a parade down Main Street. Thousands came to watch.
[132] Among them were Fence Viewers, Cullers of Hoops and Staves, Vinegar Tasters, and Weighers of Coal, Hay and Ice.
[133] Everett did not abandon its bi-cameral system until 2011.

13

Protests and Politics

-1975

Throughout the war in Vietnam, college towns across America had ringside seats to watch and listen as young people rose up and demanded peace and new rules to live by. In Waterville, where spectators could pick and choose among many causes – and sometimes join the fray – issues of the day were put in sharper focus by having their adopted son, Ed Muskie, square in the nation's spotlight.

Muskie had already earned the title of statesman by 1968, when protests to save the environment, assure civil rights, and escape the war began to escalate and converge like a thunderstorm, shaking the nation to its roots. Maine's junior senator had been a leader of the new national environmental movement, and such were his oratorical and legislative powers that his controversial Clean Air Act (1963) passed the Senate without a single dissenting vote. In 1974, his Clean Water Act, often considered the crown of international environmental policy, also passed unanimously in the Senate on its way to becoming law. Along the way, he had taken on J. Edgar Hoover and the FBI, and played a key role in the passage of the Civil Rights Act of 1964. And while he approved sending troops to Vietnam, his support for the war was growing tepid.

When Martin Luther King, Jr., was killed that April (1968) in Memphis, Waterville people did as they had often done in times of mourning, gathering at the Opera House to find solace and share their sorrow.

Students came from both campuses to join them. One of the speakers was Henry Thompson, the first black president of Colby's student body, who warned that although Dr. King would not approve, the preacher's killing could "cause many to cross over to the militant policies of violence."[134] He was right. A month later, the front-runner for the Democratic nomination for the presidency, Robert Kennedy, was assassinated as well. The young people had lost three treasured heroes in a mere five years, and their bitterness helped to fuel a summer of violence.

Frustrated by the growing protests, President Lyndon Johnson declined to run for re-election, and with Kennedy gone, war opponents felt betrayed when Democrats, slugging it out at a riotous convention in Chicago, narrowly chose Hubert Humphrey to oppose Richard Nixon in the fall. The activists preferred the most outspoken opponent of the war, George McGovern, and when he was rejected, Humphrey's choice of Muskie as running mate did not appease them.

On Election Day, with hordes of reporters tagging along, Ed and Jane Muskie cast their votes at the old South Grammar School. Protesters lined Silver Street, a hundred yards away, chanting "free elections now," and "one, two, three, four, we won't fight your dirty war!" Across the street, counter-demonstrators heckled the protesters and yelled for them to take baths. Riots elsewhere had proved that a police presence only made things worse, and during the face-off in Waterville, Mayor Donald Marden kept the cops around the corner, out of sight. (In the aftermath, he asked the City Council to buy them riot gear.) When the votes were counted, Maine had given the Humphrey-Muskie ticket a whopping 55 percent of its vote,[135] but Nixon won 32 states and the Presidency, and the war slogged on.

---

[134] Colby president Robert E.L. Strider used the platform to encourage donations in King's memory to the United Negro College Fund. Locally, more than $16,000 was raised.

[135] It was the last time a Democratic Presidential candidate carried Maine until 1992, when the state embraced Bill Clinton.

Jane and Ed Muskie, with son Stephen, presidential election night at the Waterville Armory, November 1968

By 1969, U.S. forces in Vietnam had reached a peak of 350,000, and more and more bodies were coming home. That October, students from Colby, Thomas, and Waterville High organized a rally in Monument Park as part of a national "Vietnam Moratorium," aimed at forcing Nixon to end the war. Some 1,000 citizens, heads bowed in silence, listened as students read from the list of war dead. A month later, Colby's Lorimer Chapel was packed for a "sympathy vigil," sponsored by local churches and the student Moratorium Committee. It was clear the demonstrations would not stop until the war came to an end.

With voices well practiced in protest, students on the Hill had already taken up the growing tactic of occupying buildings to draw attention to their causes. The previous spring (1969), a shifting crowd of student dissidents occupied the chapel for 16 days, insisting on changes in college rules.[136] When it came to sit-ins, local opinion was often divided between those who condemned the brashness outright and those whose support for the cause outweighed their wariness of civil disobedience. In this instance, observers had little interest in broadening the rights of students. Many felt they were coddled too much already.

A year later (March 1970), 18 black students went into the chapel, tied the doors shut behind them, and issued five "demands" centered on increasing their numbers and improving their lives as students. The local *Sentinel* gruffly opined that the protesters had more sympathy from those they were protesting than from the people in town, but fellow students smuggled in food, and a local restaurant owner sent milk shakes and hamburgers.

The occupation lasted eight days before local attorney and Colby trustee Robert A. Marden (the recent mayor's brother) went to the chapel door with a message from President Strider: vacate the building by 12:30 p.m. or face legal action. Charles Terrell, leader of the occupiers, courteously explained the sit-in would continue. By noon, Superior Court Justice James L. Reid had signed a restraining order, saying he had "adequate reason to believe a riot of serious proportions might result" if the occupation were to continue. Some 300 gawkers watched from nearby lawns when Kennebec County Sheriff Horace Drummond delivered the order at 6 p.m. It gave the protesters until 10:30 p.m. to vacate the building, and they left by the side door an hour before the deadline.

The tumultuous spring wore on. President Nixon intensified the war in hopes of achieving what he called "peace with honor," and the protests multiplied. Nixon called the student protesters "bums," and then sent troops into Cambodia to protect the pro-American government. His action was denounced as illegal, and the crowds of dissidents grew. In one of the countless outbursts across the country, students at Kent State University in Ohio buried a copy of the U.S. Constitution and set off four days of rioting. The National Guard was called in, and on Monday, May 4, as the troops set about dispersing a crowd of some 1500 protesters, four students were inexplicably shot and killed. Another dozen were wounded.

---

[136] The demands ranged from allowing scholarship students to own cars to providing radios for campus security officers, and from allowing upperclass students to live and eat off campus to staffing the college switchboard around the clock.

That night, rallies were held on campuses across the country. Colby students called for a "peaceful and nonviolent" shutdown of the college. In the morning (Tuesday) Student Government president Steven Orlov telephoned his counterparts at ten Maine colleges and the six campuses of the University of Maine, seeking their endorsement of a telegram to Senators Edmund Muskie and Margaret Chase Smith, insisting each "return home and address yourself to the people whom you represent." At a noontime rally, the U.S. flag in front of Miller Library was lowered to half-staff in memory of the dead students, and some 300 faculty and students began a "march against death," carrying four mock coffins into town. Police Chief John MacIntyre hastily issued a parade permit, and sent cruisers to bracket the marchers,[137] who gathered support as they wound down Mayflower Hill to Post Office Square, down Main Street to Silver Street, and back up Elm Street to the post office, where one of the dissenters lowered the flag. An irate postal worker quickly put it up again, and the protesters wandered away, leaving the coffins on the lawn. On Wednesday, both students and faculty voted to strike, and classes were halted. Faculty members led "counter-curriculum" workshops while federal, state, and local officials scrambled to make preparations for the Muskie-Smith appearance on Sunday (May 10).

The day arrived, bright and sunny, and by early afternoon more than 3,000 young people jammed the entire mall from the library to Mayflower Hill Drive. The scene could have been taken for a rock concert – bandannas, psychedelic tie-dye tee shirts, sandals, beads, and the unmistakable odor of pot wafting in the warm spring air. Up close, it was all business.

Muskie spoke first, and was greeted with long applause when he appeared on the library steps. He already had his eyes on the 1972 presidential election, and had seen the handwriting on the wall. He used the moment to announce he would introduce a Senate resolution for the immediate withdrawal of all U.S. forces in Cambodia.

Smith was late, and some of the crowd had begun to drift away when she appeared at four. Orlov towered over her frail form when he introduced

---

[137] MacIntyre was no stranger to the dissidents. A month before, he had dealt with a dozen students who peacefully picketed the Internal Revenue Office on College Avenue in opposition to the use of tax revenue to support the war.

Protesters gather on the lawn of Miller Library, awaiting appearances of Senators Muskie and Smith, May, 1970

her. Her reception was cool. Unlike Muskie, she had no prepared remarks, and immediately invited questions. When someone asked if there were U.S. troops in Cambodia's neighbor country, Laos, she turned to her longtime aide, General William Lewis, and repeated the question. When she turned back, she said she was not aware of any troops in Laos. The crowd booed, and several could be seen encouraging a young man as he limped his way to the podium, stood beside the senator, and introduced himself as Brownie Carson,[138] a Marine infantry platoon commander. He pointed to his leg and said he was wounded in Laos. He then asked how the ranking member of the Senate Armed Services Committee could not know that Americans were

---

[138] Carson was a 22-year-old Bowdoin graduate. Two years after chastising Smith on the Colby stage, he made an unsuccessful bid to unseat Maine Congressman Peter Kyros (1967-75) in the Democratic primary. He was to become one of the state's leading environmentalists and executive director of the Natural Resources Council of Maine.

in Laos, "and if you do know," he said, "how could you lie to us?" That was enough for Smith. The booing turned to screams, and she turned and skulked back into the library.

With that riveting day over, Waterville was still not out of the headlines. Muskie was a favorite presidential candidate of the Democratic establishment in 1972, and campaign news coverage often focused on his hometown. At the same time, the war and the protests continued. On April 21, more than a dozen students took over the Colby ROTC offices in Averill Hall and vowed to stay until the military training program was abolished.

Three days later, the college threatened the occupiers with suspension, and that morning, seven Waterville police officers, accompanied by Chief Ronald LaLiberty and assistant county attorney and former mayor Marden, arrested them and charged them with "refusal to vacate," a misdemeanor under Maine's new, untried "sit-in law." The students were hauled off in a school bus, and arrived at City Hall to discover that sympathetic faculty members had already posted bail of $100 each.

By nightfall, in light of the "dignity and concern" the students had displayed, the college shortened their suspensions to a single week. Mayor Carey, although an outspoken opponent of the war, called the punishments a "wrist-slap," and said the next time the college needed help from the police they should call Oakland.

Among the demonstrations, sit-ins, and vigils, the period brought to Waterville a number of key national and international figures, who more often than not, were enlightening on issues of the day. United Nations Under Secretary **Ralph J. Bunche** came to lecture in 1962 and again in 1965, a month before his son's Colby graduation. **Henry Kissinger**, Kennedy advisor and soon to be Nixon's Secretary of State, spoke the same year, as did **James Jackson**, editor of the Communist newspaper *The Worker*, who squared off in a colorless debate with Senator Muskie. Michigan Congressman **Gerald Ford** had been named to the Warren Commission investigating the Kennedy Assassination when he came to speak in the fall of 1964, and he emboldened dissenters when he said "it will be an evil day in this country when it is wrong to say no." That same week, **James Meredith**, who two years before had become the first black student to integrate the University of Mississippi, addressed an overflow crowd in Runnals Union at Colby and warned that the current crisis in race relations was "more explosive than the issue of slavery."[139] The next spring (1964), as Meredith graduated from Ole Miss and the Rev. King began a march from Selma to Montgomery, Alabama, the U.S. ambassador to United Nations, **Adlai Stevenson**, gave the Colby commencement address. He commended students for their participation "in the great struggle to advance civil and human rights," and he was prescient when he said, "perhaps we are destined to see in this law-loving land people running for office not on their stainless records but on their prison records." U.N. Secretary General **U Thant** of Burma was the commencement speaker in 1965, and the following year, two Presidential hopefuls dropped into Waterville for a visit: former Vice President **Richard Nixon** held a press conference at the Fenway Maine Hotel on Upper Main Street, and **Jimmy Carter** huddled with local Democrats at the Silent Woman restaurant near the Interstate exit on KMD. In 1970, two weeks after the black students vacated the Chapel, the junior class sponsored a lecture by **Muhammad Ali**. The Colby gymnasium was not big enough, and the overflow crowd stood on the sidewalk and listened to loudspeakers. **George McGovern**, with an eye on the 1972 Democratic presidential nomination, spoke at Colby's commencement later that spring, and locals began to complain that the college's list of public lecturers was trending altogether too far to the left.

Maine was proud to have elected two of the most influential members of Congress, and prouder still that Democrat Muskie and Republican Smith worked together despite a chasm of political disagreement. Waterville's particular claim on Muskie put the city in a rare and unusual place following his narrow vice presidential loss, and his hundreds of friends reveled in being able to call a presidential contender by his first name.

Muskie was the clear favorite to win the Democratic nomination leading up to the election of 1972, and polls showed he would handily lick Richard Nixon in the fall. Often compared to Lincoln, the craggy faced 6-foot-4-inch Maine senator was both physically and intellectually imposing. He had turned against the war, the liberals loved him, and his voting record made him a favorite of black Americans. It seemed the script was already written, but then it all fell apart.

In February, before the New Hampshire primaries, the *Manchester Union-Leader* published a letter, attributed to Muskie, which contained disparaging

---

[139] Shortly before his lecture, a pickup truck pulled up in front of the Union and a man got out, raced up the steps and stood at the back of the auditorium, yelling racial epithets. There was a scuffle before he was subdued and arrested. Police found a 30-30 rifle and ammunition in his truck, together with handmade racist posters.

150

remarks about French-Canadians.[140] A week later, the paper smeared the Senator's wife Jane, alleging she drank too much and liked dirty jokes. Muskie called a press conference on the newspaper's front steps, and railed against the publisher, William Loeb. Some said the drops of water on Muskie's cheeks were melted snow; others said they were tears. It didn't matter. Muskie narrowly won in New Hampshire and Iowa, and his support faded. By April, he was out of the race, and it became South Dakota Senator George McGovern's fate to lose to Nixon in the fall.

Muskie's popularity at home never waned. In Waterville, no one thought there could ever be anyone else like him, and then, against all odds, the small city sent into the political arena a second statesman whose accomplishments would soon be revered, first around the country, and then around the world.

George Mitchell grew up as one of five children in the Head of Falls riverfront neighborhood near the Wyandotte Woolen Mill, where his mother worked. His father, a janitor, was Irish. Young Mitchell attended Waterville High and played on basketball teams dominated by his older brothers. Following his graduation from Bowdoin in 1954, he served in the U.S. Army for two years before earning his law degree at Georgetown University in 1961. He worked as an attorney in the Department of Justice for a short time before becoming Muskie's executive assistant, a post he held for the last four years of the Senator's first term. He would later claim that it was during that stint that he learned the art of politics and became infected with a passion for public service.

Mitchell was serving as assistant county attorney of Cumberland County in 1974 when he defeated Portland lawyer Joseph Brennan to receive the Democratic nomination for governor. Pundits were sure Mitchell would win in the three-way race with Republican James Erwin, who had been Maine's Attorney General (1967-1971), and Independent James Longley,[141] a Lewiston insurance man known for his work as head of the money-saving Maine Management & Cost Survey Commission. They were wrong. For the first time, in a pattern that would become a habit, Maine voters displayed

---

[140] A subsequent FBI investigation revealed that the so-called "Canuck letter" was a hoax, and part of Nixon's "dirty tricks" effort to discredit Democratic candidates.
[141] Longley had been a Democrat and endorsed Ed Muskie in his first run for Senate. He entered the gubernatorial race after the deadline for filing as a major party candidate had passed and signed up as an Independent.

their vaunted independent streak, and Longley topped Mitchell by 10,000 votes. Erwin ran a distant third.

Like Muskie, who lost his first election in a bid to become Waterville's mayor, Mitchell had lost his first race as well. And, like his mentor, he would never be defeated again.

IN THE EARLY MORNING OF APRIL 30, 1975, the last Americans withdrew from Saigon, with the North Vietnamese army nipping at their heels. By noon, the enemy's red and blue flag was flying over the capital, and Saigon became Ho Chi Minh City. Another long war ended almost where it began. At home, there were no fireworks, no parades, and no public celebrations. The nation's disdain for the war was too often wrongfully extended to include those who fought it. Returning veterans were puzzled and hurt.

Fifty-eight thousand Americans died in the war. Thousands more suffered wounds of body and mind. Maine lost 343; six were from Waterville: Army PFC George Belanger and SP5 Robert Clukey; Marine PFCs Rodney Delisle and Lawrence Peters, Cpl. James Pomerleau and Sgt. Eldon Smith.

The youth had done more than anyone to bring an end to the war, and along the way, had made great strides to improve social justice. As time would tell, the work on both fronts was far from done.

14

Shifting Tides

1976 – 1988

Waterville has never been bashful about throwing parties, and on the Fourth of July 1976 the city pulled out all stops to celebrate the nation's Bicentennial. It was a good time to cheer. A bruising stretch of economic stagnation had all but ended, the pain of the Vietnam War was healing, and agonies of the Watergate debacle and the resignation of a president were over. In Waterville, the dust and clutter of Urban Renewal had mostly disappeared, industries were hanging on, and the future seemed entirely bright.[142]

The Fourth was a Sunday. That night, 10,000 revelers jammed the road to LaFleur Airport to watch an air show sponsored by the Rotary Club. Along with the aerobatics, the R.B. Hall Band played while spectators ate hot dogs and gawked at an array of antique automobiles. The next morning, the Jaycees served breakfast to 5,000 youngsters in advance of a 75-unit parade that took more than an hour to pass a single spot as it marched from Elm Plaza Shopping Center to the Hathaway factory on Water Street. The crowd, estimated at 20,000, stood 15 rows deep along the parade's last leg

---

[142] The state's unemployment rate in 1976 was 7.3 percent. Waterville's was closer to 5 percent.

down Main Street. The grand party ended that night, with a street dance on the Concourse.

Two weeks later (July 20), the American spacecraft Viking I landed on the moon, and the earth suddenly got a whole lot smaller. Globalization was already felt in the industrial cities of America, but Waterville had survived, even boomed, first during the long-ago transition from river to rails, and more recently, from rails to roads. Surely, it could face up to the coming competition and the rise of mega-corporations. More than a dozen trains rumbled through town every day, each with more than 100 freight cars carrying away new products and bringing in raw materials, chemicals, and fuel for the mills. With 1300 employees, Scott Paper Company had streamlined its operations and was set to make pulp at the new mill in Skowhegan and finish paper in Winslow. Wyandotte Industries had rehired 350 workers who were making textiles at its modern mill on the West River Road.

On College Avenue, Keyes Fibre had already faced the new challenges by partnering with firms in six states and eleven countries around the world. With 1000 workers, the company's sales had doubled in the last decade. In 1978, the company was purchased for $87 million by Arcata National of Menlo Park, California, but the famed Keyes and Chinet names continued. [143]

Waterville's oldest industry, C.F. Hathaway, was now a part of Warnaco, but the Hathaway name was still sewn into half of the fine men's shirts made in the U.S., and its 750 employees aimed to make a record 3.8 million more in the Bicentennial year. Its exquisite shirts (often priced up to $100 each) fairly flew out of the company's new distribution center in the industrial park on Armory Road.

Other enterprises brought both jobs and recognition. Harris Baking Company distributed its products statewide, and the Hoerner Waldorf Corporation made thousands of recycled paperboard boxes.

---

[143] Three years later the company was sold again, this time to the Van Leer group of the Netherlands, which in the late 1990s was taken over by the Finnish company, Huhtamäki.

Newspapers were still the most reliable source of national, state, and local news,[144] and with a circulation of 24,000, the *Waterville Morning Sentinel* employed more than 100 editors, reporters, pressmen, and delivery people to help inform some 90,000 readers in four counties. A bevy of correspondents in area towns covered everything from ball games to birthday parties, and from fender-benders to barn fires. Among the most popular and beloved local writers was Gene Letourneau, whose daily *Sportsmen Say* column captured thousands of devoted readers with its plainly written tales of the Maine outdoors.

The city boasted nearly 250 retail stores, and while downtown had fewer shops than before the sweep of Urban Renewal, 50 stores were lined up along Main Street and in the new Concourse. Elsewhere in town there were 8 hotels and motels (385 rooms), 25 restaurants, 11 banks and branches, and six outlets of national chains.

In ironic coincidence with the celebration of the past, the city's classical post office was abandoned in 1976 for a new and inelegant brick-box federal building on College Avenue. Three years later, the granite and limestone edifice on Post Office Square at the head of Main Street sold at auction for $112,000.

Two of the city's best-known eating places closed in 1977. In January, the old YMCA hotel and restaurant, the Hotel Emma, was razed in a two-alarm fire and that summer, not far up College Avenue, the Hotel Jefferson declared bankruptcy and shut its doors. Within a year, the Jefferson reopened under the ownership of Portland restaurateur John Martin, and soon after, locals welcomed a new drive-through place called McDonalds, where people could eat without even leaving their cars.

Even as the city slid down from its population high, housing expansion continued. Single-family homes went up in new neighborhoods the full length of First Rangeway, from Aubrey Street to Cherry Hill, and up and down the West River Road, from Franklin Street south to the Sidney line. Since the creation of the Waterville Housing Authority in 1967, more than 150 units of low-income and elderly housing had been created in the South End (Water and Gold streets), at Elm Towers in the center of town, and for families in the North End on Chaplin Street, and Hillside and Drummond avenues. Private developers built an additional 350 low-income and elderly

---

[144] Change was coming. A 1975 survey showed 83 percent of central Maine homes had their television sets turned on an average of 4.64 hours a day.

housing units, including the conversion of the old Hathaway Shirt Factory on Appleton Street, the new Crestwood Apartments on the West River Road, and a residential complex on the Quarry Road.

As a follow-up to Urban Renewal, the city was participating in a $3.1 million federally-funded Community Development Block Grant Program, and led the way in the creation of the Kennebec Sanitary Treatment District, organized like the once unique Kennebec Water District and located on the west bank of the river at the end of Water Street.

Public schools still overflowed, and officials had eagerly anticipated the completion of a new junior high school on West River Road. It snowed hard for two days before the $2 million facility opened February 9, 1978, and students were no more than settled in their new seats when a section of the roof collapsed. No one was hurt, but more structural deficiencies were found in the follow-up investigation. The junior high was moved to Averill School, which, together with the old junior high and South Grammar School, had been slated for closure. The repaired building was opened in the fall of 1979, and the city's 3500 students were grouped in senior high, junior high, Pleasant Street and Brookside elementary schools.[145]

WATERVILLE HAD BEEN IMBUED WITH A SPIRIT of ecumenism since the Protestant founders first absorbed the tide of immigrant French Catholics from Canada, then a stream of newcomers from Syria, and a ripple of others from many parts of Europe. By the mid-1970s, the community had some 20 churches and congregations. An area Council of Churches met regularly, and public occasions customarily had two or three clergy on the platform.

Three of the early churches celebrated landmark anniversaries in the Bicentennial year. The First Baptist Church on Elm Street, not only the city's oldest church but also the city's oldest public building, turned 150, and the Universalist-Unitarian Church marked the 150th anniversary of the Universalist Society. St. Marks Episcopal Church celebrated its Waterville centennial. Eight congregations had new buildings. The Lutheran Church of the Resurrection on Cool Street – one of the few "Missouri Synod" churches in Maine – was new altogether. Catholic parishioners at Notre

---

[145] In 1994 the Pleasant Street School was renamed in memory of Albert S. Hall, a beloved teacher and administrator who served 11 years as superintendent of schools. The Brookside School was renamed in honor of Senator George J. Mitchell in 1995.

Dame had outgrown the second-floor sanctuary above the classrooms on Water Street and wanted space to better accommodate the reforms of Vatican II. The affiliated St. Joseph School was torn down in 1970, and a year later, a modern Notre Dame with a half-circle sanctuary was dedicated on Silver Street.

The new Notre Dame church was opened barely a year in 1972 when parishioners celebrated the ordination of one of its own as a priest. Donald Edmund Pelotte was born in Waterville in 1945. His father, Norris, was a member of the Abenaki First Nations tribe, and his mother, Margaret (LaBrie) Pelotte, was of French-Canadian descent. A graduate of Fordham University, he made his first vows at the nearby Chapel of the Blessed Sacrament, home to a community of contemplative nuns,[146] and in 1978 became provincial superior of the U.S. men's community of the same order. In 1986, he was named by Pope John Paul II as the bishop of the Diocese of Gallup, New Mexico, making him the nation's first Catholic bishop of Native American descent. Bishop Pelotte returned to Notre Dame Church in 1999 to preside over the ordination of his twin brother, Dana. He served 22 years as bishop before suffering a traumatic brain injury in a mysterious incident at his home in Gallup in 2007, and was replaced in 2009. He died a year later, at age 64.

While the city's schools were being reconfigured, the Assembly of God, Calvary Temple (now Centerpoint Community Church), set about to provide a school for the Christian education of its children. In 1976 construction began on the private Temple Academy on West River Road. With emphasis on Bible teaching and academic excellence, the academy that began with three tiny classrooms reached out to students outside the church, and rapidly grew both in reputation and enrollment.

IN THE VERY MIDST OF THE 1976 BICENTENNIAL CELEBRATIONS, Mainers were keeping a close eye on news from Plains, Georgia, where Ed Muskie was meeting with Jimmy Carter. After winning the Ohio primary in June, Carter was set to receive the presidential nomination at the upcoming Democratic National Convention in New York City. He met with his final four choices for vice president on the July 4th

---

[146] The chapel at 101 Silver Street was the former home of George F. Terry, founder of the Kennebec Boat and Canoe Company (1909-1941), and became the first U.S. community of the Servants of the Blessed Sacrament in 1947. The second and only other women's community of the order is in Pueblo, Colorado.

weekend. Muskie was one of them, but Minnesota Senator Walter Mondale was chosen. Carter went on to easily defeat the incumbent unelected president, Gerald Ford, that fall.

Carter had a little more than a year left in his first term in November 1979, when his administration was frustrated as 52 American diplomats and citizens were taken hostage after radical students stormed the U.S. embassy in Tehran, Iran. Five months later, with negotiations for their release at a standoff and presidential elections looming, Carter ordered a military rescue, and it failed. Eight American servicemen were killed. Carter's Secretary of State, Cyrus Vance, resigned in May, and Carter turned to his old friend, Muskie, who agreed to serve.

Earlier that spring, Carter asked Congress to renew the law requiring all 18-year-old males to register for the draft. As the Senate set to hold confirmation hearings for Muskie's appointment as Secretary of State, more than a dozen Colby students staged a sit-in at Muskie's Main Street offices.[147] Aides explained that the senator was at the moment in a delicate spot and would not be getting into the fray. When a few protestors left the next day, one of them took the food, and the sit-in became a hunger strike. On the campus, several hundred held a sympathy rally and chanted: "No draft, no war, no way!" A day later, with the media paying close attention, students were told the cops were coming, and the occupation abruptly ended.

Muskie had served 21 years in the Senate and had two years remaining in his fourth term when he became Secretary. It fell to Democratic Governor Joe Brennan to fill the seat, and he didn't need to look far. George Mitchell had paid his party dues,[148] and following his defeat in the race for governor, had served as U.S. Attorney for Maine (1977-1979) and as a federal judge on the U.S. District Court of Maine (1979-1980).

Both Muskie and Mitchell were sticking their necks out. To avoid being a footnote in history, Mitchell would have to win at the ballot box in 1982. Muskie was 65 and might not have run again, but Carter's chances of re-election were growing slim, and Muskie's tenure as Secretary was likely to be measured in months. Still, the invitation was tempting. Maine had claimed

---

[147] The door with lettered glass announcing Muskie's Main Street office has been untouched and can still be seen at the top of the stairs on the third floor of the Key Bank building.
[148] Mitchell had defeated Brennan in the bid for the Democratic nomination in the gubernatorial race in 1974.

only one U.S. Secretary of State, and that was exactly 100 years before, when James G. Blaine accepted the call of President James Garfield. [149]

Ronald Reagan won the White House in a landslide (the Iranian prisoners were released two hours after his January 1981 inauguration), and Muskie was out of political life for the first time in 35 years. Having just received the Presidential Medal of Freedom, he returned home to a gala welcome, including a Colby reception with old friends and politicos. He reminded those gathered that he had once been a member of the local Chamber of Commerce, and joked that if he had stayed in Waterville, he might actually have become an elected president. He expressed gratitude to those who had given him a political start, and said, "no one could ask for more than to serve the people of this city and this state."

Mitchell validated his Senate appointment in 1982 by defeating Republican David Emery, and quickly rose to leadership as chair of the party's Senatorial Campaign Committee, which helped secure eight new seats in the 1984 elections and regain Democratic control of the Senate (55-45). In 1986, Mitchell won 81.3 percent of the vote in a resounding victory over Maine Christian Civic League president, Jasper Wyman. The margin was the widest of all the U.S. Senate races that year and the largest ever in Maine. It was also the last time Maine would send a Democrat to the Senate for the next three decades, and more.

---

[149] Blaine, a Republican, served in the U.S. House of Representatives from 1863-1876, and as Speaker of the House from 1865-1875. He was elected to the U.S. Senate in 1876, and later served twice as Secretary of State, under Presidents Garfield, Harrison, and Arthur. As the Republican nominee for President in 1876, he narrowly lost to Grover Cleveland.

PHOTO BY JUDY MICOLEAU
GEORGE J. MITCHELL PAPERS, MITCHELL DEPARTMENT OF
SPECIAL COLLECTIONS & ARCHIVES, BOWDOIN COLLEGE LIBRARY

Muskie and Mitchell celebrate Mitchell's Senate election victory, 1982

The galaxy of Waterville stars added another name in 1980 when local attorney Morton A. Brody was appointed to the Maine Superior Court. A native of Auburn and a graduate of Bates College and the University of Chicago Law School, Brody began private practice in Washington, D.C., in 1958. A devoted husband and father, he came to make his home in Waterville in 1961 and soon became engaged in local causes, many of them concerned with youth. He was made Chief Justice of the Superior Court in 1985, and five years later, Democratic Governor Brennan named him associate justice of the Supreme Judicial Court of Maine. His professional climb was not over. In 1991, when a new seat was added to the U.S. District Court, Republican President George H. W. Bush nominated Brody, who served until his untimely death in 2000, at age 66. The playground on North Street is named in his memory, and a Brody Distinguished Judicial Service Award is given biannually at Colby.

OF THE MANY PROTESTS CALLING FOR POLITICAL AND SOCIAL CHANGE, the loudest had brought an end to the war. Civil rights – albeit far from achieved – made progress, and there were many new initiatives to protect the environment. The cries for women's rights had been the most subdued, and the movement towards a balance of the sexes crept more slowly. Still, there were now signs that more women were willing to step forward, and more men were discovering that they were feminists.

Lyndon Johnson, ten years out of the White House, helped pave the way for Texas Congresswoman Barbara Jordan, who enthralled the country as keynote speaker at the 1976 Democratic National Convention.[150] Ronald Reagan named Sandra Day O'Connor the first woman on the U.S. Supreme Court (1981), NASA sent Sally Ride as the first American woman in space (1983), and Walter Mondale picked New York Congresswoman Geraldine Ferraro as the first woman candidate from a traditional party for vice president (1984).

Closer to home, women continued to fill the rosters of booster clubs, committees, and church groups, where the work needed to be done, but changes in the status quo were slow and often subtle. A handful of women began to move into leadership circles through the 1970s. Laura Nawfel, director of personnel at Hathaway, began as the "token" woman on civic boards and commissions, and sometimes ended up in charge. A Girls Club counterpart to the Boys Club was formed in 1972, holding programs in the elementary schools and at a child development center on Water Street, until the two clubs merged under one roof at Main Place in 1976.[151]

The first cracks in the local glass ceiling were made in the political arena. Ruth Loebs was a stalwart on the School Board, and Sally Parsons was elected to the city council as early as 1962. Louise Smith was on the first seven-person council following the charter change in 1967. Ann Peters and Germaine Orloff followed on her path. Through the period, Naomi Giroux worked with the party boss Gabriel Giroux to keep a tight wrap on the organization of the heavily Democratic Ward 7 in the city's South End.

---

[150] Jordan first came to fame as a member of the House Judiciary Committee during the impeachment proceedings against Richard Nixon.
[151] There were symbolic changes as well. In 1979, when Bill Cotter was inaugurated as the new Colby president, he gender-neutralized the college alma mater with a stroke of a pen. He changed the second line of the anthem from "thy sons from far and near," to "thy people far and near."

In 1981, the ceiling was smashed altogether when Ann "Nancy" Gilbride Hill, a Democrat, was elected Waterville's first woman mayor in a line of 41 men dating back 94 years to the founding of the city. An Irish woman from Boston, Hill was steeped in rough-and-tumble politics and was easily a full match for the boys who played hardball at City Hall. She took office in 1982 during the worst recession in 40 years,[152] when the city was $300,000 in debt. After two terms of careful management, she left of her own accord in 1986 with the city books

Ann "Nancy" Hill

$800,000 in the black. Her service opened the top city office to other women. Thomas Nale followed Hill (1986-88) before Judy Kany, who had already served in the Maine House, was elected to both the mayor's job and a seat in the Maine Senate (1988-1989).

The year Kany was elected both mayor and senator, popular Waterville native Marilyn Canavan was named director of the Maine Commission on Governmental Ethics and Election Practices, a post she held for ten years before being elected to four terms in the Maine House of Representatives.

Even more women leaders were on the way. Barbara Woodlee was director of adult education at the Kennebec Valley Vocational-Technical Institute when founding director, Bernard King, died in 1984. At age 36, Woodlee became the first woman to lead a Maine technical school. The growing Institute had moved from shared space at the new high school to a place of its own in the vacated junior high on Gilman Street in 1977,[153] and two years later it merged with the Maine School of Practical Nursing.[154] When Woodlee took office, the Institute had just acquired 60 acres of land

Barbara Woodlee

---

[152] In November 1982, national unemployment hit 10.4 percent, the highest since 1940. By year's end, more than 11 million Americans were out of work.
[153] The Institute straddled two campuses for six years before completing the move. The 1913 Gilman Street structure was renovated and then re-opened as workforce housing (Gilman Place) in 2011.
[154] A descendant of the Sisters Hospital School of Nursing.

for a new campus in Fairfield, and construction was about to begin on the first classroom building, soon to be named for King.

The Maine technical institutes formed their own autonomous system in 1986, renaming themselves as colleges three years later. In the spring of 2003, Kennebec Valley Technical College joined the new state system of seven community colleges, and Kennebec Valley Community College, with an enrollment of 3300 students – and the only woman president – became the sixth and fastest growing institution to join. As she was about to retire in 2010, the college acquired a second 700-acre campus on the site of the former Good Will-Hinckley School in Hinckley, and she stayed on for two years to lead the move.

Throughout her 27-year tenure, Woodlee brought creativity and energy to a job requiring nimble responses to the ever-changing needs of area employers to find skilled workers. Almost every graduate found immediate employment, and collectively the college made a strong positive impact on the area economy. Of her many achievements, none was greater than the example she set as a consummate role model for legions of young women.

In the steps towards gender equality, some institutions moved faster than others. In 1987, the U.S. Supreme Court upheld the Rotary Club of Duart, California, whose charter had been revoked by Rotary International for having admitted three women. That same year, Waterville Rotary president Kenneth Viens forced the issue in Waterville. Not every man got on board. Two quit in a huff. The first two women members were physician Sherry Oldham and real estate executive Joanna Dennis, who, five years later, became the club's president.

BY THE MID-1980s, A NATIONAL TIDE OF BANKRUPTCIES, takeovers, and mega-mergers had begun. A worldwide recession had ended, but high interest rates and unemployment were left in its wake. Signs of the slump were everywhere. Waterville Hardware, at the foot of Main Street, closed in 1979, and the blight became contagious. Vacant storefronts appeared up and down the street.[155]

Despite its modern plant, the Wyandotte mill on the West River Road suffered the same woes as other northern wool makers, and collapsed in

---

[155] Among those that closed in the 1980s were Dunhams, Emery Brown, McClellans, Sterns, and Alvina & Delia. Butlers was sold to Beshara and Juliet Saliba, but it did not last.

bankruptcy (1980).[156] The following year, Maine Central Railroad, once the lifeline of the area, was bought by United States Filter Corporation and quickly re-sold to Guilford Transportation Industries, which then gobbled up the Boston & Maine Railroad, as well. By 1985, fully a third of the MCRR tracks had been eliminated or abandoned, and the Waterville repair shops were closed. In order to skirt union rules, Guilford reorganized under an obscure subsidiary called Springfield Terminal, an action that led to years of union strife.[157]

The steady march of reversals went on. The poultry industry disappeared in a mere two years (1979-1981), moving south almost en masse to find lower feed, energy, and transportation costs. Lipman Poultry in Augusta and Fort Halifax in Winslow shuttered their doors, and the only reminders of the once vigorous enterprise were dozens of abandoned and decaying poultry houses that would dot the rural landscape for years to come. Following suit, Diamond Match Company in Oakland closed in 1983, and Zayre, the anchor store in the still-new Concourse, went bankrupt in 1988.[158] Radio station WTVL boosted its FM signal to 50,000 watts in 1986 and was broadcasting statewide when four years later it succumbed to the wide-open competition that came with deregulation.

Even in the worst of the slump, not every enterprise was suffering. Evariste Laverdiere and his son Reginald continued to expand their drugstore chain throughout New England, and after some wrangling, the City Council agreed to let Shaw's build a super store on Kennedy Memorial Drive. The development of a new chicken vaccine in 1980 (Bursal) allowed Ken Eskelund to expand the Maine Biological Laboratories, and by mid-decade, his Winslow facility was producing immunizations for half the hens in the world.

One of the most remarkable ventures to buck the tide was Mid-State Machines. In 1971, Douglas Sukeforth left his job as night foreman at Keyes to begin his own tool making business, working part-time in his garage. Within a dozen years he had built and then added to his own plant in Winslow, and with the help of Kennebec Valley Technical College, had 100

---

[156] In 2013, the Maine Department of Environmental Protection declared the two long-unused 2.5-acre wastewater lagoons an "imminent threat" because of a concentration of heavy metals. The state paid $200,000 to drain and cap them.
[157] Guilford became a part of what is now the Pan Am Railways network.
[158] Ames discount stores bought the bankrupt Zayre and went bankrupt itself in 2002.

skilled employees filling orders for precision industrial equipment for customers around the globe. In 1987 sales topped $20 million, most of it from the Department of Defense.

Those who built empires from scratch were known for sharing, and dozens of local causes profited from their generosity. Sukeforth built an indoor ice arena in Winslow, and later he and his family established the Festival of Trees, a popular annual holiday event that drew hundreds and helped sustain local charities.

The Chamber of Commerce was increasingly challenged, not only to juggle the competing interests of downtown merchants and those in the outlying malls, but also to raise awareness that the fates of area towns were inextricably linked. In 1983 the Chamber incorporated as the Greater Waterville Chamber of Commerce,[159] and in 1985 further adjusted its name and scope to become the Mid-Maine Chamber of Commerce.[160]

The expanded organization quickly formed the Mid-Maine Economic Development Steering Committee, which in 1986 heard a sobering report from the Maine Development Foundation. Between 1979 and 1985, the area lost 700 manufacturing jobs and another 200 at the railroad. Paper industry losses were barely offset by 1,000 new jobs at Scott's S.D. Warren mill in Skowhegan. Most astonishingly, 1800 government positions in the 15 area towns had disappeared. In a half-decade, jobs in service (education, health, retail and wholesale) had come to outnumber those in manufacturing, and Mid-Maine Medical Center (1200 employees) became the area's largest employer.

Scott, Hathaway, and Keyes were the three remaining major industries, and the only one that would survive was the first to get in trouble. In 1983, Keyes' books were $2 million in the red, with losses caused by a crippling electricity bill topping $6 million a year, and labor costs that were the highest among the many affiliated mills. In April of 1985, after failed labor negotiations, news came that the plant would close.

---

[159] All the while, the Chamber itself kept moving, first from College Avenue to upstairs at 57 Main (over Larsen's Jewelers), then to the second floor at 131 Main, and in 1986 to a place of prominence in the old Post Office building at the top of Main Street, where it would remain for nearly a quarter century.
[160] Eventually encompassing Albion, Belgrade, Benton, Burnham, China, Clinton, Fairfield, Hinckley, Oakland, Rome, Shawmut, Sidney, South China, Thorndike, Unity, Vassalboro, Waterville, Weeks Mills and Winslow.

Joseph Ezhaya, representing the new Chamber, joined Mayor Hill and State Senator Kany to work with Governor Brennan and others to see what could be done. A month later, the state offered Keyes a subsidy of up to $10 million if it would stay, and Fairfield and Waterville each chipped in offers of $6 million loans. Labor agreed to take lower wages, the company was forgiven taxes on electricity, and area citizens began saving old newspapers for recycling into paper plates. In late June, Keyes CEO W. Walker Rast published an open letter saying the plant would remain open. He commended local workers for their "character and determination" and thanked them for their sacrifice.

The industrial alarm bell had been heard, loud and clear, and the broadened Chamber membership set out to find new businesses, while at the same time promoting the ones they had. An annual *Summerfest* began in 1981, with artist displays, concerts, and sidewalk sales that drew thousands. Robert and Cynthia Cloutier had taken over the old Opera House for a program of summer musicals, and that same year launched what would become a 30-year campaign to restore one of the country's last surviving Victorian theaters. The Two-Cent Bridge, deemed unsafe and closed in 1974, was repaired and rededicated in 1985,[161] kicking off *Two-Cent Days*, an annual summer attraction.

AS WARY EYES WERE FIXED ON THE REMAINING INDUSTRIES along the Kennebec, the river itself went on a rampage. By late March 1987, the snow had already gone from Waterville, and the river was clear of ice. Up north, the clinging snowpack was six feet deep, and the river was still solid. In the last days of the month, a low-pressure mass moved northeast, bringing more than six inches of rain into Maine, swelling the river valleys. On April Fool's Day the waters rose up with a fury that hadn't been seen since the epic flood of 1936.

Roaring over the dams at 194,000 cubic feet per second, the water finally crested at 36 feet, a record 23 feet above flood stage, and in the lowlands, the water went where it had never gone before. In Waterville, the freshet washed over the new floorboards of the Two-Cent Bridge, snapping its anchor cables. Water filled the Hathaway parking lot and lapped at the

---

[161] The Maine Historic Preservation Commission provided $50,000 to insert steel beams in the towers and to replace the floor beams and cables.

factory steps, flooding its bargain basement shop. Lower Water Street was evacuated, and Mayor Thomas Nale moved quickly to assure the city would provide housing for dozens of displaced families. Winslow's Lithgow Street went completely under water; six houses were carried down the river. The famed log blockhouse at Fort Halifax simply disappeared.

Towns all along the big rivers were crippled. The road from Farmington to Quebec was washed out in dozens of places and closed. Merchants everywhere sold out of sump pumps and film. Secretary of Transportation Elizabeth Dole came to visit and declared a disaster.

> Officials hoped the historic Fort Halifax might simply have snagged up on a banking nearby and could be retrieved, but it had been completely torn apart. Pieces of its timber were found as far downriver as Swan Island, Days Ferry, and Woolwich. The blockhouse had been renovated many times, and by 1987 very little of the 1754 structure was original, in any case. It was agreed to build another replica, using whatever timbers from the washed away structure that could be found. Two local men, State Representative Donald Carter and history teacher and contractor Stanley Mathieu were put in charge.

The area dried out and recovered in plenty of time for Waterville to mark the 1988 centennial of becoming a city. Nothing would do, of course, but to throw another party, with a big parade and plenty of fireworks.

15

Bridges Falling Down

1990-2002

The new decade had barely begun when Waterville's penchant for throwing parties led to a misadventure that became a harbinger of more ruinous things to come. On the 4th of July 1990, some 5000 people converged at Head of Falls to attend "Maine's largest free concert" and an evening of fireworks. There were too many people for such a small space, and far too much beer for a warm day. In the resulting melee, the Two Cent Bridge got damaged and was closed.[162]

At the same time, a greater calamity was looming on the other side of the bridge, where Scott Paper Company was in trouble. The owners had misgauged the market, expanding its mills and production at a time when new competitors were driving prices down. By 1993, Scott profits had dropped more than 60 percent off their ten-year high. The losses called for restructuring, and the following year the company called in Al Dunlap to do the job. His reputation preceded him, and his nickname "Chainsaw Al" said it all.

Within nine months, the new CEO divested more than $2 billion in assets, firing 11,000 workers company-wide, including nearly 300 in Winslow. Determined to return to the safer market niche of making toilet and tissue paper, the company retreated from producing fine paper. The

---

[162] Once again, the Waterville Rotary Club jumped into the breach and spearheaded the redesign and rebuilding of the bridge, reopened in 1997.

S.D. Warren Skowhegan mill was put up for sale, and a South African conglomerate, Sappi, bought it.

Dunlap's slashing doubled Scott's stock prices and made the company ripe for acquisition. In 1995, the Texas paper giant Kimberly-Clark paid $9.4 billion to take it over. Dunlap put $100 million in his own pocket, and the new owners set about to further consolidate operations, product lines, and workforces.

Winslow still had five working paper machines and three finishing rooms, but much of the equipment was outdated,[163] and the mill was plagued with high costs of energy, transportation, and raw materials. Kimberly-Clark had things sorted out by 1997, and elected to close 18 of its plants worldwide. The 73-year-old Winslow mill, with its 264 remaining workers, was among the first to go.[164]

THE NATION HAD SEEN SOME $3 TRILLION worth of mega-mergers since 1980, and while the national economy was moving upward, most of Maine north of Portland was sinking. River towns that had been long reliant on their industries were hit the hardest. The year the Kimberly-Clark closed its Winslow mill, the 114-year-old Cascade woolen mill in Oakland surrendered to foreign competitors and shut down as well. On North Street, the Harris Baking Company briefly emerged from bankruptcy, only to close again.

The decline slowly ate at the city's tax base, and to make ends meet, the City Council eliminated its economic development program arm at a time when it would have been most helpful. Democratic Mayor David Bernier (1990-1993)[165] soldiered on by himself, and helped to found the Mid-State Economic Development Corporation (1991), the first of several regionalized growth-seeking consortia designed to find jobs in the increasingly competitive world.

AS IN EVERY PERIOD OF HISTORY, there was more to fear from other nations than what came from economic rivalry. Tensions with Russia had been escalating since the end of World War II, when the former ally

---

[163] The No. 4 machine still had some wooden gears, as did the water wheels under the digester that brought river water into the mill. A regular application of pork fat was required to keep them greased.
[164] Kimberly-Clark continued to use the Scott brand. Scott's Canadian interests were sold to Kruger, LTD.
[165] Lawyer son of Albert Bernier, mayor from 1958-1961.

became its most feared adversary. Through the 1980s, ordinary citizens in both countries were alarmed by the Soviet-American saber rattling, and were afraid of a nuclear holocaust. In 1983, President Ronald Reagan reinforced these worries by calling the Soviet Union the "Evil Empire."

The fears were put aside for six days in June 1990, when area citizens rolled out the red carpet for four strangers from Russia. For Winslow scientist Peter Garrett and many others, the visit marked the culmination of a decade-long struggle to build a bridge of understanding and peace. Believing in the power of friendships among ordinary citizens, in the early 1980s Garrett set out to find a Russian "sister city" for the Waterville area. He chose another river city, called Kotlas, 500 miles northeast of Moscow, a manufacturing center of some 100,000 people.

Calling itself *Our Peaceful Russian Connection*, the committee first sought local government approvals. Fairfield bought in quickly. Waterville and Winslow were more cautious and delayed their votes. Oakland refused to consider the matter at all.[166] Public approval grew when the Waterville Rotary Club provided money to publicize the dream, and local governments eventually signed on.[167] A "resolution of peace" with an invitation to pair as sister cities was sent to the Chair of the Executive Committee (mayor) of Kotlas by Waterville mayor Nancy Hill. The response was polite, but noncommittal. Undaunted, in 1996 Garrett and Hill sent further pleas to Kotlas, as well as a letter to Politburo General Secretary Mikhail Gorbachev. Waterville Russian-American Natalia Kempers began correspondence with a Kotlas boatyard engineer, Vyacheslav Chernykh. Two years went by before a package arrived at Waterville City Hall, filled with paintings, carvings, and other items made by the children of Kotlas. Not long after, a Kotlas teacher wrote to suggest the children of the two places become pen pals.

In the spring of 1989, Winslow schoolteacher Mary Coombs led a group from Winslow Junior High on a ten-day tour of Moscow and Leningrad (now St. Petersburg). Garrett, his daughter Jessica, and Kempers went along. A Moscow man who knew of the peace pairing effort offered train tickets to Kotlas, and on April 20 representatives of the two far-flung places finally came together. The warm reception prompted Mayor Judy Kany to

---

[166] In the process, Garrett was labeled as "a Red."
[167] A citizen's initiative forced a Town Meeting vote in Oakland, where it passed 60-43.

write the new Kotlas mayor, Viktor Zverey, in July, inviting him to bring a delegation to Waterville. He replied in November, saying he would come and bring with him the pen pal organizer, the boatyard engineer and a local journalist.

Kany formed a reception committee, led by high school teacher Philip Gonyar, for the historic first official visit in June. By any measure, it was a huge success, and in the fall the committee made plans to send a nine-member delegation, led by Mayor David Bernier, to Kotlas the following June (1991). The brave adventure for understanding and peace had come full circle, and the doors were open. The Waterville group sent cargo containers of humanitarian aid to Kotlas, and going forward, the Mid-Maine Chamber joined every succeeding mayor in hosting the Waterville end of exchange visits by teachers, students, musicians, and artists.

CITY LEADERSHIP SUFFERED HICCUPS through the second half of the decade. In 1995, Mayor Thomas Brazier went to jail for embezzling private funds. Former superintendent of schools Nelson Megna stood in for a year before the election of Ruth Joseph, a Democrat who worked tirelessly through one of the city's bleakest periods, but found herself in a political crossfire and was recalled by voters in a pique over several issues, including rising taxes. Thomas College professor Nelson Madore served as mayor through 2003 and vowed to put Waterville on the map as the "city of festivals."

The discount Goliath Wal-Mart, came to town in 1992, and while many pledged to boycott the place to protect the hometown merchants, most soon had their wallets overcome their willpower, and independent downtown stores continued to close. Sterns Department Store, at the very heart of Main Street, had shut its doors in 1988, and a brief flirt with Ward Brothers of Lewiston amounted to nothing. The building was reopened as the Sterns Cultural Center, but the owners soon faced foreclosure, and in 1996 Colby President Bill Cotter headed a group of community leaders seeking to turn the building into the Waterville Regional Arts and Community Center (WRACC). The price tag was a million dollars. Colby and Mid-Maine Medical Center made lead gifts of $100,000, and eight others, including Thomas College and Inland Hospital, pitched in to raise more than $500,000 before the public campaign. More than 2,000 citizens contributed to meet the goal.

The sign over the new Sterns Center had just gone up in 1996 when Levines joined the parade of closings. The oldest establishment on Main Street, "the store for men and boys" also had the best known personae. Percy "Pacy" and Lewis "Ludy" Levine, heirs to the store their father opened in 1904,[168] had a huge following, including many who stopped by just to talk. The brothers were Colby graduates, and for more than 70 years were the college's biggest sports fans. Parents no longer able to stretch out clothing bills without paying interest mourned the closing as well.

Hardly a month went by without the shuttering of other familiar stores, and by the end of the 1990s, vacant places outnumbered those that were filled. Area residents moved out of nearby neighborhoods, transient renters moved in, and the deteriorating downtown saw a rise in crime, ranging from petty vandalism to illegal drugs. The changes made it even harder for those who dreamed of a Main Street revival, and the Chamber put up an informational kiosk in Castonguay Square so no one would forget where things once were.

IN WATERVILLE, THE SAD LOSSES OF THE DECADE included the death of Ed Muskie, who died of heart failure in Washington D.C. in March, 1996. Sixteen years out of elected office, he was still revered around the country as a paragon of passion, integrity and accomplishment. At his funeral in Bethesda, Maryland, former President Jimmy Carter said, "Of all the people I've ever known, no one was better qualified to be the president of the United States."

Muskie had lived long enough to see his protégé and fellow Democrat George Mitchell complete 15 years in the U.S Senate, the last six as Senate Majority Leader. What Muskie did not know, but it would not have surprised him, was that Mitchell's reputation for non-partisan fairness and devotion to the truth would lead him to a second career that re-shaped world history and improved American institutions. In 1994, he declined President Clinton's invitation to be considered for a seat on the Supreme Court, and in 1996 became the President's Special Envoy for Northern Island. Two years later, he was lauded as a principal architect of the Good Friday Agreement (1998) that brought peace to the land of his father. While

---

[168] William Levine opened his first store on Ticonic Street, and then moved to 91 Main (later Wards, then Sterns), before opening the store at the end of the street. Pacy, at age 91, died the year the store closed. Ludy, 95, died a year later.

Chancellor of the Queen's University in Belfast, he accepted President George W. Bush's appointment as vice chair of the 9/11 Commission in 2002, and from 2009-2011 was President Bill Clinton's Special Envoy for Middle East Peace. Along the way, he investigated and wrote the "Mitchell Report" on the use of performance-enhancing drugs in Major League Baseball.[169]

> Bad news was never far away, but on January 28, 1996, no one could grasp the enormity of the discovery that a knife-wielding, deranged man had entered the convent and chapel of the Servants of the Blessed Sacrament on Silver Street and attacked four nuns, killing two of them. A spokesman for the State Police called it "one of the most heinous crimes ever committed in Maine." Mark Bechard, 37, suffered bipolar disorder and alcoholism, and had been in and out of the Augusta Mental Health Institute (AMHI). The *Sentinel* editorialized that the crime made it "painfully apparent that Maine's much-vaunted deinstitutionalization effort is an utter failure." The city grieved for the beloved nuns – Sister Marie Julien Fortin and Mother Superior Edna Mary Cardozo – and for Bechard and his hapless family.

BY THE END OF THE DECADE, Waterville's census had dropped 3000, to 15,600, the lowest since before World War II. The Chambers of Commerce in Waterville and Augusta met to form an entity called The People of the Kennebec, charging it with leading a regional development effort.[170] Some communities had already planned to build business parks, but few had the willingness, capital, or infrastructure needed to make one work. Governor Angus King joined the Chamber of Commerce in supporting the idea of having regional parks instead, and in 1998 the Legislature created a state authority to govern "super parks," and offered $1 million Community Development Block Grants to help build them. Chamber leaders Peter Thompson and Craig Nelson of Augusta and David Savage and Charles Gaunce of Waterville worked to bring one into the area. Mayor Joseph wanted it to be in Waterville, but a 285-acre place just off the Interstate in Oakland was chosen, and Oakland Town Manager Michael Roy (who became Waterville's city manager in 2004) worked with others to get

---

[169] Mitchell raised money to augment the unused portion of his last Senate campaign funds to establish The Mitchell Institute, which awards some 130 continuing college scholarships to Maine public high school graduates each year.

[170] The People of the Kennebec worked with Senator Susan Collins to create a "micropolitan statistical area" to improve the eligibility for support from various federal programs. The group was instrumental in supporting the creation of MaineGeneral Medical Center and the single Augusta-Waterville telephone network and directory.

24 area communities in Kennebec and Somerset counties to sign on.[171] The resulting collaborative investment from the Kennebec Regional Development Authority created the only such entity ever approved.

When the park opened in 1996, L.L. Bean promptly purchased two lots and began clearing for construction of a new call center to replace its facility in the JFK Mall. Soon after, T-Mobile announced it too would move into the park and would provide 600 jobs at a call center of its own. L.L. Bean withdrew, fearing a shortage of workers to support them both.[172] By the turn of the century, nearly 1,000 people were employed at FirstPark, but many were hospital employees, transplanted from other locations in the area after the merger. At the beginning of the 21st century, the park was still short of its planned potential, but well poised for what might come.

Business corporations weren't the only ones consolidating. Non-profits were doing the same thing, and for many of the same reasons. Church attendance worldwide had dropped precipitously. Most young people of all faiths were not as devout as their parents, and many Catholics were disaffected by the growing revelations of sex scandals in the church. In 1996, dwindling parishioners and a shortage of priests in Waterville led to a consolidation of Sacred Heart, Saint Francis, and Notre Dame into a single Parish of the Holy Spirit. A decade later (July, 2007), seven area churches, a summer chapel in Belgrade Lakes, elementary schools in Winslow and Fairfield, and a Newman apostolate at Colby merged as the single Corpus Christi Parish. Despite pleas to the Diocese in Portland to save it, the city's oldest Catholic church, St. Francis de Sales (1874), was razed in 2012 to make way for low income senior housing.

The loss of iconic local church structures began in 2008 when the Universalist Unitarian Church at the apex of Silver and Elm streets lost much of its Gothic Revival appeal by having its handsome clock tower removed. It had been deemed unsafe, and there was no money to save it.

---

[171] Augusta decided to go it on their own, and voted not to invest.
[172] Five years later, L.L. Bean left Waterville, citing high costs and the challenges of operating in the mall setting.

A 2012 winter snowstorm decorates St. Francis de Sales Church on Elm Street the year before the church, its rectory, and parish hall were demolished.

AS MEDICAL COSTS ROSE, HOSPITALS WERE LOOKING for more efficiency, as well. Seton and Thayer hospitals had already broken Waterville's political and parochial barriers with the 1975 creation of Mid-Maine Medical Center (MMMC). Five years later, the Augusta and Gardiner general hospitals joined as Kennebec Valley Health Systems (KVHS), and in 1997 the two merged to become MaineGeneral Health Care. The new entity moved rapidly to develop a regional health care system, expanding and

175

introducing new services and absorbing private practice physicians throughout central Maine.[173]

Weird and fast-changing weather was nothing new in Maine, but few had ever experienced the strange convergence of systems that occurred in the winter of 1998. On Monday, January 5, a series of low-pressure areas in the south brought heavy rain into Maine. Temperatures in the mountains were warmer than in the frozen towns and cities below, and for two days the rain made ice, in some places three inches thick. On Wednesday, residents awoke to cannon-like sounds of trees and power poles falling under the weight. Half of the state's population, including most in central Maine, was without electricity. Governor Angus King declared a state of emergency and called out the National Guard. Waterville had a disaster plan, but the city was not prepared to have all of its designated city shelters lose power at once. Colby took its electricity from the nearby Central Maine Power's Rice's Rips station, and its lines were all underground, making Mayflower Hill an oasis of heat and light. Mayor Joseph called Colby for help, and the college field house quickly became the area's principal shelter. Shivering residents began arriving before the cots were set up, and over the next week the college took in more than 1000 residents who either came and went for meals or stayed for the duration. Working with students, the city's hospitals set up a round-the-clock first-aid station at the field house, and other students went into town, knocking on doors, looking for anyone in distress.[174] Local power was out for a week – in some places two and three – while CMP, reinforced by crews from around the country and Canada, replaced more than 3000 utility poles and restrung a million feet of wire throughout the state.

As the city came to the end of its most trying decade since the Civil War, its beleaguered residents were easy prey for the hysteria that overshadowed the coming of the new millennium. Many feared computers had not been coded to recognize all four digits of a year, and that the midnight rollover would send the world back to 1900 (not an unworthy idea, considering the moment) or bring on an apocalypse by eating ATM cards, tumbling satellites, and melting power lines. Y2K turned out to be a false alarm, which prompted fretters to believe that, hereafter, people would pay no heed to warnings of disasters that were sure to come. Indeed, one was just around the corner.

---

[173] By 2018, MaineGeneral had 262 physicians on staff.
[174] Two lives were saved, maybe more.

MANY BELIEVED THE FATE OF THE CITY'S OLDEST and most notable industry, C.F. Hathaway, had been sealed in 1960, when Warner Brothers took over and management decisions were taken out of town. In fact, even after Warner Brothers grew to become Warnaco in 1968, the local maker of what fashion gurus called the finest of men's shirts made in the entire country thrived almost another 20 years. The first sign of trouble came in 1985, when a former division executive at Warnaco, Linda Wachner, engineered a $550 million hostile takeover of the massive company.

Every bit as ruthless as "Chainsaw" Al Dunlap, Wachner proceeded to expand and streamline, buying up license agreements with the fashion labels everyone knew. By 1991, the company was dripping in profits, and while Wachner continued on a buying spree, she also let it be known she would part with those companies that weren't performing. Hathaway, she said, was one: the year before, as evidence of her skepticism, Wachner had discontinued the Hathaway national advertising campaign and retired the classic logo of the man with the eye patch.

In January 1995, Wachner came to Waterville and met with the company's 500 employees, 95 percent of whom were women doing piecework and averaging $6.50 an hour. She brashly promised she would not close the plant if they would do quality work and at the same time find ways to bring down the cost of the finished shirts. Some of the Waterville women had already contributed by helping train Warnaco workers at its new plant in Honduras, and now, eager to preserve their jobs, they set about to cross-train: collar women learned to make cuffs, and stitchers pitched in with the packing. None of it mattered. Six months later, in May 1996, Wachner announced Warnaco would sell or close the Waterville factory. The division is not making money, she said, "and we're in the business of operating for a profit."

With the end in sight, in 1997 Governor Angus King went looking for a savior to buy the factory, while former Governor John McKernan helped establish a Maine investment group to finance a bailout. The group's name – Made in the USA Foundation – described its purpose. Windsong Alliance (Westport, Conn.) bought the factory in the fall of 2001, but by the next spring, conceded that Hathaway would have to close in June. A last-minute $5 million contract with Wal-Mart gave a six-month reprieve, but when a bid to make shirts for the U.S. Air Force was unsuccessful, the closing became certain. There were 235 workers left when the 165-year-old plant closed its doors on October 18, 2002.[175] After the final shift, many of the women lingered for a time in the parking lot, clutching each other and openly weeping.[176]

---

[175] Windsong continued to use the Hathaway label on sportswear made abroad.
[176] United Way executive director Mary Derosier led an effort to find social services and other assistance for the dismissed workers.

16

The Shoe Man

-2018

There have always been men and women of means who give generously to improve the places where they live, but it is unlikely that any small place in America ever benefited more from the philanthropy of one person than the Waterville area and the gifts of Harold Alfond.

By the 21st century, the Alfond name could be seen everywhere, recognized and admired as a sign of seemingly endless altruism. In 1950, hardly anyone knew him. He and his wife Dorothy "Bibby," a sister of the well-known clothiers, Pacy and Ludy Levine, lived on Silver Street (No. 127), where they raised four children.[177] Alfond was president of Norrwock Shoe Company, an idle factory in Norridgewock that he and his father purchased for $1000 in 1940, just as World War II began. The company prospered – in part by making footwear for the armed forces – and in 1948 was sold to Shoe Corporation of America for $1.1 million. Alfond continued as president, and two years later established the first private charitable corporation in Maine.[178] The first Harold Alfond Foundation gifts

---

[177] In 1950, Ted was five; Susan, four; and Bill, two. A third son, Peter, was born in 1952.
[178] In 1996, he founded Dexter Enterprizes, Inc., to manage his family's philanthropy, investment, legal and business interests. Attorney Gregory Powell, whom Alfond had known since Powell was a child in Waterville, was put in charge.

were made in 1951, to build two baseball fields for Waterville's new Little League.[179]

Like many other American legendary entrepreneurs, Harold Alfond built his own empire from the ground up. His success came not from good luck, but from rare business savvy, a competitive spirit, and hard work. Born in 1914 in Swampscott, Massachusetts, he went directly from high school to work with his father at Kesslen Shoe Company in Kennebunk (makers of the Goodyear Welt shoe), becoming plant superintendent at the age of 22. In 1939, he sold his car for the cash, and with help from his father, bought the shoe company in Norridgewock. He sold Norrwock Shoe in 1944, but continued on as president until 1969. At the same time, in 1958 he paid $10,000 to purchase a vacant woolen mill in Dexter where he was joined by his nephew, Peter Lunder, and later his sons, in the operation of Dexter Shoe Company, which at its peak made 36,000 pairs of shoes a day. In 1971, Dexter became one of the first U.S. manufacturers to retail its own product, and within 20 years there were more than 80 of the familiar log-cabin style stores across the country. In 1993, Dexter Shoe was sold to Warren Buffett for $433 million in Berkshire Hathaway stock, making Alfond and his family the company's second largest shareholders.[180] Alfond, his sons, and nephew stayed on until 2001, when Dexter was merged with the H.H. Brown Shoe Company.

Alfond had already funded three more local athletic fields by 1955, when the Colby ice arena became the first facility to bear his name. The college planned a covered outdoor rink, but Alfond's gift made it possible to close it in. When he spoke at the dedication, he said he hoped "to be granted the resources, the ability, and the life blood" to enable him to continue helping. No one could have then imagined the prescience of his words.

A firm believer in the developmental value of teamwork and competition, Alfond financed numerous other athletic facilities over the next three decades, including ones at both Colby and Thomas colleges. His crowning gift to area youngsters came at the end of the century. The city

---

[179] The American League field was near Thayer Hospital on North Street, near the bank of the Messalonskee. The National League field was on the flat below a sand pit on Water Street, across from the Lockwood mills.
[180] Buffett said Dexter Shoe was one of the best-operated companies he had ever seen, but he also later confessed to investors that he should never have paid for it in Berkshire stock.

Parks and Recreation Department, the Boys-Girls Club, and the YMCA separately sought his support in building new youth recreation facilities, and he offered to help if they would agree to join together, as one. The Alfond Youth Center, opened on North Street in the spring of 1999,[181] was and remains the nation's only merged Boys-Girls Club and YMCA. Speaking at the dedication that fall, General Colin Powell called it "the biggest and best" in all the land.

PHOTO BY CHRISTA LAVENSON

The North Street Alfond Youth Center, 2018

A key figure in the unique merger and its subsequent success was Kenneth Walsh, who came to manage the Boys-Girls Club in 1992. Under his leadership, the Alfond Youth Center continued to expand, reaching thousands of youngsters in more than 100 towns. New initiatives included the renovating and reactivating of a summer youth center at Camp Tracy on nearby McGrath Pond, aided by a challenge grant from the New Balance Foundation. The camp is adjacent to Maine's only licensed replica of the Red Sox's Fenway Park, named for Alfond. Walsh also led in building a scale model of the Chicago Cubs's Wrigley Field on Matthews Avenue, completed in 2017 and named to honor Francis Purnell, a life-long supporter of Waterville youth baseball.

---

[181] Alfond's initial gift was $3 million. The Alfond foundations subsequently gave $11 million more for enhancements, including the construction of a second story to make an overall 72,000 square-foot facility.

Over time, there was hardly a local educational or charitable institution that did not profit from Alfond's generosity. Although his formal education ended with high school, colleges were high on his list. Colby, the alma mater of his son Bill, was at the top, and by 2018 the college had received more than $47 million in Alfond gifts. Major grants at Thomas College included an academic building, and a business and career development center. His support of higher education often came in quiet ways, as well, as he often paid the tuition of children of his factory workers and others.[182] Hundreds have also received official Alfond scholarships, made possible by his insistence that student support be included with his gifts.

From the beginning, he placed two conditions on nearly all of his donations: the resulting program or facility must be open to all, and advocates would have to rally support to make a reasonable match of his gifts, a stipulation that not only leveraged additional funds but also assured the full engagement of the organizations' leadership. His gifts and the energy they created helped sustain and improve a number of area institutions, including the Maine Children's Home for Little Wanderers, an adoption agency warmly embraced by his wife; the Good Will-Hinckley School, Kents Hill School, the Belgrade Community Center, the Waterville Opera House, and the Waterville Area Humane Society.

Grants from his children's separate foundations were sometimes combined with his own, but often reflected their separate interests. The Bill and Joan Alfond Foundation helped establish Educare of Central Maine, a model learning and development center that opened on Drummond Avenue in 2010, serving 200 pre-school children each year. Gifts from son Ted and his wife Barbara strengthened the holdings of the Colby Art Museum, and the Peter Alfond Foundation supported many of the ventures of the others, including the Maine Film Center.[183]

Alfond was never self-indulgent, but he took great pride in his limited partnership with the Boston Red Sox (1978), and also in an acclaimed 18-hole golf course he built in Belgrade Lakes (1997), near the Great Pond complex where his extended family enjoyed their summers.

---

[185] As a tribute to his support of education, in 2013 the directors of the Harold Alfond Foundation announced that it would award and invest a $500 Alfond Grant for every baby born in Maine, to be later used, together with earnings, for their higher education expense.

[183] Tragically, Peter died from complications of malaria in 2017. He was 65.

At the end of his life, Alfond, a cancer victim, made possible a $42 million outpatient center for cancer care on MaineGeneral's new 162-acre campus near the interstate highway in northern Augusta. Following his death at the age of 93 in 2007,[184] the Alfond foundations made the lead gifts to allow the hospital to consolidate its inpatient care at the Augusta site. The 192-bed, $312 million Harold Alfond Center for Health opened in 2013. (Waterville's Thayer unit on North Street was renovated and expanded to become an outpatient center, and Seton Hospital on Chase Avenue, along with the old Augusta General Hospital, was sold.)

Under the umbrella of Dexter Enterprises, the Alfond foundations continued to make exceptional gifts in the Waterville area. A gift of over $10 million in 2012 allowed Kennebec Valley Community College to expand onto a second campus, together with the Good Will-Hinckley School in Hinckley, which was able to continue on as Maine's first charter school.

Throughout his life, Alfond shied from the limelight, but when a dedication required his participation, he usually spoke briefly and without notes. In those moments, with his round face wreathed in smiles and his eyes twinkling, it was easy enough to tell that his greatest joy came from giving. Although his benefactions were scattered across the country, by 2018 he and his foundations had given more than $144 million to improve lives in the Waterville area.

---

[184] Bibby Alfond predeceased him in 2005.

17

A New Dawn

- 2018

As the new century began, Waterville went in search of a new identity. Those who had clung to dreams of an industrial recovery had conceded that the factories were not coming back, and it was simple enough to see that nearby Augusta had captured the medical center prize and the lion's share of the region's retail trade. Even so, beyond the discouraging signs were many clues of promising things that could return the city to distinction and vitality.

A fondness for education, arts, and culture had been manifest from the beginning. In 1802, a mere handful of taxpayers scraped together $146 at the first Town Meeting to buy books for a library. Soon after, citizens gave land and money to secure a college of their own, and in 1902 rallied to build a magnificent theater within their new city hall. Waterville's reputation as a center for learning had steadily grown, and there were now three strong colleges nearby, each with its own inviting niche.

The growing galaxy of women educational leaders added yet another bright star in 2012 when Laurie LaChance was named the fifth – and first woman – president of Thomas College. Trained as an economist at Bowdoin (B.A.) and Thomas (M.B.A.), LaChance led the Maine Development Foundation and served as Maine State Economist for three governors before coming to Thomas. She learned the world of academe on the run, and she surprised no one when she began to take the college several rungs up the ladder of excellence with new and influential friends, added facilities, and burgeoning academic programs, including the Alfond-sponsored Entrepreneurial Institute.

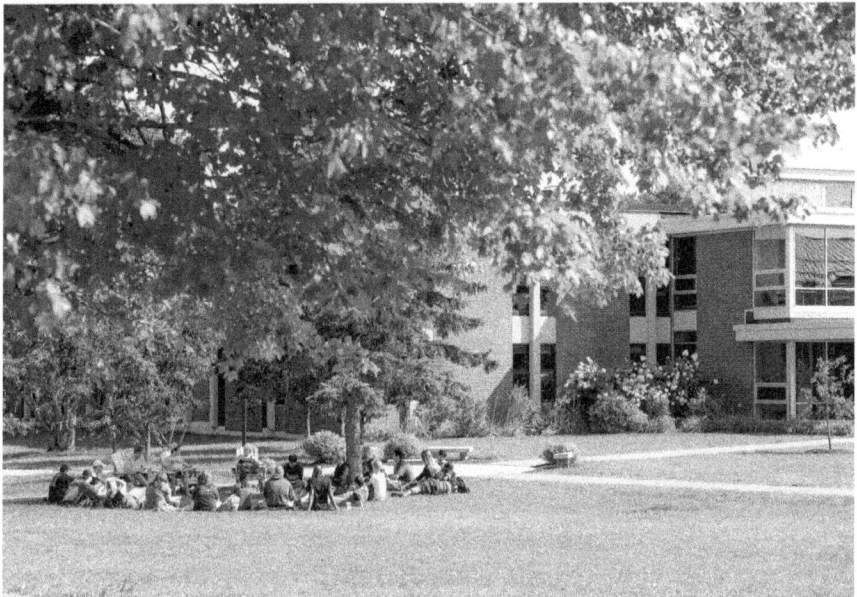

Thomas College on its handsome, ever growing campus

Beyond arts and education, the Alfond largesse and the dedication of volunteers had given the area a leg up in its attractiveness as a place to live and work. Medical services – albeit now spread out – were broad-ranging, and the city's youth programs and facilities were unmatched.

Much of the task of pulling these many positive factors together fell to the Chamber of Commerce. Its activities and influence had ebbed and flowed since it began as the Board of Trade in 1859, but now the organization had moved beyond its historic mission of pamphlet-producing and ribbon-cutting to become a confederation that melded many other civic initiatives and made them work. Representing all of mid-Maine since 1985, the Chamber's wheel of activities had spokes in every direction, from economic development to political debate, from business breakfasts to leadership luncheons, from trade shows to major fund raisers. At the hub was Kimberly Lindlof who became president in 2001[185] when all the member towns were suffering. Waterville was seeing its steepest population decline ever, off more than nine percent in a decade (to 15,605), and the city's downtown area was filled with empty storefronts. A downtown Waterville committee of the Chamber had broken off to become the Waterville Intown Business Association (WIBA) that was replaced when the city helped to fund Waterville Main Street, a merchant group bent on restoring business.[186] It was an uphill battle, and the Chamber remained the unifying element.

Lindlof's talents and energies enabled her to bridge the broad range of personalities and persuasions of the area's mostly male prime movers, and she was able to triple Chamber membership to 650 in less than two decades, and sponsor events that mushroomed to more than 60 a year.[187] Its most popular programs included a spring awards ceremony honoring community leaders, an annual golf tournament, the Taste of Waterville that began in 1993 and became an annual summer showcase of local restaurateurs, a fall raffle and dinner; and a spring Business-to-Business Showcase, drawing thousands to displays of more than 140 regional enterprises.

Despite competition from the capital nearby, commercial development was not stagnant. In 2002, a new shopping center opened on Rosenthal land north of Elm Plaza and closer to the interstate highway. Designed as a smaller version of the Augusta Marketplace, Waterville Commons brought both new jobs and traffic jams. Three years later, Wal-Mart moved across town from Kennedy Memorial Drive and opened a "supercenter" in Waterville Commons, joining Home Depot as an anchor.

---

[185] Lindlof was the second woman leader of the Chamber. The first, Gale Donald, stayed only eight months in 1983.
[186] Formed in 2001, Waterville's was one of the state's first four Main Street programs, designed to energize downtown areas and funded in part by the Maine Development Foundation. When it was disbanded, its most meaningful programs, including the Farmers Market, Common Street Arts, and the popular Kringleville.
[187] The Chamber also regained solid financial footing and was able to move, yet again, to inviting new headquarters on historic Elm Street (No. 50) in August 2010.

The vacated Wal-Mart store on Kennedy Memorial Drive was taken over by Marden's, a surplus and salvage store that was, far and away, the area's most unusual retail enterprise. Harold "Mickey" Marden was a rural mail carrier in Albion in 1964 when he began a second and more exotic career by opening a small auction house on Main Street in Fairfield. Neighbors were soon beating on his doors looking for all manner of things, and the gregarious entrepreneur began buying goods from bankruptcy courts, train wrecks, floods, earthquakes, and fires, and selling them at discounted prices. Bargain hunters flocked to see what was new and then boasted of making brand-name purchases at a fraction of their intended cost. Within ten years, he moved his eclectic business onto College Avenue (No. 184) where he sometimes stopped traffic to roll rugs into the road to measure for cutting. With five children and assorted livestock, he quipped that he would buy and sell anything at all, as long as he didn't have to feed it. A truckload of slightly damaged caskets sold out in days, and faulty windows removed from Boston's Hancock Tower made backyard greenhouses throughout Central Maine. Marden died in 2002, but his family business grew to encompass 14 stores in Maine.

The defunct Mid-State Economic Development Corporation was reborn as the Central Maine Growth Council in 2002, and 12 years later was placed under the Chamber's wing. The Council (briefly called Central Kennebec Valley Growth Council) was formed as a public and private partnership of Waterville, Winslow, Fairfield and Oakland, and it slowly but successfully expanded the regional economy through collaboration among municipal governments and businesses. Its clout helped to attract a new information-technology company to Waterville in 2016, and to support the Chamber in convincing the state highway department to create a new I-95 interchange at the Trafton Road, a combined public-private effort that opened a thousand contiguous acres for development in Waterville and Sidney.

MOTORISTS WAITING AT THE TRAFFIC LIGHTS to make their way through the maze of roads at the foot of Main Street were long accustomed to gazing at the forlorn Lockwood mills. The giant complex had been a beehive for 82 years until the cotton textile production stopped in 1955, and it got an extra 45 years when the C.F. Hathaway shirt company carried on in the lower mill until it closed in 2002. After that, the hulking mills were silent except for the old Lockwood entrance wing, used by Central Maine Power for offices; and a part of the abandoned factory, used by Marden's for industrial sales and storage. Otherwise, the view from the circle by the bridge was one of crumbling brickwork and vacant windows with broken glass.

Many New England river mills had been converted to other uses by 2006, when Rhode Island developer Paul Boghossian led a partnership that would give the local factory another life. Boghossian, who found an affinity for Waterville and its people during his undergraduate years at Colby, planned to begin by renovating the 130,000 square feet of the former Hathaway plant, and then move on to restore the rest. In 2008, in the midst of a crushing worldwide market slump, the Hathaway Creative Center was opened, featuring 67 apartments, many with striking views of the Kennebec. The apartments leased quickly, but accompanying business ventures came more slowly. The remaining half-million square feet of the old Lockwood mill, one of the largest surviving 19th century industrial sites in Maine, would have to wait, not only for backing but also for a solution to the traffic snarl that had both physically and psychologically isolated the south end of town for decades.

Waterville's long list of distinguished jurists grew in 2009, when Joseph M. Jabar was named by Governor John Baldacci as the city's fifth attorney and third native of the city to serve on Maine's Supreme Judicial Court.[188] The son of the late union activist, George Jabar, Joseph graduated from Colby and the University of Maine School of Law before becoming a federal prosecutor in the U.S. Justice Department. Returning to private practice in Waterville, he became District Attorney for Kennebec and Somerset counties and was twice elected to the Maine House of Representatives. He served two governors as Chair of the Executive Clemency Board and was a member of the Board of Governors of the Maine Trial Lawyers Association. Governor Angus King appointed him to the Maine Superior Court in 2001.

While the city pondered traffic solutions (including the possible return of two-way traffic on Main Street) private citizens were already at work to revitalize the city, including the South End, where nearly 70 percent of the residents lived below the poverty level. In 2001, Kimberly Hallee assembled a group that became known as the South End Neighborhood Association

---

[188] Others were Warren C. Philbrook (1913-1918), Frederik Harold Dubord (1956-1962), Harold C. Marden (1962-1970), and Morton A. Brody (1990-1991).

(SENA) that drew help from city planner Ann Beverage in engaging various city departments and the Kennebec Valley Community Action Program (KVCAP) in an array of programs to protect and improve the area. Later led by Jacqueline Dupont, SENA arranged for stepped-up policing, neighborhood gatherings, cleanup programs, a neighborhood park and garden, a bicycle swap program for youngsters, and, with KVCAP, a center for teens.

The creation of the Waterville Community Land Trust in 2012 built upon SENA's efforts and was able to help stabilize South End neighborhoods through buying and rehabilitating homes that were then made available to low-income families. The brainchild of Nancy Williams, the local Trust used grants and donations to acquire a number of properties, including a two-acre common lot along 350 feet of riverfront on Water Street.

There were others who imagined a revival and were not content simply to dream. Faye Nicholson had created an organization called REM (Realizing the Energy of Maine) in 1996, and with the help of her husband James, by 2018 had built successful partnerships to improve the quality of life in central Maine. Its broad aims included efforts to encourage patronage of local businesses and to build a sense of community through arts and entertainment.

Dreams were coming true in the North End as well. In 2007, local dentist John Koons rallied support for the development of a recreation park along the old Quarry Road off North Street. Once known as Mountain Farm, the area had been an attraction to outdoor enthusiasts off and on for nearly a century. Running from the west side of Upper Main Street down a steep slope to a plateau bordering the Messalonskee, the place featured an outcropping of stone, locally called The Devil's Chair. Koons's vision for a fourth resurrection of the land was the broadest yet. A joint venture with the city, The Quarry Road Recreation Area became an instant popular success as a four-season area, providing 200 acres for six miles of cross-country skiing and snowshoeing in the winter, and for walking, running and biking in the other three seasons.

Horatio Russell (H.R.) Dunham, owner of the land and operator of the state's largest ski equipment store on Main Street, opened the first Mountain Farm slope in the early 1900s. It featured a 400-foot vertical drop in barely 1400 feet, and had a 1700-foot rope tow – Maine's longest.[189] It was closed during World War II and re-opened in 1949, when the new Colby Ski Club – all freshmen and returning veterans – asked the new owner, Dr. Charles Vigue, if they could fix it up.[190] They built a tiny lodge with boards rescued from a barn being razed to make room for Thayer Hospital, and then cleared brush, laid out two slopes, and built a wooden jump with an outrun precariously close to Messalonskee Stream. It lasted only four winters. Following Vigue's death, in 1963 his sister, Mildred, gave the property to Colby. The college built a new lodge and added a 1280-foot T-bar lift, a 32-meter ski jump, lighting, and snow making equipment. It was dedicated as a community recreation area in 1964. This, too, was doomed. The slope faced the melting winter sun, and ever-expanding trails at Sugarloaf USA stole the local skiers. It was closed in 1973.

THE CITY'S LOVE OF BLUSTERY POLITICS had not faded by 2003, when 53-year-old Republican Paul Richard LePage was appointed mayor and went on to serve two elected terms before becoming Waterville's fourth governor of Maine.[191] Both as mayor (2004-2011) and as governor (2011-2018), he was a political enigma. His supporters often disputed him, and his detractors occasionally agreed. His unbroken chain of election victories came by a coalescence of voters drawn to his "give 'em hell" style, his reputation as a fiscal conservative, and his compelling life story.

The oldest of 18 children from a poor and dysfunctional Lewiston family, he left home at the age of 11 and lived on the streets. At 13 he

---

[189] Dunham died during the war and the slope was closed. Ronald Brown took over the store, which became one of the country's first retail catalogue merchants, selling Hathaway Shirts over the counter and through the mail.

[190] The Club's first faculty advisor was John Koons's father, Donaldson, a Colby geology professor.

[191] The others were William T. Haines (R), 1913-15; Edmund Muskie (D), 1955-59; and Clinton Clauson (D), 1959.

was taken in by two supporting families, and went on to earn a business degree at Husson College and an MBA at the University of Maine. He was general manager at Marden's during his time as mayor when he was able to reduce property taxes each year, while at the same time add $9 million to the city's reserves. In 2005, he created a charter commission that led to a council-manager form of government that staggered and increased council terms to three years, and established the manager as the city chief administrative officer.

Tea Party activists helped give LePage the edge among seven Republicans for the party's nomination for governor in 2010, and again that fall, when he took 37.6 percent of the votes in a three-way race to become Maine's first elected Franco-American governor.[192] Bangor attorney Eliot Cutler, once an aide to Senator Muskie, was a close second. Democratic candidate Libby Mitchell of Vassalboro finished third. LePage won re-election in 2014, defeating Democratic congressman Mike Michaud (48 to 43 percent), with Eliot Cutler again the spoiler.

In his time as governor, LePage vetoed a record number of bills in battles with the Legislature that often involved spending and social issues. He openly warred with the press and often offended special-interest and minority groups, who frequently called for his impeachment. Despite stalemates and conflicts, he achieved much of what he set out to do. Over objections, he reformed the state's welfare program, reduced cumbersome business regulations, repaid the state debt to hospitals, and paved the way for establishing charter schools. With the help of a recovering national economy, he was also able to lower the income tax rate, reduce unemployment to a record low of three percent, and recover from a billion-dollar budget shortfall to regain Maine's financial stability.

IF ONE WERE TO MARK THE MOMENT Waterville moved to center stage in the world of art, it would have to be in May of 2007, when Colby president William "Bro" Adams announced the promised gift of 500 world-renowned works of art from local residents Paula and Peter Lunder.

---

[192] Alonzo Garcelon, a Franco-American Democrat from Lewiston, received 22 percent of the popular vote in a three-way race for governor in 1878. Republican Seldon Connor got 45 percent, but no candidate had the required majority, and the Democrats joined the third-party Greenbacks to give the election to Garcelon, who served the customary one year.

The nephew of Harold Alfond, Peter Lunder became the president of Dexter Shoe Company not long after his Colby graduation in 1956. When he and Paula were married and raising their family near the campus on Mayflower Hill, Paula became a museum volunteer and patron. The couple purchased art together for more than a half century, and while few ever knew of it, amassed one of the finest private collections in the country. Embracing works by outstanding 19th and 20th century American artists – George Inness, John Singer Sargent, Edward Hopper, Georgia O'Keeffe, Winslow Homer, and the sculptor Paul Manship – the gift included the largest collection of James McNeil Whistler etchings and lithographs ever given to an American academic museum. Appraisers estimated the gift to exceed $100 million, making it the largest single charitable donation in Maine history.

The works would have been welcomed by any of the world's major museums, but the Lunders wanted them regularly displayed and used for teaching, and Colby was the perfect place. Its museum was open without charge to a growing number of visitors; the faculty was using the collection in almost every discipline; and an ambitious college program was bringing busloads of Maine schoolchildren for visits and instruction every year. Beyond that, the museum's American holdings were already exceptional, and under the skillful guidance of head curator and museum director Sharon Corwin, the scope of the collection had begun to expand in important new directions.

The museum had seen remarkable growth since its beginning in 1959, when a small gallery was carved out of the new art and music center named for retiring president J. Seelye Bixler and his wife Mary. In 1950, Bixler had brought James Carpenter from Harvard as the college's part-time curator and only art professor. C.F. Hathaway president Ellerton Jetté and his wife Edith were early supporters, and in 1956 they added focus to the collection with a gift of 100 American folk paintings. The gift prompted others to enrich the specialty, and ten years later, spilling out of a new gallery soon to be named for the Jettés, a summer show titled *Maine and Its Artists, 1740–1963* vaulted the tiny museum onto the national stage.[193] From there, the collection grew mainly through the work of a single man. Hugh J. Gourley III came as the first full-time director in 1966, worked the first 18 years by himself, and went on to a 36-year career, all the while making friends across the art world and building the museum's strength and reputation. The family of American modernist John Marin

---

[193] The show featured stunning works of Maine artists and was a smashing success. *Time* magazine said it was one of the world's 12 most outstanding exhibitions of the year, and listed New York, Paris, London, Brussels, and Waterville, Maine, among the premier cities to visit that summer.

gave 24 of his works in 1973, and in 1975, the Jettés followed with 100 paintings by American impressionists.[194] By 1991 the collection had far outgrown the space, and Shaw's Supermarket founder Stanton Davis and his wife Elizabeth built a 1600-plus-square-foot gallery with storage space in the new basement below. In 1996, in the midst of other gifts, art collector and philanthropist Paul Schupf built an entirely new wing dedicated to the work of the Maine modern realist Alex Katz.

The Lunder's jaw-dropping gift catapulted the collection to nearly 6,000 pieces, and although they had made the naming gift for a new 13-gallery wing in 1999, it was time for the museum to grow again. The Alfond-Lunder Family Pavilion opened in July 2013, and the once tiny museum mushroomed to include 38,000 square feet of gallery space, making it the largest museum in Maine. Through a wall of glass, the new pavilion displayed a colorful and inviting three-story rendering of a wall drawing ("#803") by the American conceptual artist Sol LeWitt.[195]

COLBY COLLEGE PHOTO

The Alfond-Lunder Family Pavilion, Colby Art Museum

---

[194] Ellerton Jetté died in in 1986, and Edith in 1992. Their estates left $5.7 million for the Colby museum. At the time, it was the largest gift the college had ever received.
[195] Before long, the Lunders again bolstered the museum's prestige by endowing the Lunder Institute for American Art, a program designed to engage students and the greater community through extended visits by noteworthy artist-scholars.

WITHOUT KNOWING OF THE LUNDER FEAST, the city had already begun to set the table in preparation for its re-invention as a center for the arts, education and culture. The venerable Waterville Public Library, lending books since 1896, was renovated and re-opened in 2011. Spruced up and expanded without harm to its distinct Romanesque style, the new facility had much more than books to offer. That same year, library director Sarah Sugden established a Business, Career, and Creative Center that offered counseling and computers to assist job-seekers, career-changers, and small business entrepreneurs. The Carnegie Corporation and the *New York Times* recognized Sugden's work in 2014 when she became one of ten Americans to receive the I Love My Librarian Award, and in 2017 the library was one of ten nationwide winners of the National Medal for Museum and Library Services.

After a 30-year effort to renovate the Opera House, $5 million was raised to complete the project and the rare beaux-arts theater was reopened in its former splendor in 2012. Led by Tamsen Brooke Warner, a volunteer board partnered with local businesses and institutions to resume a vibrant program of live theater, dance performances, concerts, and public celebrations that often filled its 810 plush seats.

IT WAS LOVE AS WELL AS MONEY that led to the creation of what was to become Waterville's most significant annual attraction. The Maine International Film Festival, first held in 1998, grew from a seed planted 20 years before when the indefatigable Ken Eisen, five years out of Colby, partnered with four other independent-film aficionados to create a tiny theater in an abandoned beverage warehouse near the tracks in the center of town. [196] When Railroad Square Cinema opened, all three of the city's small movie houses had succumbed to television. A multiplex cinema on Kennedy Memorial Drive offered only the standard Hollywood fare, and VCRs were yet to come. Eisen and the others saw their theater as the only way to see and share the best of American and international cult classics and new releases. The theater's patronage was slow at first, but fiercely faithful, and few ever challenged its claim to having "the best popcorn in the world."[197]

The Cinema established a nonprofit wing, which became the Maine Film Center in 1987, and in ten years began producing the ambitious ten-

---

[196] The others were Lea Girardin, Gail Chase, Alan Sanborn, and Stuart Silverstein.
[197] The Cinema moved briefly onto the Colby campus following a fire in 1994, and it was quickly rebuilt.

day summer showing of independent, restored, foreign, and retrospective films, honoring some of their makers and featuring world-renowned guests including Terrence Malick, Ed Harris, Sissy Spacek, and Glenn Close. The festival steadily grew to attract broad industry and popular notice, and in 2016 the *Boston Globe* declared it "the best curated film event in New England." In 2012, the Maine Film Center, originally a partner, became the nonprofit parent organization of both the Cinema and the Festival.

In 2002, Colby professor and Waterville author Richard Russo won a Pulitzer Prize for his fictional novel, *Empire Falls*. Working with the Chamber and the Maine Film Office, the motion picture TV giant HBO shot a movie version of the work, starring Paul Newman, Joanne Woodward and others. Much of the filming was done in the local area, and the movie premiered to a packed Waterville Opera House in the spring of 2005.

By 2014, Waterville's many creative arts and cultural initiatives were sometimes getting in each other's way, and it was time to focus the many of the separate efforts that were aimed at the single goal of strengthening the region's vitality. Waterville Creates! (with an exclamation point for graphic shock) was established in 2014 as a collaborative consortium to sort out calendars, coordinate fundraising efforts, improve marketing, and provide volunteer leadership development. When Shannon Haines was named CEO in 2016, she had already provided exceptional leadership for the Maine Film Center, the Maine International Film Festival, and Waterville Main Street, three of the six principal partners of the new consortium.[198] The others were Waterville's Opera House and Library, the Colby Art Museum, and Common Street Arts, a program of Waterville Creates![199]

---

[198] Haines was also instrumental in founding KV Connect, a successful and enduring association of young professionals, providing volunteer, leadership development, and networking opportunities in a program coordinated by the Chamber.
[199] Support for the umbrella organization came from the Unity Foundation, established in 2002 by Bert and Coral Clifford of Unity. A World War II Navy veteran, Bert returned to serve as the postmaster of Unity Plantation and was an early investor in the Unity Telephone Company, becoming the majority owner in 1963. It became UniTel in 1990. The couple was the motivating force and principal donor in the founding of Unity College in 1969. Among their many other gifts were Unity's spacious Field of Dreams and Center for the Performing Arts.

18

Homecoming

-2018

The long-ago campaign that kept Colby in Waterville brought good fortune all around. Freed from the shackles of the railroad tracks and the river, the college flourished; and despite the Depression, the city grew in new directions. It all seemed right, except no one had given much thought to the hidden cost of uprooting an entire college from the middle of town and moving it a mile away.

At the time of the move, town and gown had been as one for more than a century, sharing the Baptist church and meeting place of their founders, and facing ups and downs together. Students and faculty lived in nearby neighborhoods and shopped in town; the college supplied most of the local teachers, and more often than not, community and college leaders were the same. It wasn't until the college was settled on its new campus that the space between downtown and Mayflower Hill suddenly seemed a very long mile. For some, it might as well have been a hundred.

Every mayor since Richard Dubord and every Colby president since Franklin Johnson had worked to bridge the gap, and the records show many examples of city and college reaching out to each other in meaningful ways. Still, time wore away memories of the once-close ties, and an odd aloofness grew. Adding to this uneasy contrast, by 2014 when David Greene became

Colby's 20th president,[200] the college was growing by leaps and bounds, while the city was suffering.

Greene had done his homework and knew Waterville's plight before he arrived, and he also knew the city and the college were symbiotic. Colby needed a vibrant community to attract the best faculty and students, and Waterville relied on the college for its economic health.

When Greene's appointment was announced, former mayor and city booster Karen Heck wrote to invite him on a tour of downtown. He accepted, and on his first day as president, a walk scheduled to last a half-hour stretched on for two. When it was over, Greene was certain of the need for "significant economic intervention," and in his inaugural address that fall he was prescient: "We can never forget that we are a Waterville institution first," he said. "We are of this place and we were formed by the generosity of its citizens. The ingredients are here for a renaissance of this proud city, and Colby College should partner with and support local leaders to accelerate the pace of improvements and stimulate economic growth and prosperity."

Former Mayor Karen Heck tours Main Street with the new Colby president, 2014

---

[200] William Adams had been Colby's president for 14 years, and he went on to serve as chair of the National Endowment for the Humanities under President Barack Obama.

Greene was well equipped to face the challenge. In his previous post as executive vice president at the University of Chicago, he had led a venture to revitalize the nearby Hyde Park neighborhood, and in the full range of his academic and civic work, he had earned a reputation as a persuasive and effective leader. Moreover, as his new colleagues up and down the Hill were soon to discover, he was not good at sitting still.

With a grant from the Alfond Foundation, Greene commissioned a comprehensive downtown study and presented it, together with an action plan, to the college trustees, where he found strong support from leadership. Board chair Robert Diamond exhorted his colleagues to go "all in," as anything less might fail. He was joined by both former, still-serving chairs, Joseph Boulos and James Crawford, as well as chair-elect Eric Rosengren, president of the Federal Reserve Bank of Boston who was deeply involved in the bank's successful collaborative program, Working Cities, designed to help post-industrial cities recover. All of them understood the power of the promise Colby was about to make. The full board agreed.

With the support of Mayor Nick Isgro, Greene took the plan downtown for a series of open meetings, where city officials, business leaders, and community advocates expressed their views and offered suggestions. A smaller steering group took the revised scheme and set out to make things happen. Initially, Greene hoped to find a developer who would take the risks and manage the projects, but when none came forward, the college struck out on its own.

Colby's buying spree began in July 2015 with the purchase of two long-vacant buildings at opposite ends of Main Street. Levine's store (No. 9) became the site for a proposed college-owned boutique hotel; and the old Waterville Savings Bank building (No. 173) was slated for renovation. [201] Before fall, the college bought two more buildings. Waterville Hardware (No. 416 Main), vacant since being gutted by fire in 1981, was set for demolition, as was the Elks Club-cum-church building on Appleton Street (Nos.13-15).

---

[201] The gray, brick-and-limestone bank building first opened in 1904. Designed by Waterville architect William Butterfield, it was the first structure in Waterville made with reinforced concrete, intended to be fireproof. In 1947, soon after the bank moved across the street, attorney Lewis Lester Levine purchased the building, taking the third floor for his offices and leasing the floors below for professional offices, a billiard parlor, and the headquarters of the Maine Christian Civil League. Robert Hains bought the structure in 1986, and it remained mostly unused and neglected until the Colby purchase.

In December, Greene called stakeholders and political leaders to a meeting at Colby where he announced that the Boston-based technology firm Collaborative Consulting (CC)[202] was coming to Waterville with some 200 new jobs, and the newly acquired bank building would be made ready for them.

> In testimony to Greene's dogged persistence, eyes popped when CC's founder and chief executive William Robichaud stood to speak and blithely admitted he had actually intended to take his firm to Bangor. "But," he said, smiling at the Colby president, "this man just won't take 'no' for an answer."

The regeneration effort got another boost in October 2016 when, under a crowded tent in Castonguay Square, Senator George Mitchell spoke of growing up only a few hundred yards away, at Head of Falls. He applauded the initiatives to restore the heart of his hometown, and when he finished, Greene and Gregory Powell of the Alfond Foundation announced that the college and the foundation would each commit $10 million toward the effort.

In the spring of 2016, work began on a new college Main Street building on Main Street. Standing on the corner of Appleton Street, in the parking lot where the Concourse met Main Street, the 100,000 square foot, five-story brick structure was to transform the face of downtown. With public meeting rooms and retail space on the glass-fronted street level, the building has apartments for students and faculty on the four floors above.[203] Bill and Joan Alfond made the naming gift, and when Alfond Commons opened in the fall of 2018, there were nearly 200 students living downtown, almost half the number that had resided there in the years before the move. Under a new program of civic engagement introduced by Greene, all Alfond Commons residents were pledged to engage in local volunteer service.

---

[202] Collaborative Consulting was later acquired by the Montreal firm, CGI.
[203] Camden National Bank, which had long occupied the art deco Federal Trust building on lower Main Street, elected to move into the Alfond Commons, and Colby purchased its old building to join the property with its planned hotel.

Artist's concept, Alfond Commons, Main Street

Colby's initiatives were not universally embraced. Grumbling over the loss of parking spaces with the construction of Alfond Commons harkened to the days of Urban Renewal, when a fondness for asphalt had led to the almost total paving of the Concourse. Some were also anxious about what they saw as the college's intrusion into city affairs, and with a tinge of resentment, began calling the city "Colbyville." ("Green[e]ville" was taken.)

Paul Boghossian and a small cadre of local entrepreneurs had a head start on downtown rebuilding,[204] and now the list of investors grew with each promising headline. In a single year (2016-2017), the city's real-estate market went from cold to hot as downtown property values escalated and citywide home sales jumped nearly 30 percent.

THE INFUSION OF YOUNG PEOPLE INTO THE DOWNTOWN MIX was bound to enliven all sorts of things, including the arts, and amid the flurry of other changes, the community focus on shaping its new

---

[204] Among them were insurance man Bill Mitchell, son of the late Urban Renewal chief Paul, who purchased and renovated the former Masonic building on Common Street and opened a restaurant (The Proper Pig) at street level; and the inveterate Waterville cheerleader, Charlie Giguere, son of the late downtown supermarket proprietor, Lionel, who renovated his Silver Street Tavern and built offices and modern apartments upstairs.

identity was not lost. With key help from the city's colleges and hospitals, the old Sterns Department Store on Main (No. 93) had been purchased in 1996 and had since served as home to various community endeavors. In March 2018, Waterville Creates! and Colby announced that the building would be part of an overall project to establish a compelling downtown center for arts, arts education, theater and film. Plans called for building alterations to afford a better view of the Opera House from Main Street, and to create a modern art gallery that would be an inviting downtown "front door" to the museum on the Hill. Former Colby trustee Paul Schupf, a discerning collector and faithful Colby benefactor, made the $2 million naming gift for a ground level, glass fronted gallery of contemporary art facing Castonguay Square.

The Square, known as the Common from its 1796 origin until it was renamed to honor World War I soldier Arthur Castonguay in 1919, was last improved in 1986 by a citizen's group called GROW (Great Revitalization of Waterville). With leadership from Mayor Thomas Nale, the project expanded the green space by eliminating Common Street westbound from Front Street to Main and improved its appearance with the installation of cobblestone walkways, new lighting, and plantings. (All the while, the city continued its aggressive program to save one of the Elm City's last and oldest elms, appropriately located near City Hall, from Dutch elm disease.) With Main Street in a swirl of redevelopment, in 2018 Waterville Creates! received a grant from the National Endowment for the Arts to initiate another facelift for the Square.

Before it began, the striking weathervane sculpture titled *Ticonic*, created by well-known Maine artist Roger Majorowicz, was uprooted from the Concourse in a move that was cheered by motorists who had been plagued by the work since its installation in the middle of a tiny traffic island in 1997. Its awkward and irritating placement had done little to endear it to locals, especially those already disinclined to care for modern art, but when the work was re-installed on the riverbank near the Two Cent Bridge, it became a striking harbinger of good things to come.

Head of Falls, the tract of land close by the bridge, had lain barren since 1976, when the last of the factory buildings, as well as the homes that had sheltered generations of French and Lebanese workers, were razed by the bulldozers of Urban Renewal. Generations of city leaders had pledged to make good use of the old neighborhood, but none had succeeded, and for a half-century the forlorn stretch of land served no purpose other than to collect snow from the plowed streets and provide crude off-street parking places that hardly anybody wanted.

Making something of the empty stretch along the river seemed key to every effort to make downtown attractive to visitors, and in 2016 the city joined with the Kennebec Messalonskee Trails organization to develop plans for a project named RiverWalk.[205] Focused on the venerable and often-restored Two Cent Bridge, the project called for a lighted walkway along the river, with a gazebo at one end and an outdoor amphitheater at the other, a children's playground, and connections to the city's extensive network of walking trails. Headed by City Manager Mike Roy and Lisa Hallee, the $1.5 million project got a head start with handsome lead gifts from Kennebec Savings Bank and the ever-reliable Waterville Rotary Club, and by the summer of 2018 it seemed certain that the proud city would at last have a fitting monument near Ticonic Falls, at the very place where it all began.

---

[205] Kennebec Messalonskee Trails was founded by Peter Garrett who first proposed the Head of Falls section in the early 1990s and spearheaded a regional effort to develop more than 40 miles of walking trails.

Acknowledgments

The only previous comprehensive history of Waterville was published in 1902 by the Rev. Edwin Carey Whittemore, pastor of the First Baptist Church, to mark the 100th anniversary of the establishment of the town. For his *Centennial History of Waterville*, Whittemore called upon community leaders to write the several topical segments, all of which helped inform the early parts of this story. Although this work is entirely my own, I also have relied upon assistance from others along the way. Most especially, I want to thank City Planner Ann Beverage, who supplied much valuable information and advice, and who, with her husband Parker, scoured every chapter to make them better; Charles Ferguson, an ever-faithful friend and most skillful copy editor; Patricia Newell, the splendid publisher at North Country Press; Anne Nelson, a talented and thorough proofreader; and as always, my wife Barbara. Thanks as well to the Mid-Maine Chamber of Commerce and its president Kimberly Lindlof, who first proposed that this history be written; to Waterville's Redington Museum and its most helpful curator Bryan Finnemore; and to the accommodating professionals at the Waterville and Colby College libraries. I must also acknowledge the people whose names are listed below in a tiny type size that belies my enormous gratitude. This book could not have been written without them.

E.H.S.
Belgrade Lakes, Maine
August, 2018

William Alfond	David Friedenreich	Crista Lavenson	Marie Paradis
Sara Barry	Denise Gallo	Maggie Libby	Abraham Peck
Christopher Bernier	Peter Garrett	Ben Lisle	Wayne Pelletier
Daniel Bernier	Henry Gemery	Constance Lizotte	John Picher
Margaret Bernier	Charles Giguere	John Marden	Nancy Rabaska
Eric Bloom	John Goodine	Wesley Marden, Jr.	Frederick Robie
Nicholas Boutin	David Greene	Stanley Mathieu	Robert Rosenthal
Sarah Bowen	Darlene Hallee	Joy McKenna	Michael Roy
Allison Brochu	Lisa Hallee	Stana Short McLeod	Tina Serdjenian
David Brown	Karen Heck	Laura Meader	Tanya Sheehan
Jennifer Buker	Margaret Hemphill	James Meehan	Earle Shettleworth
Patricia Burdick	Edward Hershey	Thomas Meucci	Benjamin Smith
Amy Calder	Buffy Higgins	Wendy Miller	David Smith
Marilyn Canavan	Joseph M. Jabar	Julie Miller-Soros	Kelly Smith
Katherine Carlisle	Ruth Joseph Jackson	Kirk Mohney	Louise Smith
Robert Chenard	Frederic Johnson	Scott Monroe	Jack Sutton
Sharon Corwin	Diane Johnson	Caroline Moseley	Gerald Tipper
John Dalton	Janice Kassman	Jack Nivison	Richard Uchida
Susan Damren	Pearley Lachance	Kate O'Halloran	Kenneth Viens
Sanderson Day	Felicia Lambert	Steven Orlov	Meta Vigue
Patti Dubois	Caitlin Lampman	Regina Ouimette	Janet Weymouth
Kenneth Eisen	Cathy Langlais	Anne Owens	Arthur White
Sidney Farr	Elizabeth Leonard	Jennifer Pare	Barbara Woodlee
Ryan Fitzsimmons	J. Alfred Letourneau	Ernest Paradis	

203

NOTES

ABBREVIATIONS

BTJ   *Board of Trade Journal*, Vol. XXIII, Portland, Maine, 1910

CHW   *Centennial History of Waterville, Maine*, Rev. Edwin Carey Whittemore, 1902

CM   *Colby* Magazine

CMH   *A Chronology of Municipal History and Election Statistics, Waterville, Maine*, Clement M. Giveen, Maine Farmer Press, Augusta, Maine, 1908

HCC   *The History of Colby College*, Ernest C. Marriner, Waterville, Maine, 1963

HFD   *History of the Waterville Fire Department*, 1995

KJ   *Kennebec Journal* or *Daily Kennebec Journal*

MH   *Mayflower Hill, A History of Colby College*, Earl H. Smith, University Press of New England, 2006

WPH   Waterville *Postcard History*, Earle G. Shettleworth, Jr., Arcadia Publishing, 2013

SHW   *A Short History of Waterville, Maine*, Stephen Plocher, Colby College, 2007

WM   *Waterville Mail*

WS   *Waterville Sentinel* or *Waterville Morning Sentinel*

1. ALONG THE RIVER

Informed by *The Centennial History of Waterville*, written by the Rev. Edwin Carey Whittemore and published in 1902; and by *A Chronology of Municipal History and Election Statistics*, compiled and edited by Clement M. Giveen and published in 1908; John Smith writing: *The Portraictuer of Captayne John Smith, Admirall of New England*, (sic), London, 1616; "That there majesties subjects …" Giveen, Clement M., *A Chronology of Municipal History and Election Statistics, Waterville, Maine*, Maine Farmer Press, Augusta, 1908; Arnold's greeters: Ibid. p. 36; "in the spring season .." CHW, pp 53-54; Petition wording: CMH, p. 53

2. WATER VILLAGE

"The only pollution concern …" CMH, p. 62; "In all, the stream would …" Hayward, *New England Gazetteer*, 1839; "The closest the local …" CHW, p. 58; "agreeably affected" Ibid. p. 59

3. PLENTY OF NOISE

Informed by *The History of Colby College*, written by Ernest C. Marriner and published in 1963, and from Lovejoy files in Special Collections at the Colby College Library. Also taken from the author's *Mayflower Hill, A History of Colby College*, published in 2006; Davis: BTJ, pp. 181-182; several thousand, BTJ, p. 44; "to persons to sell …" CMH p. 86; Temperance laws: ibid, pp. 92. 94, 95; "I found the …" CHW p. 230; "The college did not embrace …" Rowe, Amy. *A People's History of Colby College*, 1999; "Even as Late" .. Marriner, Ernest, *Kennebec Yesterdays*, 1954: To the lasting glory .. SHW p. 13

4. QUICK TO ANSWER

Benjamin Butler: Taken from text accompanying the Butler portrait at Colby College, written by Elizabeth Leonard, John J. and Cornelia V. Gibson Professor of History; "to give tone and energy ..." *History of the Work of the Board of Trade*, Portland, Maine, 1887; Work of first City Council: BTJ, p. 146-47

5. FULL STEAM AHEAD

Hollingsworth & Whitney: Madden, James L., *A History of Hollingsworth & Whitney Company, Waterville, Maine*: Colby College Press, 1957; Keyes background: Marriner, Ernest C., *A History of the Keyes Fibre Company, Waterville, Maine*, Colby College Press, 1958; The story of Nelson: Informed by Stephen D. Thompson, *When Waterville was Home to Nelson*, 2009; "The story explained ..." KJ, Jan. 3 & 19, 1900; "If he won't try to walk ..." *Complete Works of Theodore Roosevelt: Memorial Edition*, State Papers and Addresses, 2007; "Across America ..." *U.S. Census and Maine Register;* Levines, informed by Arnon, Sara Miller, and Miller-Soros, Julie, *The History of Levine's: The Store for Men and Boys*, 2011; Giguere, Sentinel: WS, Mar. 28, 1921; Johnson quote: BTJ, Vol. XXIII, 1910, p. 617

6. MOST BEAUTIFUL CITY

"prettiest city ..." BTJ, ibid; "for maintaining the honor ..." ibid; "not for the intellectual ..." CHW, p. 93
"the place to get oiled up ..." BTJ, 1910; Ursuline Sisters: *U.S. Catholic Special Collections*, Dayton, Ohio, 2010
"one of the handsomest ..." BTJ, 1910, p. 629; "put it on the highest ..." ibid. p. 615; "The subject of the address ..." CMH, p 183; "promised the most fastidious ..." Maine Memory Network; "charming spots ..." BTJ, p. 571; "It went on to ..." ibid. p. 609; "a central organization ..."; www.uschamber.com/about/history

7. SHRINKING WORLD

"financial success ..." WS, 7/7/14; "The building housed ..." WPH, p. 28; Fire Department: HFD; Abanaki Golf Course: Robert Rosenthal interview, 10/17, and his book, *LJR*, undated; Taft remarks: WS, 2/16/17; Pershing: WS, 6/5/20 p. 1; Libby Hospital: WPH, p. 42; Sisters Hospital: Daughters of Charity, Province of St. Louis Archives, Emmitsburg, Maryland; Physicians: CHW, Ch. XXIII; Prohibition laws: CMH, p. 103, 130

8. AGAINST THE TIDE

Keeping Colby, informed by HCC, Ch. XXXVI; MH, p. 35 ff; "In the general hullabaloo .." MH, p. 47; Airport: Air Festival program, 1969; Dean Field: Jack Nivison research; Earhart quote: WS, 8/10/33; George Averill: MH; Keyes Fibre: Marriner, *History of the Keyes Fibre Company*, Colby College Press, 1958
"Asked if he was .." MS, 7/2/33; "A day later .." MS, 7/23/33; "Despite changes ..." informed by Bernier study, 1981; "Violence erupted ..." MS, 9/20/34; George Jabar: Bernier, op cit.; "the communists ..." MS, 9/5/34; Paul Dundas: Waterville Annual Report, 1939

9. ALL IN THE SAME BOAT

First news: *The Glory and the Dream*, 1974, William Manchester, p. 257; "The country's largest .." ibid. p. 293; "The few local people ..." MH, p.54; Roosevelt memorial, Waterville: MS, 4/16/45; "Waterville counted ..." Pearley LaChance archives; Bourque-Lanigan: Commander Ernest Paradis; Osteopathic: MS, 10/20/78; WTVL: David Brown archives

10. SUNSHINE AND SHADOWS

Downtown description: MH, p. 64 ff; "While Main Street held …" Statistics from Manning's 1952 Waterville City Directory; Eaton writes: ibid; Chamber incorporates: Incorporation document, Maine Secretary of State; Coburn: Archives of John C. Nivison; Scott Paper: including fundinguniversity.com; Lockwood strike: WS, 4/55; Highway: MH, p. 112 ff; "Ogilvy took credit ..": MH p. 142; Roberts-Toynbee: ibid. p. 113

11. URBAN RENEWAL

The story of Waterville's Urban Renewal is informed the website acad.colby.edu/mappingwaterville/, assembled by Prof. Ben Lisle and his American Studies students at Colby College; "Once cited as .." Johnson: BTJ, Vol. XXIII, 1910; "Experts were predicting .." Planning and Renewal Associates, *Downtown Plan for Waterville*, 1960; "Most striking .." Ibid.; Genesis, Elm Plaza: op. cit. Robert Rosenthal interview; Lewis Rosenthal: ibid and WS, 3/27/86 and 4/3/86; Joly was discouraged: MS 2/8/64; Head of Falls plans for reuse: *H.A. Manning City Directory*, 1967; "The city and the URA insisted .." Rose Warren v. Waterville Urban Renewal Authority, Supreme Judicial Court of Maine, 5/12/65; "From before the Charles Street …" Myron U. Lamb, *Waterville, Maine Comprehensive Plan*, The James W. Sewell Company, 1969, p. 2-14

12. SCATTERED CLOUDS

"strong participation and support .." MH, p. 137; "some 9000 came …" WS, 10/20/78; Air service, MacPhee: Air Festival dedication booklet, 1969; Keyes: Marriner, op cit., *History of the Keyes Fibre Company*; Earth Day, Koons: WS 4/22/70; Grant and Fogg: Woodlee interview, December 1917; Ford Foundation: Colby archive; Time, art show: *Time* magazine 7/23/62; Strider, CBB: Strider interview, Aug. 2002; Simcock, Day: Gallagher

13. PROTESTS AND POLITICS

1968 presidential campaign and election: from MH, p. 171ff; Henry Thompson: WS, 4/9/68; Election day: Colby ECHO, 11/8/68; Sentinel opined: WS editorial, 4/5/70; Kent State rally, 3000 people: Associated Press, 5/11/70; Brownie Carson: author interview, November 2004; Carey, wrist slap: *Portland Evening Express*, 4/25/72

14. SHIFTING TIDES

1976 setting informed by *Waterville 1976*, bicentennial booklet; industry: ibid, Glenn Turner; shops: ibid, Robert Pricer; housing: ibid, Frederick Vigue; religion: ibid, Ernest Marriner; Muskie quotes, retirement event: WS, 1/16/81; "That spring, Carter .." MH, p. 243; "half the hens .." WS, 3/7/81; Mid-Maine Economic Development report: John M. Joseph, Jrs., Economic Consulting Services of Hallowell, 1986; Walter Rast letter: WS, 6/28/85; Mid-Maine Machines: WS, 7/23/82 and 11/19/87

15. BRIDGES FALLING DOWN

"Maine's largest .." WS, 7/6/90; Scott history: www.kimberly-clark.com, MH 324; "The local tax base …" MH, 325; Kotlas: including, *Kotlas Connection's* newsletter, Aug., Oct., Dec., 1992, www.kotlas.org, Jean Ann Pollard and Gregor Smith; Brazier caused a stir: author chair of citizens' committee; WRAAC, MH 327; "A spokesman said …" WS, 1/29/96; *Sentinel* editorial: ibid; FirstPark: including Paul Keonig, centralmaine.com, 4/19/04; ice storm response: MH p.323 f; "In January, Wachner …" *New York Times*, 5/15/1996; Honduras: ibid; Wachner quotes: ibid.

16. The Shoe Maker

Alfond, "hope to be granted" Colby *Alumnus*, Spring 1955; Powell, biggest and best: WS, 10/19/99; Alfond gifts and amounts: Maine Corporations Annual Reports and Ryan Fitzsimmons, Dexter Enterprises.

17. A New Dawn

Marden's: in part from John Marden interview, 3/20/18; Hathaway Creative Center: including *Maine Biz*, 1/7/13; LePage bio from Laurie LaChance introduction, Chamber breakfast, 3/18; Lunder gift: in part adapted from *With the Help of Friends, The Colby College Museum of Art, The First Fifty Years 1959-2009*, Earl H. Smith, Colby Museum, 2009; Film Festival, Railroad Square: Ken Eisen interview, 4/18; "When it was over .." Greene interview, 11/17; Trustee approval was unanimous: ibid; "The City's real estate market .." *Maine Life Real Estate*, 2018.

18. Homecoming

Greene had done his homework: Heck, email, 11/23/17; "significant economic intervention" CM Winter, 2017; Colby board: Greene interview, 11/8/17; Colby needed to be all in: ibid; hoped to find a developer, ibid; cold to hot, home sale: *Maine Real Estate* magazine, 2018.

BIBLIOGRAPHY

Allen, Frederick Lewis. *Since Yesterday: The 1930s in America*. Open Road Media, 1986

Bangs, Issac S. *Military History of Waterville, Maine*. Augusta, Maine, 1902

Beard, Frank and Smith, Bette. *Maine's Historic Places*, Down East Books, 1982

Bernier, Margaret. *Labor Study of the Franco-American Community of Waterville, Maine*. Colby College Senior Scholars Paper, 1981

Fecteau, Albert C. *Community of Waterville, Maine*. University of Maine, Master's Thesis, 1952

Giveen, Clement. *Chronology of Municipal History & Election Statistics, Waterville, Maine*: Farmer Press, Augusta, Maine, 1908

Hayward. *New England Gazeteer*. 1839

Marriner, Ernest C. *History of the Keyes Fibre Company, Waterville, Maine*. Colby College Press, 1958

Madden, James M. *History of Hollingsworth & Whitney Company, Waterville, Maine*. Colby College Press, 1957

Manchester, William. *Glory and the Dream*. Little, Brown & Co., 1973

Marriner, Ernest C. *History of Colby College*. Waterville, Maine, 1963

Plocher, Stephen. *A Short History of Waterville, Maine*. Colby College Independent Study, 2007

Rowe, Amy E. *An Exploration of Immigration, Industrialization, and Ethnicity in Waterville, Maine*: Honors Thesis, Colby College, 1999

Shettleworth, Earle, Jr. *Waterville Postcard History*. Arcadia Publishing, 2013

Smith, Earl H. *Mayflower Hill, A History of Colby College*. University Press of New England, 2006

Sleeper, Frank. *Around Waterville, Images of America*, Arcadia Publishing, 1995

Whittemore, Rev. Edwin Carey. *Centennial History of Waterville, Maine*: 1902

Witherell, James L. *Ed Muskie: Made in Maine*, 2014

Board of Trade Journal, Vol. XXIII: Portland, Maine, 1910
Downtown Waterville Plan, Planning and Renewal Associates, 1960
Historical Sketch of Waterville, Maine, Boston: Mercantile Publishing Co., 1889
History of Waterville Fire Department: 1995
History of the Work of the Board of Trade: Portland, Maine, 1887
Neighborhood Analysis for Waterville, Maine: Hans Klunder Assoc., 1966

INDEX

211

212